MISSOURI HERITAGE
VOLUME II

By

LEW LARKIN

Printed by
The School of the Ozarks Press
Point Lookout, Missouri

ASSEMBLING OF THE FIRST LEGISLATURE
ST CHARLES MO. 1821

MISSOURI HERITAGE

TO

LUANNE AND GAIL

Other Books by *Lew Larkin*

BINGHAM: FIGHTING ARTIST

VANGUARD OF EMPIRE

GENERATIONS OF MILLSTONES

MISSOURI HERITAGE, VOL. I.

FRONTISPIECE - The Assembling of the First Legislature at St. Charles is the cover picture. The original painting, approximately 12 by 6 feet in size, is over the door to the governor's elevator at the Capitol in Jefferson City and was done by Richard E. Miller of Provincetown, Mass. The artist has depicted the moment when these picturesque pioneer legislators are assembling in the square at St. Charles in front of the building where the legislators are to convene. The Flag designates the room where the legislators will meet. Costumes and accessories here are true to life and to the time. Gerald R. Massie, assistant director of the Missouri Division of Commerce and Industrial Development, who has won numerous national honors for his photographic achievements the past 25 years, took this photograph of the original painting.

BACK COVER - The Lake of the Ozarks at 10,000 feet taken by Massie.

PREFACE

The dynamic story of the historic role Missouri and Missourians, played in the last century in the creation of a new world power, has been told in various textbooks. The first 100 columns that appeared in The Kansas City Star, presenting a different format in the delineation of history, were reproduced in "Missouri Heritage, Vol. I." The second 100 columns are presented here.

The author wishes to thank Paul V. Miner, President of The Kansas City Star, for permission to reprint these columns. Dr. Floyd C. Shoemaker, Secretary Emeritus and Consultant to the State Historical Society of Missouri, and Dr. Richard S. Brownlee, Director and Editor of the Society, for their warm encouragement and help, and Mrs. Mary K. Dains, the Society's Research Director, and her staff for excellent technical assistance. Again, Dr. David D. March of the Northeast Missouri State College was most helpful in historical research.

Three of my original supporters of Volume I also gave encouragement to this one, Dr. Everett Keith, Executive Secretary of the Missouri State Teachers Association, and Miss Mabel Burrill and Mrs. Robert E. Cullers of Trenton.

I am also grateful to several members of The Star's staff, Buck Martin, director of the Editorial Art department; Edward J. (Hap) Donnell of the Photographic department, John Doohan, The Star's librarian, and Frank Spurlock, Director of Editorial Page features, and his staff

Lewis Clark Shepherd Larkin
Kansas City, Mo., Jan. 1, 1972

VI

TABLE OF CONTENTS

VII

VIII

ILLUSTRATIONS

IX

LABOR ORGANIZATION

In the first 40 years of statehood, Missouri had little or no labor trouble, and no labor legislation.

The year before it became a state, 1821, Missouri had a population of 60,000 whites in 15 counties, of whom about 12,000 were regarded as able-bodied men. Slave labor was used. The first mine in Missouri, Mine LaMotte, about 1723, was manned by almost 500 slaves. A century later 11,000 slaves worked in the state, planting, tending and harvesting crops, felling trees, helping build homes and working in the mines.

When Missouri was admitted to the Union in 1821, white laborers could move around the state or nation at will, whereas in England they were prohibited from forming trade unions or changing jobs except by government permission.

In 1817 the Mechanics Benevolent Society was organized, but it was concerned mainly in the mutual welfare of the members and parading on patriotic occasions such as the Fourth of July with its own brass band. The St. Louis County Agricultural Society was formed in 1822 for social and educational pursuits among farmers and functioned for several years, but it had no relationship to a labor union.

In 1835 the Typographical Society was functioning and about the same time the Society of Carpenters and Joiners, and the Cabinet Makers Society were organized. They also met and paraded on July 4 and had almost no labor objectives as understood today.

In 1836 the St. Louis barbers organized and staged something close to a strike, demanding 10 cents for a shave. The so-called "dandies" of the time, who were clean-shaven, and others just let whiskers grow, and the barbers took a trimming!

Some of the working men in St. Louis the same year began agitating for a ten-hour day, but made no progress. In 1837 the Tinners Society and the United Journeymen Cabinet Makers Society were organized. Their efforts, too, were limited mainly to patriotic parades.

The panic of 1837 set back any progress that labor organizing might have made in St. Louis (there being no labor problem anywhere else in Missouri), but the Journeymen Carpenters and Journeymen Tailors joined for a strike in May of 1837 seeking higher wages and a 10-hour day. There was no affinity between the two groups in a labor union sense, and a newspaper commented:

1

"This strikes us as a very indiscreet movement. Few houses will be put up this year and people will wear their old clothes until times grow better."

By 1840 the Journeymen Laborers and Mechanics in St. Louis were organized into trade unions but progress was small. But on May 1, 1867, a Missouri law became effective making the 8-hour day legal for some crafts. An Illinois law became effective about the same time. The Brookfield, Mo., Gazette commented:

"We cannot but consider the action of the legislatures of both states as unwise in the extreme and entirely uncalled for. We believe that everyone should have time for recreation and the improvement of the mind. It is manifestly absurd to suppose that employers will pay the same wages for eight hours of labor that they will for 10. If employees will work but eight hours they must submit to a reduction of one-fifth of their wages."

In 1877, when a national railroad strike hit St. Louis, the Globe-Democrat proclaimed:

"Down with all mobs and up with the law—no compromise with rioters."

Three days of mob rule ended when 5,000 armed men broke up the headquarters of the strike. When labor leaders proposed a demonstration in St. Louis and other cities on July 4, to create sentiment for an 8-hour day, there were demands that the parade be stopped. The press was divided; the Globe-Democrat upheld the right of labor organizations to parade peacefully. The parade took place without disorder.

In 1885, street car operators in St. Louis struck for $1.75 for a 12-hour day and conductors $2. There were some disorders but little progress.

The shop workers of the Wabash railroad suffered a wage cut that year. Thousands quit their jobs, and for the first time in the Middle West a "sympathy strike" occurred, in that workers on the Missouri Pacific and Katy railroads also left their jobs. Engineers, firemen, brakemen and others followed, and what began as a local incident became a national strike.

The wages were restored, then cut again in August, 1885. The strike was resumed. Jay Gould, one of the railroad kings in the nation, had no love for strikers but beheld the national chaos and bankruptcy for the railroads, and intervened. By the time it was over, laboring men had learned what could be accomplished by striking together on a national scale.

The Knights of Labor, started in 1869, reached into St. Louis the same year. It had 700,000 members by 1885, but a decline set in and five years later the membership was 100,000, due partly to the fact that the new American Federation of Labor was beginning to gain strength.

The Missouri State Federation of Labor was organized in a convention held May 4, 5, and 6, 1891, in Spillane's hall, Kansas City. F. F. Davis was elected treasurer and Edward J. Stein, secretary; both were Kansas Citians.

July 6, 1968

BENJAMIN HOLLADAY

Benjamin Holladay was born in Kentucky in 1819 and as a boy learned about horses and transportation. His father, who had fought with George Washington, had a fine stable of racing horses and when the son didn't ride one correctly once the father gave him a whacking. The father operated stagecoaches and a chain of flatboats between Louisville and New Orleans.

The young man arrived in Liberty about 1837 and moved to Weston the next year. He did some trading with the tribes in that area and in the War with Mexico he sold supplies to Col. Alexander Doniphan's army.

Following that he was an almost constant trader with Santa Fe, freighting goods of all kinds there and returning donkeys and silver dollars. He was trusted by other merchants and in 1849 took goods valued at $70,000 to Salt Lake City. He formed a partnership with Theodore F. Warner of Weston in 1849 and it soon became a million-dollar operation.

He built a 16-room mansion in Weston.

Russell, Majors and Waddell, for years the leading freight company, began to lose money and Holladay bought them out for $100,000 in 1862.

Holladay early had foreseen that speed would pay off. His stages could travel from Atchison, Kas., to Denver in three days, 11 hours and 15 minutes, and an advertisement bragged, "Ben Holladay's coaches can make almost as good time as a railroad train." Frequently they raced one another across the prairies.

Holladay carefully selected the strongest and fastest animals and used the Concord coach, structurally one of the best. For those who wanted speed at the sacrifice of some comfort he used carriages without springs. He invented a day seat that could be changed into a bed, the forerunner to the Pullman, and even established restaurants along his route.

3

With such conveniences, he competed for awhile with the railroads even though the fares were high. The fare from Atchison to Virginia City was $350 in 1866 and $525 to Helena, Mont.

The Border Times of Weston on May 14, 1864, commented, "Over 1,400 passengers have been conveyed across the plains since the first of February last by the Overland Stage company. The whole route will soon be stocked with fresh and superior horses, and passengers may expect a speedy and safe transit across the plains to the mines, Oregon and California."

It was a constant battle with the iron horse competitor. Both faced similar hazards—robbers, Indians, breakdowns and bad weather—but the advantage was with the trains. Holladay even put horns on his stages to announce their arrival in towns along the way.

Holladay hired drivers who were expert rifle shots and thus could afford a measure of protection for passengers. When the complaints about holdups and killings became too numerous, he hired a professional gunman who reportedly killed 26 marauders.

His company once controlled 5,000 miles of stage lines, more than any competitor. He had a million-dollar contract with the government for handling the mails. But in 1866 he sold out to Wells, Fargo & Co., and the following year he organized the North Pacific line of 16 steamships. Shortly afterward he built a railroad in Oregon and a hotel in Portland.

Within several years he sold his steamship interests to bolster the railroad project, was caught in the panic of 1873 and lost the line to his bond holders.

July 13, 1968

FERRYBOATING

Ferryboating was big business on the Missouri, the Mississippi, the Kaw and other streams in this area in the last century.

The territorial and state Legislatures passed regulatory laws about ferry operations, and local courts had licensing powers. In 1806 the license was $50, depending on innumerable requirements. Bonds were required and rates had to be posted. Usually rates were 25 cents a person, 50 cents for horse or cow, $1.50 for a wagon and 12½ cents a hundred pounds of lumber.

A later act provided some kind of penalty for ferrymen who refused to make a trip without a good and valid reason.

There is some doubt about the date of the first ferry but it is believed to have been on the Meramec River before 1780.

4

In 1820 ferryboats, pulled through the water by horses on a tread-mill were launched in St. Louis.

One of the first commercial ferries at St. Louis was in 1808 when the Missouri Gazette ran an advertisement, "To Travellers," and "Rates of Ferriage as established by law, from St. Louis to the Opposite Shore."

In 1821 Capt. William Jack established "Jack's Ferry" across the Missouri near what is known as Lexington. In 1816 a ferry was established at Arrow Rock, and a short time later it became important in the Santa Fe trade route.

There were several enterprising operators in the last century. One was Maj. John Stemmons who operated at Rocheport. The Missouri Statesman of July 28, 1848, in an advertisement, said about the "New Horse Boat Ferry" that could carry three wagons or 40 horsemen across the Missouri in four minutes:

"The traveling community will rely, that they will meet with no detention, as no pains will be spared by the proprietor in expediting the crossing of all persons who may favour us with their patronage. The proprietor having STRONG OPPOSITION is from the very nature of the case, full of accommodation and compromise, the consequence is, charges will be reasonable.

Teachers and preachers, engaged in their duties at the time, would be taken over free.

With the Kaw and Missouri Rivers at Kansas City it was natural that ferrying would be a major business. Peter Roy cut a road in the town of Kansas down to the waterfront where his ferry docks were established about 1837.

There also was a Caleece ferry here that ceased in 1830. The Wyandotte Indians established their own but it lasted only a few years.

The Grinter ferry over the Kaw was successful and popular for many years. It was the first over that river. Moses Grinter, a regular army man at Fort Leavenworth, started it in 1831. Many others were established here, one by William Chick, whose ancestors are civic leaders in Kansas City today.

By far the most expansive and ambitious ferry operator in Missouri was Samuel Wiggins, who persuaded the Illinois Legislature that no competing ferry could be built within two miles along the Illinois side of the Mississippi.

In the 1850's the railroads began to arrive. They had to use the ferries to cross the river at first. Then construction of the Eads bridge began, and while this actually sounded the death knell for the Wiggins operations, the fight lasted many years. Wiggins tried many moves to prevent construction of the bridge but it was dedicated July 4, 1874.

Wiggins placed barrels of free whisky on his ferries and cut fares in half. The bridge countered with free ice water, three free band concerts a week, ice cream and "extra kerosene lamps."

July 20, 1968

WILLIAM SHERLEY WILLIAMS

The lanky man was bearded and unkempt. His gnarled fingers picked at the foliage to check how many hours before Indians had passed the spot. His bony nose was hoisted like that of a foxhound. He listened for a moment and then he dropped to the ground.

He smiled and he said to himself, "Thar's Injins about. Blackfeet. But this chile intends to do some trapping."

This was William Sherley Williams, one of the best mountain men in American history. He was born January 3, 1787, in North Carolina and the family moved to Missouri.

Sketch credited: Buck Martin

He became an itinerant Baptist preacher in the wooded country around St. Louis, and then he moved farther west as a missionary to the Osages along the Marais des Cygnes river. He even translated part of the Bible into the Osage language.

There are varied stories as to why he quit the ministry. One is that one day during a service he found himself unable to take his eyes off an attractive girl in the front row. Another is that he was disappointed in love and turned to drink.

Just when Old Bill became a loner is not known. Experienced trappers and scouts were few. They would team up with Old Bill, although it might be three days before Old Bill would even say, "Howdy."

Old Bill never worried about Indians too much until they started trailing him. Then he might circle around and end up trailing the Indians. In most cases they were friendly so they would sit down and roast buffalo meat together.

After marrying a beautiful Osage maiden, he gravitated more to the Indian habits and customs.

The Osages worshiped the sun, moon, earth, stars and rain. The dormant missionary spirit frequently popped up in Old Bill and he would attempt to convert them to Christianity.

Old Bill served as an interpretor at Ft. Osage in the summer of 1817, did some trading with the tribes, helped Nathan Boone and others in negotiating treaties, and a few years later assisted the government party that surveyed the Santa Fe trail.

Old Bill always felt the Indians were his brothers, except for the Blackfeet. In Blackfeet country he was very wary, except one night. He felt in an expansive mood and roasted beaver tails, his favorite. He made the one mistake of not putting the fire out shortly before dusk.

The Blackfeet rushed him as he slept. He escaped, but they wounded him in the calf, and took his provisions, rifles, ammunition, his horse, Santa Fe, and his mule, Flop Ear.

The patience of Job was needed by a successful scout and pathfinder in that era. Old Bill nursed his leg along, using poultice leaves and water. He walked and he stumbled and he pulled the old leg along, and he finally arrived at the camp of his attackers. He had only a knife, left by his previous looters.

Old Bill stabbed two to death. Then, some say, he scalped the two Indians and waved one scalp in front of the third, who fled.

Years later he was asked why he didn't kill the third, he replied, "Ef I'd kilt that Injin, thar wouldn't have nobody left ter tell them Blackfeet how them bucks had gone under nor who rubbed them out."

Old Bill Williams may not have been fully appreciated when he was alive, but his name has been memorialized. In various parts of the West, mountains, streams and towns have been named for him.

July 27, 1968

JOSEPH SMITH

Jospeh Smith, founder of the Church of Jesus Christ of Latter Day Saints, and his followers settled in Independence in the early 1830s. In 1835 the church's apostles were selected and one was Brigham Young.

But the Missourians, called "Gentiles" by the Mormons, forced the latter out of Independence.

Not all Missourians were antagonistic towards the Mormons. A Liberty lawyer, Col. Alexander Doniphan, went to their aid by pushing a bill through the Missouri Legislature that set aside a part of Ray County for a Mormon town to be known as Far West.

Far West was planned to be the central city of the church organization and the county seat of a new county, Caldwell. There were other towns such as Salem and Haun's Mill.

Plans were made to build a great temple in the center of the city. The main avenues would be 132 feet wide, and the cross streets 82 feet wide, and many parks and playgrounds.

Within two years Far West was the largest city in Northwest Missouri, with a population of 3,000, eight stores, two hotels, six blacksmith shops, a school, four dry goods stores, three groceries and hundreds of log cabins.

A ceremony to lay the cornerstone of the great temple was July 4, 1838. One of the speakers was Sidney Ridgon, a silver-tongued orator. He proceeded to castigate the "Gentiles," some of whom were in the audience. Rigdon's speech triggered trouble for the Mormons.

Historians refer to subsequent events as the "Mormon war." There were frequent fist fights, sniping, looting and destruction of property, and at Crooked River the Mormons routed a detachment of the state militia.

In the fall of 1838, a group of Missourians attacked the Mormons at Haun's Mill and 20 Mormon men and boys were killed.

On October 27, 1838, Gov. Lilburn Boggs, who despised the Mormons, issued his famous "extermination order." It stated that the Mormons must be driven from Missouri and those who would not leave must be summarily shot.

Once again the Mormons' defender was Colonel Doniphan, who

8

was not a Mormon, but in charge of 500 Missouri militiamen. He refused to carry out the order.

The Mormon leaders realized that staying in Missouri would be futile and undoubtedly would lead to more bloodshed. They went to Illinois and founded a new city, named Nauvoo. Peace reigned only a short time. The Illinois "Gentiles" arrested Joseph Smith and his brother, Hyrum Smith, and other leaders and put them in jail at Carthage, a few miles from Nauvoo. On June 27, 1844, a mob stormed the jail and killed Joseph and Hyrum Smith.

Mormon Leaders finally realized that many persons in the Middle West never would accept them, and under the leadership of Brigham Young they went west and founded what is now Salt Lake City.

Just why the Missouri "Gentiles" hated the Mormons has never been fully explained. Maybe the Mormons pursued their religion a little too aggressively. They opposed slavery. Perhaps they worked harder in the fields, built stronger barns and produced larger crops. Militarily they were not belligerent, and in fact, epitomized the Biblical phrase, "Turn the other cheek."

In any event, if it had not been for the oppression of the Mormons by Missourians, this state might have continued as headquarters of the Mormon church and Far West might have become a thriving metropolis.

August 3, 1968

DUELING IN MISSOURI

The most famous duel in American history occurred in 1804 when Aaron Burr killed Alexander Hamilton. Undoubtedly the most famous encounter in Missouri was a pair of duels, the first 151 years ago Monday, between Sen. Thomas Hart Benton and the respected Charles Lucas of St. Louis.

Dueling was brought to Missouri by settlers from Kentucky, Tennessee and other Southern states, where the duel was a common recourse in arguments. But the brutal belligerence with which Benton pressed a quarrel to a fatal end caused him to suffer deep remorse the rest of his life and just before his death he destroyed all papers relating to the tragic affair.

The two men were lawyers in a court case in which they exchanged sharp words during the trial. The verdict was in Lucas's favor. The decision so angered the quick-tempered Benton that he issued a challenge. Lucas declined on the basis that differences in a court between lawyers were much different than private disputes.

The trial was in October of 1816. In the election of August, 1817, Benton sought to vote and Lucas inquired if he had paid his taxes in time to vote. An altercation occurred and Benton's language was so violent that Lucas had no recourse except to issue a challenge to a duel.

The duel was fought on an island in the Mississippi river that became known later as Bloody island. Col. Luke E. Lawless was second for Benton and Joshua Barton for Lucas. It was pistols at 30 feet.

Benton was wounded just below the knee and Lucas in the throat. Since Lucas was the challenger he was asked by Lawless if he was satisfied. He said he was not but when the bleeding from his throat increased, his physician argued against another firing. Lucas was asked if he wished a second meeting later, and he said he did not. Benton then said he was not satisfied and demanded a second meeting as soon as Lucas was able.

This occurred at sunrise September 27. A partial reconciliation had been effected by mutual friends but Benton was adamant. This time the distance was 10 feet. Benton was not harmed but the ball from his gun went into Lucas's left arm and lodged near the heart. He died within an hour but forgave Benton before his death.

The pistol Benton used was owned for many years by a family in Marshall, Mo. Benton is supposed to have borrowed it from Gen. Thomas A. Smith, a brother of John Smith T, the famous duelist who is reported to have killed 10 to 15 men in duels.

It is not known for certain when the first pistol duel was fought in Missouri, but the first of record, and on Bloody island, was in 1810 between Dr. B. G. Farrar and James A. Graham. The last is believed to have been around 1881 near Mt. Vernon between two doctors.

The name, Bloody island, was not attached until 1831 when Spencer Pettis and Maj. Thomas Biddle dueled at five feet and killed each other.

The island began as a sandbar. Then weeds, cottonwoods, willows and sycamores began to grow on it. Since it was neither legally in Missouri nor Illinois there would be no prosecution of the duelists.

However, the Benton-Lucas duel shocked the public and in 1822 the Missouri Legislature passed a law seeking to stop dueling. The law disqualified a man from office who fought a duel; required judges to instruct grand juries to investigate reported duels and duelists; required judges to bind a man to keep the peace if he was suspected of fomenting a duel and required every civil and military officer and lawyer to take an oath that he had not and would not take part in a duel.

August 10, 1968

JOHN CHAPMAN

One of the most charming, unusual and somewhat controversial personalities in America during the last century was a man named John Chapman. If that doesn't ring the historical bell, how about Johnny Appleseed?

Many historians say he never was in Missouri. Others, with perhaps more evidence, argue he was. In any case, his cause, the planting of apple trees, took hold in this state in a big way. James Stark, who arrived in 1816 with apple cuttings in his wagon, started the nursery which developed and distributed that most famous eating apple, the Delicious.

John Chapman was a strange mixture of plant nurseryman, herb doctor, military hero and religious enthusiast. Behind the legends and rumors about him are some concrete facts:

1. He did distribute apple seeds and his name was John Chapman.
2. He was born at Leominster, Mass., September 26, 1774.
3. There is a monument in Mansfield, O., with the inscription: "To the memory of John Chapman, best known as Johnny Appleseed, Pioneer Nurseryman of Richard County from 1810 to 1830."

There are stories from pioneers in St. Charles County, Missouri, that Johnny Appleseed visited them. Maturin Bouvet, an escapee from the French Revolution, who came to Missouri with several others and settled near what is now New London, related there was a knock at the fort door one night, and that when he answered a gaunt stranger greeted him in Anglo-Saxon sing-song: "I sow while others reap; be sure my warning keep; Indians will come by break of day, Indians hunting scalps I say."

Then he left. The Indians came and tried unsuccessfully to capture the fort. There are other stories that he warned whites of impending attacks by the Indians, although he wandered unmolested among the Indians, lived with them, ate their food and adopted some of their customs.

He is supposed to have married an Indian girl in Ralls County, Missouri, lived there for awhile and then suddenly disappeared.

One story is that he was engaged to marry Sarah Crawford of Kentucky, and that she died on the wedding night. His grief unbalanced his mind and in his delirium he was called by the Lord as a harbinger of peace to the West and that those who followed might reap the benefit of his sowing. So he went to the orchards, gathered a bag of apple seeds and began his mission.

11

Whatever the truth of these stories, there is no doubt John Chapman was a wandering man, friendly with all. He spread the gospel of Emanuel Swedenborg, helped pioneers in house raisings, planted corn with the Indians and was believed to have a mystic ability to converse with the denizens of the forests.

He started his first nursery six miles south of Warren, Pa., and a few years later, still in his 20s, he went to Franklin, Pa., 50 miles south. Then he began to move around, distributing the apple seeds, and now and then pennyroyal, wintergreen and hoarhound.

He liked the outdoors and cared little for his dress. At times he appeared gruff but upon learning that a teen-age lad was now the head of the family because of the father's death, Chapman not only gave many seeds of all kinds but plowed the ground and helped to cultivate the crop later.

Such writers took cognizance of him as Carl Sandburg, Rosemary and Stephen Vincent Benet, Edgar Lee Master, Vance Randolph, Louis Bromfield and Vachel Lindsay. Several poets compared him with Walt Whitman, Thoreau and others, a friendly man with a blithe spirit. They said then that he symbolized the spirit of the new democracy.

August 17, 1968

BETHEL COMMUNE

One of the major social-economic-political developments in the last century in this nation was the establishment of communes in various parts of the United States.

There were the Shakers, the Harmonists, the Separatists of Zoar, the Perfectionists, the communities of Robert Owen, Brook farm, the Icarian community, the Altruist community at St. Louis, the Home Employment company at Long Lane, Mo., the Friendship Community in Dallas County and one with the most fascinating name, the Fanatical Pilgrims at New Madrid, established in 1817.

Missouri's best known community of this type was Bethel, on the North river in Shelby County and 48 miles from Hannibal.

The main settlement in Shelby County consisted of 3,536 acres of land, and while Bethel was the major center there were nearby satellites of Elim, Hebron and Mamri. In Adair County, not far from Kirksville, 731 acres of land comprised the communal area and the major town was Nineveh.

Bethel existed from 1844 to 1879, and while there was a constitu-

12

tion drawn up and passed, the founder, Dr. William Keil, paid no attention to it.

The people were almost all Germans and there were no Jews or Catholics. They could dress as they wished. Drones and laggards did not last long. A treasurer took charge of all funds. There was a common storehouse and commissary that doled out the necessities. An overseer checked the clothing needs of every family in the spring and fall and distributed what was needed.

Bethel was self-sufficient except for drugs and medicines. There was a water mill, tailor shop, tannery, glove and shoe factories, whisky distillery, laundry, a hat factory and thousands of acres in farm land.

There was little amusement except for concerts by the Bethel band, occasional dances and observance of Easter, Pentecost and Christmas.

Keil was born March 6, 1812, in the Erfurt district of Prussia. Little is known of his childhood but as an adult he was a burly man with blue eyes, white hair and a beard. He was moody and excitable, and a scholar of the Bible.

Keil preached every two weeks, and woe to the man who did not appear in church. But there was no baptism or observance of the Lord's supper in the church.

In 1855, it was agreed that a second "Bethel" would be established in Oregon. Keil had talked about going "across the plains" and beginning a new commune. His son, Willie, obtained a promise from his father that he could accompany them.

At 19, Willie died, and his grief-stricken father carried out the promise. Willie was placed in a lead casket filled with preservative alcohol. On May 23, 1855, the cortege left Bethel. There were 24 covered wagons following the wagon-drawn hearse; 250 men, women and children, and as they left Bethel they sang, "Das Grab ist tief und stille," or "The grave is deep and still."

On December 26, 1855, between Menlo and Ramond in Washington, Willie Keil was buried with elaborate ceremonies.

August 24, 1968

MEREDITH MARMADUKE

The Marmaduke family of Saline County in the last century was well known and prominent throughout Missouri, able and industrious and possessing many other diversified attributes.

The family was the only one in Missouri in which both father and

13

son served as governors. John Sappington Marmaduke was elected governor in 1884.

Meredith Miles Marmaduke was born 177 years ago last Sunday in Westmoreland County, Va., and when the War of 1812 started he raised a regiment in his county, received a colonel's commission and served with distinction throughout the war. He was only 21 when the war started.

After the war he remained in Westmoreland County, served as deputy United States marshal and clerk of the county court. The vast and mysterious West soon beckoned, although he wasn't certain where he wanted to go. Robert S. Garnett of Essex County, Va., a friend, wrote John Scott, at Ste. Genevieve, Mo., asking Scott to give Marmaduke whatever help he could.

Garnett referred to Marmaduke in his letter as "a gentleman of great respectability." Marmaduke reached St. Louis, but instead of turning south to Ste. Genevieve he kept traveling west until he reached Franklin, Mo.

He was handsome and aggressive and could make friends easily. One of his first favorable moves was to marry Lavinia Sappington, daughter of the famous Dr. John Sappington who discovered the medical efficacy of quinine and made a fortune. Marmaduke and Lavinia had three boys and seven girls.

Marmaduke became almost instantly aware of the potentialities of Santa Fe trade, organized companies and made several trips from Saline County to Santa Fe. He formed a partnership with his father-in-law who undoubtedly advanced some money for the first few trips.

Marmaduke's diary account of his trip in 1824 told of 81 persons and two slaves, with one small cannon, numerous rifles and hand weapons, 200 horses and trading merchandise valued at $30,000, making up the caravan. He almost always came back with Mexican silver dollars, jennets, the original breeding stock of the famous Missouri mules, and some merchandise. Marmaduke had a sharp eye for business. He noted the Mexican and Spanish women liked large, black silk veils, or mantillas, and on the next trip took a batch of them and profited handsomely.

After several trips Marmaduke had become a fairly wealthy man, bought a large tract of land five miles west of Arrow Rock and began farming on a large scale.

In 1840 he was elected lieutenant governor of Missouri, Thomas Reynolds winning the top spot. On February 9, 1844, Reynolds committed suicide and Marmaduke succeeded to the governorship. Marmaduke served less than a year but he set forth many recommendations that his successors carried through.

He was a candidate to succeed himself but a serious factional fight developed within the Democratic party, and rather than force an outright split he withdrew in favor of John Cummins Edwards, who was elected.

August 31, 1968

MEREDITH MILES MARMADUKE

Credit: State Historical Society of Mo.

NATHANIEL TUCKER

Long before the Civil war erupted, a prophetic book about secession was written by Nathaniel Tucker, very likely while he was a resident of Missouri.

Tucker's book, "The Partisan Leader," made a grave impression on the South and was used by the North after the war broke out to show that Southerners long had planned to secede.

Tucker was born 184 years ago yesterday in Chesterfield County, Virginia, was graduated from William and Mary College in 1801 and was admitted to the bar. He practiced law in Viginia until 1815 when he moved to St. Louis.

Tucker, who was related to the famous John Randolph of Roanoke, Va., was a classical scholar and was regarded as a very able lawyer. Three years after arriving in St. Louis he was appointed circuit judge. He resigned this post in 1826 for some unexplained reason, then said he would run for Congress but he could not get enough party endorsements. A short time later he moved to Saline County and lived on a farm near Jonesboro.

In 1830 he married Lucy Ann Smith, daughter of Gen. Thomas A. Smith, who had lent his pistol to Sen. Thomas Hart Benton in the dueling death of Charles Lucas. Smith had retired from the Army and directed the United States land office at Franklin. Tucker's circuit was in St. Louis and St. Charles Counties and he lived at Florissant during his tenure.

On this farm he is supposed to have cut off a giant sycamore tree 10 feet from the ground and then hollowed out a space 8 by 10 feet that he used as a library or office. It is here that he is believed to have written "The Partisan Leader, a Tale of the Future," and a second book, "George Balcombe."

He returned to Virginia in 1833 to become dean of the law school of William and Mary college, a post which his father, J. St. George Tucker, had held.

The National Intelligencer began printing "The Partisan Leader" in 1835 or 1836. Then it came out in book form under the name of "Edward William Sidney." The book bore the "publication date" of 1856, which was the prophecy by the author when secession would begin. Tucker used a pseudonym.

The book predicted the formation of the Southern Confederacy 25 years (1836) before the Civil war. It predicted that Virginia would

17

NATHANIEL TUCKER   Credit: State Historical Society of Mo.

lead the secession movement and then be followed by other Southern states.

There were several basic points, one being the encroachment of federal authority upon the states which Calhoun and Randolph fought aggressively.

The book predicted a 3-term President, giant growth of federal patronage, increased power of big business in the North that gradually would engulf the South, circumvention of the Constitution and eventual eradication of states' rights.

Secession, according to the book, was the only answer, followed by the signing of a treaty with England and a favorable tariff agreement with England and other nations which would overcome the industrial advantages of the North.

The book actually portrayed secession after Federal toops had pushed to the Virginia borders to "regulate" elections. Tucker's major argument was the right of the South to self-government rather than the right to keep slavery. The book was widely circulated in the South and aroused considerable controversy.

Northern leaders knew about the book long before war started and, in fact, used it to some advantage when the war did begin. It was reprinted by some Northern publishing houses as proof that the conflict was no sudden outbreak, that it had been long (25 years at least) in planning, consideration and preparation.

The basic strategy was to convince Northerners that the South had been slyly and craftily planning to defeat the North. One explanatory introduction to the book stated:

"The reader will learn from the following pages that the fratricidal contest in which this country has been led is not a thing of chance, but of deliberate design, and that it has gradually been in preparation for almost 30 years." It went on to charge that the plotters lived in Virginia and South Carolina.

September 7, 1968

LIBERATION ATTEMPTS

George Thompson paddled his skiff close to the Missouri side of the river and watched his companions, James Burr and Alanson Work, go ashore.

Several slaves suddenly appeared along the bank and shouted to Thompson if he was a friend. He replied affirmatively. Suddenly white men appeared and arrested Thompson. His companions already were under arrest.

It was July 12, 1841, and one of the highly dramatic and emotional pre-Civil war incidents had begun.

Work was from Connecticut, Burr from New York and Thompson from New Jersey. It was only by coincidence that they happened to get together at the Mission Institute near Quincy, Ill. They were among thousands joining organizations that promised liberty to the slaves.

Missouri was not a Southern state in the sense of large plantations and numerous slaves, but some segments of the North regarded it as such.

Nevertheless, there were many attempts, and several successful ones, to free or liberate slaves from Missouri to Illinois. The Rev. Moses Hunter, a Congregational minister from New York, visited the institute, became interested and promoted an "underground railroad," which was to liberate slaves.

Thompson, Burr and Work had the same strong feeling about slavery, and were determined to do something about it. There is no record of how many slaves they brought across the river into Illinois before they were caught.

On this particular occasion they agreed to bring across slaves belonging to William R. N. Woolfolk and a "Mr. Boulware." One of the slaves told his master and the three were arrested and tried in Palmyra.

Thompson was regarded as the ringleader. They were reviled by small groups and taunted and called "nigger stealers." The three men had never been in trouble and were not criminals. J. R. Abernathy, the circuit attorney, and his assistants, J. B. Crockett and Thomas L. Anderson, were puzzled as to what charge to file.

According to Missouri law, slaves were property. No Supreme Court decision was necessary to establish that. The problem in the trial was that Missouri had no law against enticing slaves to leave their masters.

The defense attorneys contended that their clients were not guilty of larceny; no attempt had been made to carry off "property" the accused had used no force and they had no goal to profit from the incident. The legal question then turned, not on whether slaves were property, but whether the action of the three men constituted larceny.

However, they were charged with "stealing property." Samuel T. Glover and Uriel Wright of Palmyra, Mo., and Calvin A. Warren of Quincy, Ill., were defense attorneys.

The trial began September 10, 1841. The courtroom was crowded with people, and the defendants were the object of jeers and obscenities. Armed groups waited outside the courtroom to hang the three if the jury acquitted them, and the jurors feared for their lives.

The court held that an agreement to meet the slaves for the purpose of aiding them in attaining their freedom, and their meeting under that agreement, constituted a "taking," or larceny.

Incidentally, the court allowed hearsay evidence. Among the owners of the slaves were William Dingle, William Brown, R. N. Woolfolk and a Mr. Boulware.

On September 13 the jury deliberated an hour and returned a guilty verdict, assessing 12 years in the state prison to each.

The crowd shouted enthusiastic approval of the verdict. The armed men, many belonging to the Marion association, an anti-abolitionist organization in Marion County, began to disperse. The jurors were congratulated. One of them was John M. Clemens, father of Mark Twain.

The three received far better treatment in prison than they had in the Palmyra jail. They were obedient prisoners and because of exemplary behavior received special privileges.

Two governors, probably worried about public reaction, refused clemency. The third, Gov. John C. Edwards, pardoned Work, whose 4-year-old daughter had died a few months after his imprisonment and whose large family was destitute, on January 20, 1845, on the condition that he return to Connecticut. Edwards pardoned Burr a year later and on June 24, 1846, he pardoned Thompson.

September 14, 1968

AUSTIN AUGUSTUS KING

Austin Augustus King served Missouri as governor in one of its most trying periods, from 1848 to 1853, when Missourians were slowly moving from the thinking of a Southern state to that of a border state. King was one of the best examples of this tenuous change.

He was born in Washington County, Tennessee, 166 years ago today. At the age of 28 he came to Missouri, and at Columbia formed a law partnership with John B. Gordon. He was elected to the Legislature from Boone County in 1834, re-elected for a second term and then moved to Ray County, where he became circuit judge. In 1848 he received the Democratic nomination for governor and defeated a close friend, James S. Rollins, the Whig candidate.

Although King moved slowly through the transitional stage on the slavery matter, his record as governor is regarded by most historians as a good one. Some of his major accomplishments are:

1. He was the author of the Missouri code of civil procedure passed by the Legislature in the first year of his administration.

2. At a special session near the end of his term he pushed through a law granting financial aid to the Pacific, Iron Mountain and North Missouri railroads and four other lines, which help Missouri would not have developed economically and industrially as fast as it did.

3. He pushed for better educational facilities and probably was best known for this accomplishment. He and Rollins, as well as many others, worked hard for the establishment of the University of Missouri, and later for expansion of the university.

He recommended that a state department of education be established and that every county have a county superintendent of schools. He supported the the establishment of colleges for women in Columbia, and was a trustee of Richmond college in Ray County. Later a public school in Ray County was named for him.

Governor King's change of attitude on slavery was similar to that of other Missourians; but because he was a public figure, for more than two decades, he received more attention. King, a slaveholder, was elected to Congress in 1862 as a "Union Democrat." The "Union Democrats" opposed the extension of slavery. But when he voted for the constitutional amendment to abolish slavery, many constituents and friends wrote him it was political suicide.

In Congress he was one of 11 Democrats who voted for submission of the amendment abolishing slavery. His district in the Ray County area was heavily pro-slavery, and he was defeated for re-election; but he sounded a warning that the Union must be preserved at all costs.

He was a Benton Democrat and committed the same kind of "political suicide" as did the ebullient "Old Roman," Sen. Thomas Hart Benton, who was more than a decade ahead of his party on the slavery issue. His friend Rollins was of a different political party; but serving together in Congress, both supported President Lincoln in the Black Hawk war and finally found themselves agreeing on the slavery question 30 years later.

King had many other accomplishments. He pushed through the formation of a reform school for boys in St. Louis in 1851. When cholera struck St. Louis and other cities he quickly marshaled doctors, nurses and others to fight it. The plank road mania began in his administration and he gave it some impetus. When Caldwell County was organized in 1836, the first town, Kingston, was named for him.

Austin King's first wife, Nancy Harris Roberts, whom he married in 1827 in Jackson, Tenn., bore eight children. His second wife, Martha Woodson, married in 1858 at Kingston, bore two daughters.

He died in 1870, six days after being stricken in a courtroom where he was counsel for a client. His grave in a Richmond cemetery is marked by a momument the state erected in 1904.

September 21, 1968

GOVERNOR AUGUSTUS KING   25   Credit: State Historical Society of Mo.

STERLING PRICE

GENERAL STERLING PRICE

Union forces under the command of Gen. Thomas Ewing were thin in Missouri. Confederate scouts estimated them at fewer than 1,500 men. About half of them had military training.

The South decided on a gamble. Gen. Kirby Smith and others selected Price to lead an army of 12.000 men, in three divisions headed by Gen. John S. Marmaduke, Gen. Jo Shelby and Gen. James F. Fagan. They left Princeton, Ark., on August 30, 1864, marching to a brass band that was probably playing "The Yellow Rose of Texas," "Listen to the Mocking Bird" and other Southern songs.

Price marched north, foraging and living off the countryside. Union scouts got word of Price's movements to Gen. W. S. Rosecrans at St. Louis. General Rosecrans ordered Ewing and his men to Pilot Knob, near Ironton in Southeast Missouri, to fight a delaying action.

General Marmaduke's men looted Fredericktown. Price's band boomed during the day and several hundred recruits joined the Rebels. Price knew Ewing had a small force and that a quick victory by his men would have psychological effects. Then they could move through several rich counties, take Jefferson City and sweep the rest of Missouri.

Ewing reached Pilot Knob and checked the terrain. The key to his defense was Fort Davidson, just west of the Knob, and nearby was Shepherd's mountain.

Fagan's troops, coming north from Arcadia, tried twice to force a gap and were thrown back. Marmaduke gained a spot on Shepherd's mountain, then was thrown back.

The war trumpets were sounding the death knell of the Confederacy in 1864. In the East, Grant's new war strategy of feint and hold was providing dividends. General Lee was being pinned down. Vicksburg had been won, cutting the Confederacy in two. Sherman had sliced his way to the sea. Virginia was starving. There wasn't much hope left for the Confederacy.

The Union's Western flank was exposed. This was Grant's great gamble. Leave it exposed. The Eastern-Southern strategy was more important.

There were many Confederates ready to pounce on that exposed Western flank. Gen. Sterling Price, Gen. Jo Shelby and some of the other Missourians were spoiling for a fight with the North. Price's friends wanted Richmond to place him in charge of the Missouri and Arkansas forces. Some even thought Price should succeed Gen. Robert E. Lee or President Jefferson Davis.

Although Ewing had the advantage of two hills, he surprised the Confederates by sending two companies down through Ironton toward Fredericktown. They ran into Fagan, who drove them back into Ironton. Ewing then sent a stronger force, with both artillery and cavalry, and forced Fagan's army back into a gap. Fagan's troops couldn't take the fire of the more experienced Unionists.

There were other skirmishes. On September 27, Price surrounded some of Ewing's troops. But Ewings's best sharpshooters had several hundred rounds of ammunition.

Rebels died in groups trying to gain the hills. In 20 minutes more than 1,000 officers and men under Price were killed. Ewing had lost about 200 men. It ranked with the greatest carnage in the entire war, in the number killed per minute.

Unitl now it was Ewing's victory, but he realized it would be lost sooner or later. Cannon wheels were muffled, a small squad blew up the magazines and Ewing's army retreated. Near Harrison he erected crude defenses and for three days kept Price's force at bay. On the fourth day Union troops from Rolla relieved his battle-weary men and Price moved on eastward.

It was a crushing defeat for General Price. His first and last attempt at capturing the state for the Confederacy had resulted in failure. Particularly humiliating was the fact that a small army had wreaked havoc on a force considerably greater. Confederate losses at Pilot Knob probably helped the North in obtaining a victory four weeks later in the Battle of Westport.   September 28, 1968

JEFFERSON CITY

Jefferson City officially became Missouri's capital 142 years ago last Tuesday on October 1, 1826. St. Charles had been the capital.

There was some confusion among the commissioners and trustees charged with selecting and platting a capital site, and there were many maneuvers by real estate promoters to place the capital elsewhere to their own financial advantage. There was one certainty: It had to be on the Missouri river. Potential locations were Columbus, near the mouth of the Osage; Smithton, which is now Columbia; Bluffton, Persia and others.

Congress, in granting statehood, required "four entire sections of land" for the establishment of a permanent seat of government for Missouri and that a capitol be built thereon. "No place shall be selected which is not situated on the banks of the Missouri river within 40 miles of the mouth of the Osage," according to the 1820 Constitution.

After arguments about the precise meaning of "four entire sections of land," the commission chose parts of ten sections, to total four, at what is now Jefferson City. The Legislature ordered the platting of the city and Major Elias Bancroft platted the site.

Jefferson City, sometimes referred to as a "little San Francisco" because of its many hills, was platted in 120 days despite the pessimistic predictions of some that the land, because of its hills, couldn't be platted at all. The trustees were authorized to sell 200 town lots to the highest bidders and then to call for bids to build the "State—House," as it was referred to in the public announcement.

The specifications called for a "good brick building," 60 by 40 feet, the foundation "well laid in limestone, sand and mortar," and "sunk as deep into the ground as the trustees think necessary." There would be three rooms on the first floor, for state officials, and rooms on the second for the legislature; also eight fireplaces.

Daniel Colgan, Jr. and James Dunnica got the contract for $18,573. The 200 lots brought a total of $6,540.75, or an average of $32.70.

In laying off the streets, many were named after Presidents and governors. It is believed to have been the first town in the nation to be named after Thomas Jefferson. In 1829 it became the seat of Cole

31

County, so named for Stephen Cole, one of the Missouri territory's famous pioneers.

Just how many real estate disasters occurred prior to the actual selection of the site is not known, but one was of special interest. The early discussions, rumors and reports indicated the capital would be at the confluence of the Missouri and Osage rivers, several miles east of the present site. Also, the capital would be named, "Osage."

The Boonslick Advertiser published a layout of the capital showing "wide streets, large squares for public buildings and a street a mile long paralleling each river front."

The tremendous potentialities for a port and shipping center were noted partly because the Osage "flowed from the land of cotton" and therefore would be free of ice most of the time. The newspaper failed to point out that the city and port might be locked in during severe winters by ice on the Missouri river.

Nevertheless, lots for "Osage" were actually sold in Franklin and St. Louis, and among many buyers were Alexander McNair, the first elected governor; Col. Richard Gentry of Columbia, Missouri's hero of the Seminole war, Sen. Thomas Hart Benton and others.

William Scott, an aggressive real estate agent, announced on February 4, 1823, when lots in Jefferson City first were advertised, that he would sell lots just across the river and establish another city to be named Washington. This was the site of the present Cedar City.

October 5, 1968

MOSES AUSTIN

Several years before 1780 there was a paragraph in an Eastern newspaper saying that there was enough lead in the Missouri territory to furnish every nation in the world. The date and newspaper information have been lost but Moses Austin was impelled to come to Missouri to find out about the newspaper claim.

Moses Austin's contributions are many:

*He revolutionized the lead mining industry in Missouri.

*He sank the first deep mine shaft in Missouri.

*He built the first reverberatory furnace west of the Mississippi river.

*He established the town of Potosi, named after the famous South American silver mine, and it became the seat of Washington County.

*He founded Herculaneum and is supposed to have named it

32

because the edges of the limestone strata were worn away as to resemble seats of the amphitheater of the ancient city near Naples.

*And Moses Austin was the "grandfather" of Texas.

And yet, Austin died a tired and bankrupt man.

Austin was born in Durham, Conn., October 4, 1761. He became the proprietor of a dry goods firm in Philadelphia, started a branch of the business in Richmond, and in 1789 became drawn to the lead mines in Southwest Virginia. In 1784 he married Maria Brown of Philadelphia.

On his arrival in Missouri, he received a land grant of one square league from the Spanish governor of Louisiana that included the famous Mine a Breton.

Austin then showed what Yankee ingenuity could do. Mining methods were simple—spades, picks, shovels, a windlass and tub and diggings not more than 10 feet. He pushed to 40 feet or more, then 80 feet.

The town of Herculaneum grew. A sheet lead and shot factory, sawmill, flour mill, blacksmith shop, general store, furniture store, clothing store and a shoe factory employing 50 persons were built.

J. N. Maclot built a shot tower in 1809 that provided much of the lead and shot ammunition for the War of 1812. Austin built one in 1810. The limestone bluffs of 100 feet provided a shot fall. Workmen melted the lead at the top and poured it over the edge in driblets into a receptacle of water below. The lead hardened into round pellets downward and the cold water solidified the ammunition.

The largest shot, about cannon size, required a 140-foot drop, the smaller 90 feet. After the lead was prepared, one man could smelt and cast about 4,000 pounds daily.

His 80-foot mine shaft astounded miners. Some were afraid to go down that far. Most had worked only in the summer because they were afraid of Indians in the winter. Austin changed all that.

One historian has said, "During his (Moses Austin) 24 years in Missouri, (1797-1821) he probably added more to the wealth of Missouri than any other man unless it be one of the leaders of the fur companies."

By 1812 Austin had become involved in many enterprises. He helped to organize the Bank of St. Louis in 1816 and it failed in 1819. A depression followed the War of 1812. He found it difficult to collect on his deliveries of lead and shot.

Austin was financially ruined at the age of 58, an age when most men would feel it was hopeless to pursue any other enterprise.

He had heard about the Southwest, the area now known as Texas, Arizona and New Mexico. He thought it should be colonized. He rode to San Antonio and asked the Spanish governor permission to bring 300 families for colonization. His reception was cold and as he prepared to leave he encountered an old friend, Baron de Bastrop, whom he had met in New Orleans many years before. The baron interceded but promised nothing.

The almost 60-year-old Austin started home. He swam rivers and fought off wild animals, but the rigors were too much and he died of pneumonia at the home of a daughter in St. Francois County. He did not know that on the way permission for his colonization plan had been granted. Stephen Austin would carry out the plan. The latter became the founder of one of the principal colonies in the area now known as Texas or the "Father of Texas."

October 12, 1968

JEAN PIERRE CHOUTEAU

In this era there is a growing concern for disadvantaged minorities, including the American Indians. For more than two centuries a majority of white Americans regarded Indians as enemies, and obstacles to their progress.

It is worth recalling today that there were cases of trusting and brotherly relationship between a white man and Indians in the era when some pioneers said a "good Indian is a dead Indian." Take, for example, the friendship between the Osage tribe and Jean Pierre Chouteau.

Chouteau was given 38,000 acres of land belonging to the tribe for his kindness. He mastered the Osage language and in turn taught them English. The tribe expressed its thanks to Chouteau, in a document which read:

"Brother: As thou hast, since a long time, fed our wives and our children, and that thou hast always been good to us, and that thou hast always assisted us with thy advice, we have listened with pleasure to thy words; therefore take thou on the River Lamine the quantity of land which may suit thee, and no one can take it from thee, neither today nor ever. Thou mayest remain there, and thy bones shall never be troubled. Thou askest a paper from us, and our names, here it is. If our children do trouble thee, you have but to show this same paper; and if some nation disturbs thee, we are ready to defend thee. At the Fort of the Grand Osages, this 19th of March, 1792."

Jean Pierre Chouteau was born in New Orleans, October 10, 1758, the son of Pierre Laclede and Marie Therese Chouteau, who took him

JEAN PIERRE CHOUTEAU   Credit: Mo. Historical Society

to St. Louis in 1764. Most of the Chouteau family were leaders in one way or another; Jean Pierre seemed to be near the top. At 18 he was a merchant and trader. At 19 Spain granted him permission to trade with several Indian tribes, including the Osages. Chouteau traded with the Missouri tribes, then established a post in Salina, Okla., stayed for awhile and returned to Missouri.

The gift of the land in 1792 from the Osage tribe was probably the first, and certainly the largest, of its kind in the early history of the nation. Chouteau earned a reputation for fair dealing as a trader. Sometimes he told a tribe it had underpriced its pelts, and paid more. He lived and hunted with the Indians, became an honorary chief, sent them food and clothing.

In 1804 Thomas Jefferson appointed Chouteau as the first Indian agent west of th Mississippi. In 1806 he led a delegation of Osage Indians to Washington to lay the groundwork for Ft. Osage in what is now Northeastern Jackson County.

In November, 1808, Chouteau met with the Osage Indians of Ft. Osage and negotiated a treaty transferring Osage-owned lands along the Missouri river to the United States government. He also negotiated treaties between the government and the Osage in 1818 and 1825.

Although Jean Pierre Chouteau may be known best for his relationships with the Indians and fur company firm establishments (the St. Louis Fur company in 1809 and the American Fur company a few years later), he had other accomplishments as well. In 1809 he recruited the first cavalry company for the Territory of Missouri. In 1818 he contributed to the building fund of the first Catholic cathedral in St. Louis, and also to the Jesuit college which is now St. Louis University.

Another member of the family established a fur trading center on the Missouri river, at the bottom of Cliff drive; but Jean Pierre built the second brick house in the limits then of Kansas City. John McCoy built the first brick house.

Chouteau visited the land given him by the Osage tribe but did not live on it. However, his reputation with the tribe was so tremendous that there was no tinkering with the land claim. Spain confirmed it immediately after the Osage tribe sent the proper papers and so did Congress later after Missouri became a state. William H. Ashley, the first lieutenant governor of Missouri, bought the land from "Chief" Chouteau for $1.25 per acre.

The city now known as Kansas City was once termed "Chouteau's Landing." The Chouteau bridge commemorates the family. Jean Pierre Chouteau died July 10, 1849, in his 90th year, at his estate on the outskirts of St. Louis.

KICKAPOO INDIANS

One of the lesser native tribes, the Kickapoo, has an interesting but neglected history in Missouri. Some highlights:

*The tribe benefited greatly, perhaps better than any other Missouri tribe unless it be the Osages, from contact with Christianity, and Chief Keeanneekuk became a devout Christian and had a great influence on the tribe. The best authority for this observation is George Catlin, the famous artist, who visited almost all of the major tribes and did paintings of the chiefs and leading braves.

The Kickapoos were on friendly terms with their white neighbors. They hunted, trapped and cultivated land. But while not warlike, they could be fiercely defensive.

When Emmanuel Hesse and British officers began recruiting eight tribes for the assault on St. Louis in 1780, the Kickapoos were not enthusiastic although a few joined. This was when George Rogers Clark, brother of William Clark, and his hastily recruited "Missourians," whipped the British-led tribes.

Just 136 years ago last Thursday, at Castor Hill in St. Louis County, the Kickapoos signed a treaty with the United States ceding all their land in Missouri in return for 1,200 square miles of land north and west of Leavenworth.

The Kickapoos were of the Algonquin stock and are known to have become strong in Wisconsin and Illinois. One account says that in 1797 they established a village near Ste. Genevieve. Another relates that they first settled at the confluence of the Missouri and Mississippi rivers, in 1805. In 1808 there were about 20,000 Indians in Missouri—Osages, Missouris, Iowas, Sacs, Fox, Kickapoos, Shawnees, and Delawares. The French had gotten along fairly well with the tribes and so did the pioneers coming from the East.

From 1804 to 1820 there were three treaties with Indians regarding land in Missouri. In 1804 the Sac and Fox ceded land for which they received money and annuities, but no land. In 1808 the Great and Little Osage tribes ceded land for money, annuities and other considerations, and in 1819 the government ceded land to the Kickapoos in Missouri who were from Indiana and Illinois.

In 1812 a band of Kickapoos settled in what is now the southwest

38

part of Springfield, Mo., and from 1819 to 1832 they occupied the north half of what is now Greene County. In 1829-30 the first white settlers, John P. Campbell and William Fulbright, arrived to establish homes in the Springfield area.

When the Illinois Kickapoos went to Southwest Missouri in 1819 and afterward, the Osages began to complain to the government that they had sold their lands to the whites and did not like the idea of the Kickapoos coming in to kill their game and settle on the land. There were a few encounters and several Kickapoo families moved on to Kansas, many more in 1832 under a new treaty.

William Clark of Lewis and Clark fame found himself mighty busy for 31 years as federal superintendent of Indian affairs. He was friendly with the tribes, and except for some warpath "brush fires" kept the Missouri tribes from any large scale war except for an Osage uprising shortly before his death on September 1, 1838.

There were some Kickapoos in Greene County to lend a helping hand in 1838 to the Cherokees on the "Trail of Tears" tragedy, but like all other tribes the Kickapoos were gradually pushed westward and southwestward by those who taught them Christianity.

really?
The same ones?

October 26, 1968

DAVID MOORE

Missourians have made many efforts to preserve their heritage, but in one area they have been neglectful. They have failed to keep up the graves of Civil war veterans.

In visiting some of the national cemeteries, I was faintly aware of this but it was brought home more sharply at a recent meeting of the Civil War Roundtable of Kansas City.

Next to me was Dr. Leslie Anders, professor of history at Central Missouri State college, Warrensburg, and author of the recently published book, "The Eighteenth Missouri," an account of one of Missouri's most heroic Union regiments of that war. Dr. Anders mentioned the general neglect of the graves of both Union and Confederate veterans in many cemeteries and pinpointed it by an explanation he termed, "The Case of the Three Colonels." They are David Moore, Peter Madison Miller and Joseph G. Best.

"Our Missouri heritage is a rich and dramatic one," he said "and should impel everyone to see that the graves and headstones of these veterans are properly cared for. I have visited the graves of all three and their conditon is pitiful. There are surely a great many people

39

possessing family records, letters and diaries which would aid all of us interested in seeing that neglected graves, and reputations, get attention."

David Moore was a native of Ohio, son of Scot-Irish immigrants, who came to Clark County, Missouri, in 1850 at the age of 33. Seven miles south of the present county seat, Kahoka, he opened a general store and farmed.

He had been a captain in the War with Mexico and when the Civil war struck Missouri he directed formation of the 1st Northeast Missouri Home Guard and was elected its colonel. His men came from Knox, Clark, Scotland, Putnam and Schuyler Counties. Most of them were farmers and supplied their own horses and weapons.

Martin Green of Lewis County, a Confederate and brother of U.S. Sen. James S. Green, also raised a Rebel regiment in that same general area, and on August 5, 1861, the two clashed north of Athens, Mo., on the banks of the Des Moines. Moore scored a victory but only after he ordered a surprise bayonet charge that threw back the enemy in confusion.

Altough it was a minor skirmish, there were large Federal supplies stored at Keokuk, Ia.

Moore's regiment went on to distinguish itself at Corinth, Shiloh, Fort Blakely and other spots. At Shiloh, Moore's left leg below the knee was shot off. After hospitalization, he fitted himself with a wooden leg and returned to take command of his regiment. He was brevetted brigadier general for his gallantry at Shiloh. After the war he dabbled in politics and was elected in 1870 to the Missouri Senate.

He is buried at Canton, close to the grave of Senator Green, whose monument is of beautiful red granite and erected and paid for by the state of Missouri, but Moore's marker is eroded and leaning to one side.

PETER MADISON MILLER

Peter Madison Miller was born in Mercer, Pa., in 1811 and came to St. Louis 10 years later, served in the War with Mexico and was wounded at Buena Vista. In the 1850s he was elected mayor of Carondelet, became president of the Iron Mountain railroad and was elected to the Missouri Legislature in 1860.

He joined the 1st Missouri infantry as a captain, was cited for coolness under fire at Wilson's Creek and then became a colonel in the 18th Missouri infantry. He fought valianty at Shiloh and in other battles in the South and was brevetted brigadier general. He was elected

40

to the state Senate in 1864, serving at the same time his brother-in-law, Thomas C. Fletcher, served as governor.

He died in 1896 and is buried in beautiful Bellefontaine cemetery at St. Louis, the resting place for hundreds of famous Missourians. Surrounded by handsome monuments and marble shafts is the government issue marker, weather-beaten and leaning at an angle.

"It is the same, sad story with Joseph G. Best," Anders related.

He was born in North Ireland in 1838 and brought to this country as a baby, the family settling in Quincy, Ill. Later he moved to Scotland County, Missouri with his widowed mother.

He enlisted in David Moore's home guards as a private in 1861 and received a commission in company I of the 21st Missouri infantry, rising to colonel.

He also took part in some bloody battles, including Shiloh. After the war he married David Moore's daughter and became active in politics, first with the radical Republicans and then the Democrats. He was elected clerk of Scotland County in 1882. He was prominent in many organizations and activities of his general area.

He is buried in the Memphis, Mo., cemetery and his marker also is a government issue stone, weather-beaten and, like those of Moore and Miller, leaning slightly.

"These are examples of an almost wholesale neglect of our Civil war dead on both sides," Anders added. "Undoubtedly there are thousands throughout the state. I hope 'the Case of the Three Colonels' might lead to a general improvement."

November 2, 1968

BOATMEN'S NATIONAL BANK

What kind of label would you put on an organization that aimed a part of its first business service to rough riverboatmen, later opened an exclusive ladies department and now has enough valuable paintings, prints and engravings to launch an art gallery?

It's a bank! The Boatmen's National Bank of St. Louis, the oldest west of the Mississippi river, celebrated its 121st birthday recently and its general historic diversification has provided more than the usual interest in a banking institution.

Riverboatman Mike Fink didn't live long enough to become an early patron but many of his contemporaries undoubtedly did because George Budd, who launched the bank, had them in mind after learning that a young acquaintance planned to gamble one night on the levee.

"Save some of it," Budd suggested. He began to think about interest on deposits. The Bank of Missouri and private banks were unable to meet this need. Legislation was passed to allow George Budd and 14 associates to incorpoate as the "Boatmen's Savings Institution," and it opened for business October 18, 1847 at 16 Locust Street.

Budd's idea, as the name indicates, was to serve the boatmen and others who made up a large proportion of the laboring element there.

With somewhat unusual vision, the officers set aside Friday "for the female community," but Mrs. Colton marched into the bank on a Saturday, laid down $100 for deposit and thus broke the bank's first official rule. More women became patrons of the bank and many years later it opened a special department for lady depositors with a parlor, a maid in continual attendance and a special teller.

The idea of earning interest on investments was scoffed at by some bankers but at the end of the first month, Boatmen's secured a $1,000 city of St. Louis 6 per cent bond. George Budd's vision paid off and he served as director and trustee until 1873.

Since that opening day, Boatmen's bank has occupied six different locations in downtown St. Louis. Disaster struck in 1849 when the city was stricken with a cholera epidemic and a fire started on the steamer, "White Cloud," at the levee that spread to nearby buildings destroying 23 steamboats and 15 business blocks. The bank was untouched but crippled somewhat by a lack of business for awhile.

Shortly afterward it moved to No. 52 North Second street, staying for two years. Expansion brought almost all of the three moves in the first ten years. The bank stayed at Second and Pine streets from 1857 to 1891 and then built a swanky 7-story structure, regarded as one of the best bank buildings in the nation. Fire struck again in 1914 and it moved to the Monward building at Broadway and Olive.

The bank's art collection is undoubtedly the finest of any other bank or commercial business in the United States and better than many art galleries. Its value is estimated to be in the hundreds of thousands of dollars. In it are 300 separate pieces—oil paintings, water colors, engravings, lithographs, etchings, drawings and maps.

Three of the bank's best known oil painting are by George Caleb Bingham, Missouri's famous painter of the last century. They're from the artist's "Political Series,"—Stump Speaking, Verdict of the People and The County Election.

An oil painting, "Race of the Robert E. Lee and the Natchez," by Dean Cornwell, also hangs in the bank. It depicts the start of the race from New Orleans to St. Louis in 1870, won by the Lee in three days,

18 hours and 14 minutes, fastest record then for a commercial boat over that course.

The bank owns prints and engravings by John James Audubon and Carl Bodmer, water colors by John Rogers, Herbert M. Herget, Frederick Remington, Charles Marion Russell, and Alfred Jacob Miller, and numberous works by lesser known local and national artists.

November 9, 1968

COURTESY OF BOATMAN'S BANK

FRANZ SIGEL

Although historians have hung the not-too-complimentary tag of "master of retreat" on Franz Sigel, the aggressive little German played a far more important role in keeping Missouri in the union than his credits show.

He was born 144 years ago on November 18, 1824, in Sinsheim, Baden, and received a full military training.

In 1848 he took part in a revolutionary movement, served briefly as minister of war at Baden and then fled to Switzerland in 1849 ahead of the invading Prussian army. He went on to New York City and then to St. Louis.

There had been a large emigration from Germany around the middle of the last century and when war clouds threatened the nation around 1860 there were many German immigrants living in St. Louis. The Germans had fled from persecution in their native land and on that basic philosophy could not support slavery or the Confederacy. Sigel sensed a war of some sort was coming on. He began training a volunteer group of soldiers, mainly Germans. When Col. Nathaniel Lyon arrived in St. Louis he learned the small and nervous Sigel was ready to help. Sigel aided Lyon and Frank Blair in the capture of Camp Jackson and told Lyon he and his men were ready for any action necessary.

The historic confrontation occurred at Planters' House in St. Louis on June 11, 1861, when Lyon told Claiborne Fox Jackson, Missouri's secessionist governor, that "This means war."

Jackson and Gen. Sterling Price fled St. Louis aboard a special train to Jefferson City burning railroad bridges en route to forestall pursuit by Union forces. Lyon sent Sigel and his force southward to try and cut off the army under Jackson and Price and prevent a union of Missouri and Arkansas Confederates.

Sigel was too late for a complete success. In the "Battle of Carthage" that followed he was outnumbered 5 to 1. His little army hit hard but Sigel analyzed the possible outcome and staged his "masterful retreat." There is one salient facet to this "masterful retreat." If his army had been captured, he could not have joined Lyon at the Battle of Wilson's Creek.

Sigel's men were trounced at Wilson's Creek. Civil war historians have been arguing ever since whether the battle was a draw or victory for the South. Perhaps it was a tactical, but certainly not a strategic, victory for the Confederacy.

FRANZ SIGEL   Credit: State Historical Society of Mo.

Sigel was promoted to brigadier general after the battle of Wilson's Creek. This "master of retreat" never "ran" from a battle, even if he was outnumbered. And he was outnumbered several times—at the battles of Carthage, Wilson's Creek and Pea Ridge, Ark. In time Sigel was promoted to major general.

Before the second battle of Bull Run, Sigel was given command of one of the armies under General Pope. In this capacity he was given, and failed in accomplishing, the almost impossible task of dislodging Gen. James Longstreet from Bald Hill.

Sigel commanded the 11th corps in both the Antietam and Fredericksburg campaigns. In the Battle of the Wilderness he retreated from Strasburg in a tactical maneuver.

History hasn't forgotten the old "master of retreat." A monument has been erected to him on Riverside drive and a park in the Bronx has been named for him. More than two decades ago a plaque was erected at a downtown St. Louis site where the old "German Institute" once stood, a building Sigel taught in sometime in the 1850s.

November 16, 1968

CLAIBORNE FOX JACKSON

CLAIBORNE FOX JACKSON

The Congress of the Confederate States of America in Richmond, Va., officially admitted Missouri into the Confederacy 107 years ago next Thursday.

This event followed a series of actions in which the Union and the Confederacy jockeyed to win Missouri. The state had so-called "border rank" with Kentucky and Maryland, but Missouri was far more important to the contenders than the other two.

In retrospect it is difficult to understand how two of Missouri's outstanding leaders could have so badly misjudged the temper of Missourians about secession and staying in the Union. They are Sterling Price, former governor before the war and one of the state's most respected leaders, and Claiborne Fox Jackson, who was elected shortly before the war started as governor.

Jackson was born April 4, 1806, near Flemingsburg, Ky., and came to Old Franklin, Mo., in 1825. He later moved to Saline County and was elected to the Missouri Legislature in 1836. He served for several sessions, rose to political power and was elected governor in the 1860 campaign. Although Jackson was one of the Stanchest supporters of secession, probably next to General Price, he flew in the face of storm signals. He felt the pulse of Missourians and frankly admitted the state was not really secessionist, but in the next breath promised the state would secede within 30 days after the major break. His general outlook was tempered by the fact that he had lived in an area somewhat sympathetic to the South and that he had believed, as Sterling Price, that the legislative feeling was with the South.

He was tall, erect, a handsome man and fluent. He commanded respect. When President Lincoln called for Missouri troops, Governor Jackson tagged it an "unholy crusade." Neither the legislature, nor the new governor, Claiborne Jackson, paid any attention to the outgoing governor, Robert M. Stewart, who delivered some forthright ideas about the impending conflict, the best of which probably was, "The very idea of the right of voluntary secession is not only absurd in itself, but utterly destructive of every principle on which national faith is founded."

Jackson became governor shortly thereafter and said in his inaugural message, "Missouri will not be found to shrink from the duty which her position upon the border imposes; her honor, her interests and her sympathies point alike in one direction, and determine her to stand by the South."

When Mr. Lincoln requested four regiments from Missouri, Jackson said it was "illegal, unconstitutional and revolutionary in its objective, inhuman and diabolical."

Claiborne Jackson was adamant. He asked for a special assembly to determine Missouri's course. Not one delegate elected to this convention favored secession. The convention did not favor secession.

On August 5, 1861, Jackson at New Madrid, Mo., issued a proclamation that Missouri was an independent and sovereign state but the Confederate government was not quite ready to go along. Lt. Gov. Thomas C. Reynolds had issued an ordinance of secession July 31, but he and Jackson had not met nor conferred about the matter. Reynolds also gave Gen. Jeff Thompson military orders contrary to those issued by Jackson.

On August 20, the Confederate congress authorized negotiation of a treaty with Missouri, providing for admission to the Confederacy as soon as the Constitution was ratified. The secession Missouri legislature met at Neosho, October 21, took appropriate action and the following month Missouri became a member of the Confederacy.

Sometime in 1862 Jackson bought a home in Texas and moved his family there. He had set up temporary headquarters in Camden, Ark. In Marshall, Tex., he had conferred with the governors of Arkansas, Texas and Louisiana.

It is believed that Jackson had been suffereing from cancer. His condition became worse in November, 1862, and he died December 7, 1862, in a boarding house in Arkansas. He was buried in Little Rock and later reinterred in the Sappington cemetery near Arrow Rock.

November 23, 1968

COUNTY HISTORY

Missouri has an exceedingly rich and interesting history and many who write about it have lamented for many years that insufficient attention has been given it.

In the period after the Civil war, for about 25 years, there was a sort of frenzied rush by the counties to publish an official county history, and many excellent volumes were turned out. There are several gathering cobwebs either on library shelves or relegated to the junkpile.

Because there are cycles to so much human endeavor, Missouri writers of history are wondering if there is an approaching renaissance to the writing of county histories. The initial evidence is there. Will the movement continue and spread?

The first major endeavor occurred many months ago with publication of the Saline County history, a monumental 560 page, slick paper tome, 9 by 12 inches, with an attractive binding and many photographs and illustrations.

A. H. Orr, 93-year-old president of the Saline County Historical society, who was born and has lived on the same farm all his life, pushed the idea. It was a team job with four associate editors.

John R. Hall, associate editor of the Marshall Daily Democrat News for 40 years, and who died last summer at 75, wrote a lengthy contribution on Saline County government. He was from a prominent Saline County family and with Mr. Orr regarded as the outstanding authority on the county.

William Elder, vice-president in the county society and a teacher of history in the Marshall high school, and Mrs. Elder contributed the article on the history of Saline County schools.

The editors agreed that the backbone of history in a county lies in four major categories-cemeteries, churches, communities and schools, and for example, there are 100 cemeteries described, many churches, 40 communities and almost 50 schools. Among the communities there are Blue Lick, Fish Creek, Grand Pass, Pennytown, Rose Valley and White's Island to name a few with unusual names.

Two histories of Saline County have been written, the first in 1881 and the second in 1910. The material for this new one was voluminous, and Mr. Orr said in his preface, "In spite of all that has been done by the writers, they were unable to cover the county 100 per cent in their endeavor to obtain its history. It's a guess that there is enough material left uncontacted to make another volume of history."

Many counties have held off on such projects because of the enormous costs of paying writers, researchers, historians and the printers. Saline County may have paved the way because almost all of the work was done gratis. And why bring in ousiders? Mr. Orr contends, and quite correctly, that those who were born and grew up in a county or community know more about it than anyone else.

Jefferson County recently issued an attractive and interesting account of that county in a 198-page book which illustrates and documents 138 sites of importance. It has a different format than the Saline County document, going in more for pictures and illustrations of important sites with brief descriptions.

The county's history begins around 1770 with the arrival of the first white settlers, then the mining history that was started by Moses

Austin and the growing expansion. It is mainly a pictorial history showing the old Telegraph road, more than 100 homes and commercial buildings, numerous churches, and other historic spots.

A recent history was issued in Carroll County. Mr. and Mrs. Mahlon N. White, Clinton, publishers of newspapers in Clinton and Warsaw, as well as several books, recently published a Clinton-Henry County history for Haysler Poague, Clinton attorney, and also are working on the third reprint of the Henry-St. Clair County history that originally came out in 1883.

Dr. Richard S. Brownlee, director of the State Historical Society of Missouri, recently reported that many counties have re-published, or re-issued, histories written in the last century.

Some of the more interesting ones are about the counties of Buchanan, Dunklin, Gentry and Worth, Harrison and Mercer, Laclede and Lafayette. Several counties joined together almost a century ago and one of the largest was a history of Dade, Cedar, Dent and Barton Counties.

The Ramfre Press, in Cape Girardeau, has recently taken many of the old county histories and re-issued them in modern covers, type face and paper. Two have been on Jackson and Platte Counties. Another omnibus edition is on Franklin, Jefferson, Washington, Crawford and Gasconade Counties.

Dr. Brownlee, encouraged by the revival, has commented, "It is high time more Missourians, and more Missouri counties and cities, become increasingly interested in the rich background of this state."

SENATOR GEORGE GRAHAM VEST

History is sometimes fickle and will place the tag of immortality upon a person for some apparently vaporous and nebulous achievement that is completely overshadowed by a lifetime of plodding and concrete accomplishments.

Consider such a person.

He was the only Missourian to serve in both the Union and the Confederate Senates.

His first outstanding achievement in the United States Senate was the protection in 1831 of Yellowstone park from exploitation by private interests.

He insisted upon fair treatment for the Indians when the latter were gradually pushed west and southwest.

He foresaw American imperialism in the annexation of the Philippines.

Who was he? He was George Graham Vest, a lawyer whose immortality rests upon his eulogy to the dog that has been translated into hundreds of languages, and a statue to Old Drum now is a part of Warrensburg where Vest delivered the eulogy.

Vest was born in Frankfort, Ky., on December 6, 1830, received a degree from Centre college in Danville, Ky., and a law degree later from Transylvania university. A short time later he headed for California but the imp of fate, that would later co-operate with the fickleness of history, had different plans.

There was a stagecoach accident in Georgetown, then the seat of Pettis County, and the young man suffered a fractured leg. There was nothing to do for awhile, so he hung out his shingle. There are several anachronisms in his career and the first occurred in Geogetown.

The Southern-born and bred Vest defended a Negro slave charged with murder. The slave was acquitted, but he was promptly lynched and Vest was run out of town.

Vest went to Boonville, hung out his shingle and proceeded to become one of the outstanding lawyers of Central Missouri. He stumped the State for Stephen Douglas in 1860 and also was elected as Cooper County's Representative in the Missouri House of Representatives.

There was no doubt about his Southern sympathies in the Missouri Legislature. He introduced resolutions that denounced the coercion of the South and a bill that called for a state convention to determine Missouri's relations with the Confederacy.

War came. Claiborne Jackson, Missouri's elected secessionist governor, had to flee. The first Rebel legislature of Missouri was held at Neosho, Mo., and there Vest is believed to have written Missouri's Ordinance of Secession, passed October 28, 1861.

The Union forces drove the Rebels out of Missouri and the capital was established at Marshall, Tex. Vest went on to Richmond, Va., where he served three years in the Confederate House, then was appointed to the Senate.

After the war he returned to Missouri and opened a law office in Sedalia with Col. John F. Philips of the Union army. His friend, Francis Cockrell, who had distinguished himself with the Confederate army, formed a partnership with Thomas Crittenden, who also had a fine record with the Union army.

Whether this partnership started the idea of "working both sides of the street politically" is not known, but they obtained a big bag of political plums and plenty of law business.

Cockrell was in the United States Senate for 30 years and Vest for 24. Philips served in Congress, then on the state Supreme court and as United States district judge. Crittenden was attorney general and governor. Almost all held lesser offices.

Vest was about 5 feet, 6 inches tall and 110 pounds, and was called "Missouri's Little Giant" and "Missouri's Great Big Little Fellow."

Vest was a tremendous trial lawyer. His oratory could be attuned with a mellifluous finesse depending upon the background of the jury.

On the Philippine annexation he foresaw imperialism and said, "It is a wicked attempt to revolutionize our government and subsitute the principles of our hereditary enemies for the teachings of Washington and his assocciates."

He was a stanch Rebel but one of the first to introduce a bill for pensions for Union veterans in the Senate. He campaigned for free coinage of silver, opposed high protective tariffs, prohibition, woman suffrage and the direct election of United States senators.

As far as it can be ascertained, Vest was not necessarily a dog lover, nor an avid hunter, and he is supposed to have said that if he didn't win the case involving Old Drum he would "personally apologize" to every dog in the county. He of course, did win the case.

Despite the fact that George Graham Vest's lifetime achievements surpassed those of several other outstanding personalities, the cloak of immortality dropped over him at the beginning of a 5-minute eulogy before a hushed courtroom in Warrensburg when he softly intoned, "The one absolutely unselfish friend that a man can have in this selfish world, the one that never deserts him, the one that never proves ungrateful or teacherous, is his dog...."

December 7, 1968

PEDDLERS

First he came, bent over like an overfed bug, crawling through the green underbrush, seldom raising his head for directions, but pointed unerringly to his objective. He was a man, not a bug, loaded with innumerable household articles, farm tools, dress goods and many others. If he was brave in the wilderness, he either did not know it, or care.

In all probability he was one of the most important citizens of the early West. Military post leaders, Indians, pioneers, settlers and others

56

eagerly sought his counsel and information.

Today he would be called, perhaps, 'just a peddler."

Timothy Flint wrote, "There were no strangers in those days," and the peddler was a friend to all. Sometimes he helped slaughter the hogs and hang the shanks in the smokehouse and drink sassafras tea with people who were his friends and customers.

At first the peddler carried everything on his back. After selling enough merchandise, perhaps over a few years, he bought a horse or donkey. Then when affluence struck him he bought a cart. Name it and he had it; all kinds of goods such as calicoes, ginghams, silks, coffee pots, skillets and innumerable kitchen utensils, knives, forks, fancy scarves, bolts of gaily colored ribbon, handkerchiefs, razors, nutmegs, wax dolls, garden and field tools and many other articles.

The peddler was often regarded as a member of the family and stayed as long as he wished, but he seldom overstayed because he had to get on down the trail to the next family.

He never sought a quick sale. He might be a master at baking apple pies which always pleased the pioneer housewife and he could put the deft scalloped edge to the pie crust.

He helped milk the cows and went into the field to help with other chores. He was the "newspaper" of those early days, knowing everything about everybody in his general sales area, which might be hundreds of miles. He was probably the best listener of any era, and he could ask more questions than a news reporter.

He was always willing to dispense his information because he realized his was a two-way business. The family always gathered around to get his news and over tea, cider, coffee and other beverages he told them the news.

He knew the woods, the forests and the plains; the Indian tribes, when the creeks would overflow and how long ago Jim Jones's oldest child had recovered from the chicken pox.

He helped plant the corn, the peas and squash, pick the blackberries, huckleberries and fox grapes, the autumn pawpaws, persimmons, hickory nuts, walnuts, chinquapins and hazelnut.

He was the "roving ambassador" of the wilderness, a sort of legendary Johnny Appleseed.

The peddler also helped in the house raisings and house warmings, sap collections, sugaring-offs, plowing, corn shucking and sometimes judged at quilting bees and bonnet shows.

Although today's ambassador uses a diplomatic jargon that may not mean what it sounds like, the itinerent peddler spoke straight from the shoulder. He couldn't afford to lie or do otherwise.

He told settlers and military post commanders which Indian tribe was on the warpath. And by the same token he warned his own friendly tribes when their enemies were preparing for an attack on them.

With his long hair and sun-tanned swarthy skin he even resembled an Indian. Sometimes he slept overnight with a tribe. He also cooked venison, johnny cakes or fish timbales with his Indian friends.

He always had an ax or two of his own, ring mauls, wedges, niggerheads and gluts to help a new family cut down the trees, split the rails and build first an enclosure for their livestock and then a house and barn. He told them where the quail, turkey, deer and pheasant could be found nearby, which streams provided the best fish, where the ginseng weeds grew and the honey trees abounded.

These men, a breed historians have never properly and accurately catalogued historically, possessed an earthy outlook with an almost foolhardy courage and a belief that all men, white, black and red, were his friends. There was no room for hatred in his heart. Like the scouts and pathfinders, he seemed to synthesize his own brand of religion from the great outdoors and the men and animals that lived there.

Historians today cannot recall many of them. They defy identity. Historically they are faceless. They have vanished into history as casually as they melted into the forests after a sale and visit. There is no yardstick to measure their exact spot in history but they undoubtedly made many valuable contributions to the pioneers, the tribes and almost all else. In all conjecture it is a most important unwritten chapter in Missouri history.

December 14, 1968

JOHN SMITH PHELPS

Newspapermen who have covered Jefferson City are well aware of the fact than an incoming governor seldom has many kind words to say about his predecessor even though they may be of the same political faith, so when accolades are handed out there must be a disposition to regard them as sincere.

"My predecessor," wrote Gov. Thomas Crittenden, "was John S. Phelps, an able statesman, a distinguished politician, not only in Missouri but throughout our common country as he had served nine terms in Congress. It was somewhat embarassing to follow such a popular governor as he had made."

This proved, at the end of Crittenden's term, to be the

GOVERNOR JOHN S. PHELPS   State Historical Society of Mo.

compliments of one able governor about an equally able predecessor. Both men were far above the average as governors.

He was born in Simsbury, Conn., December 14, 1814 (or December 22, according to another source). He entered Washington college at Simsbury but left before his graduation. He was later awarded a degree, studied law in his father's office and was admitted to the Connecticut bar in 1835. He practiced briefly in Simsbury, married and decided to migrate westward. He and his bride stopped in the small settlement of Springfield, Mo.

It was necessary to pass the Missouri bar and he went to the home of Judge George Tompkins of the Missouri Supreme court in Cole County. The judge was sawing wood and the two sat down on a log and young Phelps passed his bar examination.

Tall and rather dignified, with a probing mind and a friendly personality, Phelps soon became a leading lawyer in Southwest Missouri. After two terms in the Legislature, he ran for Congress, was elected and later was re-elected for eight consecutive terms.

He was a popular and hard-working congressman. He pushed a bill for land grants to help build a railroad from Hannibal to St. Joseph, advocated an overland mail service to California and helped select the route. He served many years on the powerful ways and means committee and was chairman one term.

Phelps was a Douglas Democrat at the outbreak of the Civil War and a stanch supporter of the Union. He raised and commanded a regiment that achieved a reputation as tough fighters. He led it in the important battle of Pea Ridge and several other battles.

He and his men distinguished themselves at the battle of Wilson's Creek, and so did Mrs. Phelps. That was their home. She turned their home into a hospital caring for the wounded on both sides and the body of General Lyon. Congress was so moved, after the war, by her unselfish service and bravery that it granted her $20,000 with which to establish an orphanage at Springfield for the orphans of both Union and Confederate soldiers.

Phelps liked politics and sought to re-enter this arena after the war. He lost the race for governor in 1868 which did not surprise many because he had taken an aggressive stand, along with Frank Blair and others, against the odious test oath passed by the 1865 Convention and a part of the so called Draconian code.

But he bided his time, stayed around the fringes, worked for the party and tried the gubernatorial race again in 1875 and was given an overwhelming majority.

Governor Phelps seemed rather easy-going in many matters except as to crime and riots. There were labor troubles in St. Louis during his administration. He addressed a labor meeting there. He told the workers they had every right to organize but he also told them they had no right to riot, violate the laws, destroy property or attack defenseless persons.

He told certain members of the riff-raff fringe he would not tolerate such activities. They tried his mettle, this veteran of many bloody Civil war battles. He issued a proclamation demanding that "unlawfully assembled bands" promptly disband, that there must be no molestation of citizens, that the strikers and troublemakers return to work.

There was a strong citizen militia available. Phelps was ready to call out state guards. The threat passed although the workers continued peaceful picketing and organizing, but knew exactly where Phelps stood in the difficulty.

Phelps supported more money for public schools as governor, obtained an appropriation for a building to house the Supreme court, state library and office of attorney general. This was built in 1877 and occupied until the present structure was erected in 1905.

Phelps County was organized November 13, 1857, and named for him. A school and park in Springfield are also named for Governor Phelps. In 1863 Mr. Lincoln appointed Phelps military governor of Arkansas and at the same time named William F. Switzler, Columbia newspaper editor and historian, as military secretary of state for Arkansas. Phelps accomplished much in soothing war wounds and uniting the Northern and Southern factions in Missouri after the war.

He died November 20, 1886, in St. Louis and is buried in Hazelwood cemetery in Springfield.

December 21, 1968

LOHMAN'S LANDING

Missouri is rich in historical lore and memorabilia. Although now and then a building or other point of historical interest slips by us in man's quest for progress, citizens over the years have somehow managed to preserve and identify more than 100 important such sites throughout the state.

Old buildings crumble and fall. Some do so by their own accord. Others are purposefully torn down. Some that are beginning to fall are reconstructed. Others are completely rebuilt based on contemporary documents and artistic renderings of the original structure.

Lohman's Landing in Jefferson City may be an exception to this. It is one of the oldest buildings in Missouri. It's still usable.

The Missouri state department of buildings, headed by John Paulis, Jr., wants to tear it down. While state semantics usually cover an infinite number of meanings, Paulis plainly states the old building is standing in the way of modern progress, meaning he wants to use the land it occupies for a parking lot to service nearby state government office buildings.

The Cole County Historical society wants to save and preserve Lohman's Landing. Paulis insists that there is no state money available for the purchase, restoration and maintenance of the building. The society points out that restoration and maintenance would be up to the organization, that restoration would not be necessary and that it would take care of any maintenance it needs.

Lohman's Landing building is on the railroad tracks at Jefferson and Water streets in Jefferson City. It's a handsome, well constructed building with heavy stone walls and timber framing. It could become a popular museum or tourist center.

It was built in 1834. Richard Schackelford bought the property from Samuel Jamison and built the first section of the building. He sold this property, including ground and building, to Harry Colgan in 1836, who is supposed to have added some construction. The property was then sold to John Yount. By then it was the largest structure in Jefferson City. Because it was built along the water front, it was called "Jefferson Landing."

In 1852 Charles F. Lohman bought the property. He had come from Germany in 1844, stopped in St. Louis and married Henrietta Linsenbart. They planned to go to California but never got any farther than Jefferson City.

Lohman was aggressive and enterprising. He saw the possibilities of river business. He'd invested his money in several buildings in Jefferson City and when John Yount decided to sell the property Lohman bought it for $796.

He expanded the facilities of the building. He kept part of the first floor as a warehouse. On the second floor he spaced out rooms for travelers. Then he astounded the Western world by installing what would be called an elevator to the third floor. It was a chain and pulley type and the first in that part of the country.

Lohman's Landing was popular for almost half a century. It was a spot of teeming interest on the river and wagon traffic, a ferry station for traffic across the Missouri River. He charged you 12 cents to take a cow across, 37 cents with your horse.

Lohman was also a merchant. His advertisements boasted that one could buy "anything from baby stockings to shrouds at Lohman's."

There were from 25 to 50 steamboats stopping annually at Jefferson City with almost 50,000 tons of freight being loaded or unloaded on the landing plus thousands of travelers, some staying before going on to overland destinations.

In the 1850's, riverboats took off almost daily, or nightly, from St. Louis, with parties dancing, dining and drinking their way to Jefferson City. Wedding parties on riverboats were also popular affairs of the day.

Lohman's Landing was solidly built. It is 71 feet long and 47 feet wide, has limestone walls that are 18 inches thick. Its cross beams are made of hewn oak and are 13 inches wide and 8 inches thick. Still standing, sturdily constructed, there's not a single nail in the structure. It marks the heritage of a living that was both aggressive and graceful, that was productive and pleasant.

Outside of the usual day-to-day differences, the "Landing" has had a rather positive history. Yount sold it after the Monroe, a steamer, stopped with 150 Mormons, one or two with the cholera. Yount could not keep it from tying up. It was reported that 64 died in the city and that a death trench from the site of the building to the present Missouri Pacific Railroad station contains most of the graves.

December 25, 1968

REV. JESSE WALKER

The man was a complete picture of dejection, despair and discouragement. He sat limply in the saddle. His head was bowed. He was beaten. He clucked the horse to get moving and the Rev. Jesse Walker left St. Louis for South Missouri.

Walker had failed in his great goal to plant Methodism in the predominantly Catholic city of St. Louis. The man who became known as the "Father of Methodism" in Missouri had been successful in many other cities and towns of both Missouri and Illinois and St. Louis was to be his great victory.

And almost as John Wesley felt his heart "strangely warmed" at Aldersgate, England, in 1738, so something strangely inexplicable warmed Jesse Walker 18 miles south of St. Louis on that fall day of 1820.

"Was I ever before defeated in this blessed work?" he asked himself, and he answered his own question: "No! Did anyone ever trust

64

Credit: Buck Martin of the Star

WALKER

God and get confounded? Never! Then by the grace of God I'll go back and take St. Louis." He returned and "took" St. Louis. Perhaps it is one of the most dramatic stories of any religion that occurred at the beginning of the last century in Missouri.

Other than those in the larger villages and towns, there were no churches in Missouri and the circuit-riding preachers held services in the settlers' cabins. Walker didn't fear bad weather, hunger, Indians or the Devil. Many times he would rap on the door of a pioneer in a howling snow storm, enter more dead than alive, and exclaim, "I'm Jesse Walker, and I've heard there is a white family here and I wish to bring the gospel."

For many years he had made sporadic attempts to plant Methodism in St. Louis. His efforts were half-hearted. Again the grand rebuff.

A rather fearful hopelessness enveloped Walker. He murmured a silent prayer for his detractors, bowed his head and started south. That might have been the end of Methodism in St. Louis and in Missouri, but Walker decided to return to St. Louis and try preaching there again.

He prayed and then slept soundly that night. The next morning he simply began looking for a Methodist . . . just one solitary Methodist. He found one, but the man was afraid to publicly admit it. Walker left him after Biblical persuasion failed.

Then he rented an unfinished vacant house for $10 a month. He bought a few discarded benches. This he called a church. He began preaching, twice on Sunday and often in the evenings. He and his family slept on the cold floor of this house. Food was scarce.

But Jesse Walker vowed he would "take" St. Louis and this time he would not be denied. The half-dozen that began coming to listen to him swelled to a dozen and then more. Then he shocked the city by announcing he would teach the children of poor parents to spell and read five days weekly, also the children of slaves.

He asked for contributions to build a church. They began to come in. Lumber was contributed by a dealer. The women raised enough to pay for the pulpit. The stark and undaunted courage of Walker began to break through to St. Louisans.

He experienced an extremely warm feeling when a Catholic priest called him "Father Walker" on the street, stopped and chatted with him. Walker had wisely realized that the earlier opposition had not come from the Catholic leadership.

Within a short time his church was built including a chapel and school. There were 70 members.

Walker continued preaching in St. Louis, other Missouri towns and in Illinois, and did outstanding missionary work among the Indians. He died October 4, 1835.

REV. WILLIAM T. LUCKY

In any historical evaluation of Missouri associations, organizations and similar groups, the Missouri State Teachers association has made a tremendous impact upon the educational, cultural and moral life of this state in the past century.

The 112-year-old organization has been concerned with the lives of countless teachers and school pupils and has been instrumental in spending billions of dollars on public education. The association basically strives "to promote the sacred interests of education by uniting the different members, advancing their mutual improvement and elevating the profession to its just intellectual and moral influence on the community."

In Wyman's hall at St. Louis, May 20, 1856, there were 110 teachers from 22 counties gathered to form the association. It was not a propitious time to form such an organization because the so-called public education image then was neither sharply etched nor favorably received. Wealthy parents could afford to send their children to private schools and these offspring, of course, would be the future leaders. Public education then was only for the poor and it was expensive and a waste of public tax money.

Only one-third of the 300,000 school-age children in Missouri were getting any schooling. The University of Missouri was receiving no tax revenue from the Legislature. Teachers generally were just tolerated by the community and received little respect.

But there was lofty vision with earthly hopes for the future of education in Missouri among this small group. Horace Mann, the highly respected educator from Massachusetts, helped to kindle the fire in a major speech in which he advocated "normal colleges," where teachers could be specifically trained to teach. The Rev. William T. Lucky, founder of the Howard high school at Fayette, was elected president, and the small organization pushed off to a precarious future.

The organization members were practical enough not to climb on cloud 9 of that era but to advance slowly with basic objectives. Following Horace Mann's recommendations, it began promoting the idea of "normal colleges" and 14 years later the colleges at Warrensburg and

DR. W. T. LUCKY,
First President of the College.

DR. W. T. LUCKY

Kirksville were established.

Then it began thumping for a 4-year course in education at the Universtiy of Missouri. The minimum public school term in 1873 was four months. The association urged six months and over a protracted period kept pushing until the present term of nine months was gained.

The association insisted that every Missouri youngster had the birthright of a good, or basic, education, and tied this in with a resolution for compulsory school attendance in 1878. Eighteen years later it began the advocacy of child labor laws, that no youngster under 14 could be commercially employed.

The early founders aimed at helping the pupils but never forgot that happy teachers can provide the real spark to successful teaching. It began to work for higher qualifications for teachers, plus better salaries and improved working conditions.

Many public figures were shocked at an association tenet that stated teachers have a right and responsibility to participate in public affairs and to teach in a climate of intellectual freedom; much too liberal for the hide-bound conservatives then. The association added more tremors by advocating free textbooks, free bus transportation, consolidation of school districts, where economically necessary and feasible, and the eradication of politics from public education. These objectives were not realized overnight, many over half-a-century, and the vision of the founders, like the torch passed, carried over to their successors down to the present.

Over the long stretch legislatures sometimes balked, public leaders were critical and obstacles arose, but the association moved indomitably forward. What was good for the pupil was good for the teacher and what was good for the teacher was good for the pupil.

The leaders realized that improperly trained teachers could not command decent salaries. The "normal" school began to open this door. Today almost all of Missouri public school teachers are college graduated. Many have more than one degree.

From the original 110 charter members, there are now 50,000 in Missouri, which is among the top ten states in the percentage of teachers who are members of the association. In the early days a good annual convention attendance was 100. Last November in Kansas City 20,000 convened.

Today the teachers have an excellent retirement program, insurance on their lives and property, 31 credit unions throughout the state, improved certification, automatic salary hikes as they increase their own educational qualifications, a beautiful vacation spot of 2,000 acres in Shannon County and many other benefits.

71

The association in its 113-year history has either initiated or worked for legislation, urging support of school safety-bus laws, schools for handicapped children, school libraries, state support for kindergartens, promotion of vocational training and uniform courses of study for rural schools.

From a viewpoint of getting constructive legislation passed for both pupils and teachers, a sharp awareness of school needs, a large and aggressive membership and the ability to keep step with general educational progress, the Missouri association is regarded as one of the best in the nation.

January 11, 1969

HANNAH COLE

Historians, for one reason or another, have yet to deal justly with the many tremendous contributions and sacrifices pioneer women made in shaping Missouri's early history.

One woman is particularly outstanding in this regard. She was Hannah Allison Cole. Hers is one of Missouri's most dramatic pioneer stories.

She was born in 1764 in Wythe County, Virginia, where she grew to young womanhood. She and her husband, William Temple Cole, had nine children. Hannah's sister, Phoebe Allison, married Stephen Cole, a brother to William, and of this union were born five children.

In 1807 the two families moved to Loutre Island in the Missouri where her husband was killed in an Indian raid in 1810. That same year Hannah and her nine children, and Stephen and Phoebe Cole and their five children established their home on the south bank of the Missouri River near Boonville.

A fort was built on Stephen Cole's place as a means of protecting the Coles and other families from Indians. Settlers called it "Cole's fort." During the War of 1812 years Cole's fort was attacked by Indians but those who'd found sanctuary within its walls escaped safely. Hannah Cole is credited with much of the strategy involved in saving the group from the Indians.

The Indians continued to attack settlers in the Boonville area in 1813. In 1814 area settlers decided to build a fortification on land occupied by Hannah Cole. It was built on a bluff with cannon protecting it from almost every angle. It was called "Hannah Cole's fort." Christmas day, 1815, was observed in this first and probably the only early day military outpost to be named for a woman.

72

Photo credit: Gerald Massie

HANNAH COLE GRAVE MARKER 14 MI. SOUTHWEST OF BOONVILLE

But there were troubles ahead for the settlers. The fort not only became a military bastion, but also served as a hospital for the wounded. Hannah Cole served as a "Florence Nightingale" in her home area. She bandaged the wounded, administered to them, performed all menial tasks required to keep things going at the fort and in her "idle moments" cast leaden bullets for the rifles the settlers used to hold back the attacking Indians.

Howard County was organized January 23, 1816. It was named after Gen. Benjamin Howard of Lexington, Ky., congressman of Kentucky and of Upper Louisiana which became Missouri territory in 1812. Fayette became the county seat of Howard in 1823.

When Howard County was organized in 1816, Hannah Cole's fort became its first county seat.

As early as 1811 Peter Woods, a Baptist minister, held church services in Hannah Cole's cabin. In 1817 her cabin was used as a schoolhouse. History fails to record the name of the teacher who taught there, but the tuition was one dollar a month. Her cabin was one of four voting ' booths" used in the first general election in 1819. Later it became a postoffice for several years.

Hannah Cole was also one of Missouri's first business women. Before Missouri became a state, she pre-empted, bought and sold many acres of land near Boonville. In 1816 she established the first ferry service crossing the Missouri River at Boonville. The business was operated by her sons.

Her life was filled with tragedy. The last came in 1822 when one of her sons, Stephen, and his uncle, Stephen Cole, were killed by Indians on the Santa Fe trail about 60 miles from Santa Fe.

Three years later she built a cabin on land she owned 15 miles south of Boonville near the home of her son, Samuel Cole. With a faithful slave, Lucy, she lived there until her death in 1843 at the age of 79.

Hannah Cole had much to do with settling and pioneering of what is known as Cooper County, Missouri. For her many accomplishments she might justifiably be tagged "the first lady of Missouri."

Hannah Cole is buried in Criscoe cemetery, 12 miles south of Boonville. Her grave is identified by a marker placed there by Boonville's Hannah Cole chapter of the Daughters of the American Revolution.

January 18, 1969

MERIWETHER JEFF THOMPSON

Although Meriwether Jeff Thompson didn't win any battles in the Civil War, unless Fredericktown be credited to him, he did provide the Confederacy with some potent hit-and-run tactics that kept the Yankees on edge in Southeast Missouri.

Thompson, who became known as the "Swamp Fox" during the war, was born in 1826 at Harper's Ferry, Va. Unable to get an appointment to a military academy, he came west and stopped at St. Joseph, Mo.

His Virginia nickname was "Jeff." It followed him to Missouri and he legally changed his name to "Meriwether Jeff Thompson."

He showed his "chamber of commerce" abilities early by tooting the horn loud and long for St. Joseph as the jumping off place for the gold rushers. He pointed out there were four such spots: St. Joseph, Ft. Leavenworth, Westport and Independence. Westport, he said, was a "mere village." He angered the people in Independence by calling it "an old town, indebted to and still depending on Santa Fe trade for its prosperity and support."

St. Joseph, he added, was a "new town," barely six years old. Its situation was far superior to any town on the Missouri River and it had a potential for "unprecedented growth from its natural advantages and resources."

From the time he arrived in St. Joseph in 1847 he moved rather fast from dry goods clerk to a railroad president and mayor of the city. He became a construction engineer in charge of the western terminus of the Hannibal and St. Joseph railroad and reportedly rode the first train from Hannibal to St. Joseph, taking the throttle to bring it into his city.

A man of diversified talents, he surveyed land for the federal government in Missouri and Kansas and farmed out other contracts in Nebraska, became St. Joseph city engineer in 1858 and was the mayor of that city the next year. As mayor he surveyed and graded streets, built bridges and levees and slapped the rump of the first pony that inaugurated the Pony Express. Thompson had been defeated for re-election the day before the auspicious Pony Express start and the clouds of rebellion hovered over the land. His sentiments were with the South and he joined the Confederacy. Within a short time he was commissioned a brigadier general and given Southeastern Missouri to capture and defend for the Confederacy.

JEFF THOMPSON   Credit: State Historical Society of Mo.

Gen. William J. Hardee with 4,500 men at Pocahontas, Ark., and Thompson, with a smaller contingent at Bloomfield, Mo., near the great Mingo swamp, were supposed to meet and outflank the Yankees at Rolla, driving them back to St. Louis and seal off Southeastern Missouri for the Confederacy.

Gen. Gideon Johnson Pillow, Gov. Claiborne Jackson and Thompson met at New Madrid, Mo., to formulate their master plan. Hardee moved, expecting to meet Thompson but Jackson decided that Thompson and Pillow should move in different directions to first take Cape Girardeau.

It was here that Thompson showed his mettle as a "swamp fox," an ability to drive his men at a fast pace through almost inpenetrable swamps, brackish water and dense undergrowth. This he did through the Mingo and Nigger Wool swamps and encamped at Sikeston awaiting Pillow who, in the meantime, was delayed in New Madrid.

With virtually no communications between Hardee, Pillow and others, the South may have lost its first chance to seal off Southeast Missouri. Thompson was exasperated, went to Benton and Commerce, fired several rounds at Union boats on the Mississippi and awaited orders.

Then he was ordered to move toward Fredericktown, Mo., to become part of a larger offensive, planned by Gen. Albert Sidney Johnston, to first capture that area, where so much Yankee ammunition was being produced, and then go on to St. Louis.

Thompson, with another fast move, arrived in Fredericktown October 17, 1861. General Grant now was directing the Yankee strategy and moved Colonels W. P. Carlin and J. B. Plummer against Thompson. Carlin from the west and south, and Plummer from the east and north, began a pincer movement. Thompson's men intercepted a Yankee courier with information that changed the tactics of the Swamp Fox.

He pulled his supply trains out of Fredericktown. Plummer and Carlin arrived and found Thompson gone but the wily Swamp Fox, with a smaller force, had laid out an ambush a short distance outside of Fredericktown along the Greenville road.

Plummer was ambushed and forced to deploy. Carlin hurried to the spot. The battle raged for almost three hours. Both sides lost heavily, the Confederates more. Thompson staged a masterful retreat. Plummer's cavalry sought unsuccessfully to capture Thompson and his army, and then the latter's supply train, but the Swamp Fox was too wily and too fast.

Jeff Thompson was captured in Northeastern Arkansas late in

1863 and was in federal prison almost a year. He did not think much of Gen. Sterling Price's military abilities but was with him in his raid across Missouri that ended at Westport in 1864.

January 25, 1969

LOTTERIES USED BY PIONEERS FOR "GOOD CAUSES"

Yessir, ladies and gentlemen, step right up and get your lottery ticket for the grand prize of $3,000, and then there are 996 prizes left totaling $10,000. Your full ticket is only four dollars, a half for two bucks and a quarter for one little dollar...

This possible "pitch" by a "barker" is not a bit modern but occured more than a century ago. The history of lotteries and gambling in Missouri in the last century indicates the rather loose attitude by all concerned. Consider these developments:

The territorial legislature authorized the first lottery to establish and buy equipment for the fire department in St. Louis.

A second authorization was made to build an academy at Potosi.

A third was made to provide $10,000 for a building for the Sisters of Charity in St. Louis.

Another lottery was authorized for building a Masonic hall in St. Louis.

But the lottery for Franklin, Mo., and then New Franklin, seemed to skip over lines of incorporation, legislative authority and even the Missouri Supreme court.

Franklin was founded in 1816. It was the center of the Boone's Lick area. Daniel, his son Nathan, and other Boones were some of the first settlers in the area. The town had the first newspaper west of St. Louis in 1819 and was the county seat of Howard County from 1817 to 1823. Other well known early settlers in Franklin were Kit Carson, George Caleb Bingham and the "Father of the Santa Fe Trail", William Becknell. Two of Missouri's governors, John Miller and Hamilton Gamble, were also early Franklin residents.

On January 16, 1833, the state Legislature incorporated the Town of New Franklin and conferred upon its board of trustees, or city council, the authority "to raise by lottery a sum not exceeding $15,000 for the construction of a railroad from the Missouri river to New Franklin." But the railroad failed to materialize.

On February 8, 1839, the Missouri Legislature passed an act authorizing the lottery funds to be used for constructing a

80

"M'Adamized" road instead. This act provided that when the trustees had exhausted their funds they should report to the governor who had the power to raise additional funds by virtue of the lottery. On November 17, 1840, Governor Lilburn Boggs issued a proclamation continuing the lottery and later in 1853, and 1855 governors and legislatures did the same.

While the lottery law remained on the state's legal books as being illegal, newspapers in St. Louis tried to "expose" its violation. The St. Louis Republican sent a reporter to New Franklin to expose the matter. He wrote several interesting stories. Nothing was done about it, however.

The legislature passed laws in 1835 and 1842 against gambling and lotteries but then turned backs to the matter. The Supreme Court upheld the contracts by the New Franklin trustees.

It was not until 1877 when the New Franklin lottery laws were invalidated. In the meantime, several legislative sessions had crisscrossed the field, the Supreme court had been presented with several cases and the 1875 Constitution outlawed all forms of gambling that included lotteries.

For the most part the long and drawn-out New Franklin lottery lost money for every concerned. The railroad, the "M'Adamized" and plank roads failed to produce profit. The Potosi academy was not finished with lottery money. The St. Louis fire department needed more funds to complete its establishment. Additional money was also needed to finish the Masonic hall in St. Louis. The Sisters of Charity in St. Louis however, received almost enough for their building program.

February 1, 1969

COL. GEORGE MORGAN

When writing about an interesting personality of the past, historians sometimes concentrate their writing about that individual around one particularly outstanding achievement in that person's life, in the process disregarding other important happenings in their lives.

Consider, for instance, an incident that took place on August 26, 1806, at "Morganza," the family estate of the Morgan family seven miles north of Washington. Aaron Burr had requested and was granted a meeting with George Morgan, owner of the estate.

Morgan had returned to his ancestral home after founding New Madrid, Mo. Burr had been in contact with Gen. James Wilkinson, military commander of the Louisiana territory. The two apparently were planning to establish an independent nation somewhere in the central part of the territory. Burr was anxious to enlist Morgan's support in their conspiracy.

Morgan was angered at Burr's proposal. He wrote a letter to President Jefferson informing him of the proposed conspiracy. Burr eventually was arrested and tried on charges of treason. Just how much Morgan's letter contributed to Burr's downfall is not known.

The Burr-Morgan meeting was a particularly important one in Morgan's life. Most historians, however, seem to be content to overlook it when writing about him, instead concentrating on his founding of New Madrid, Mo., some years before.

Morgan was born in Philadelphia of Welsh descent. He was the son of a prosperous merchant and showed such an aptitude for business in his formative years that he went into business for himself. After Chief Pontiac's rebellion in 1763 Morgan ventured West where he began trading with the Indians. Two years later he returned to Pennsylvania where he fought in the American Revolution, eventually rising to the rank of colonel.

Morgan was "looking to the West" when he came to the attention of Diego de Gardoqui, the Spanish minister to the United States. Spain thought a buffer colony in the New World might stop or slow down American migration westward. Gardoqui offered Morgan a large grant of land in what is now Southeast Missouri on which he wanted to establish the colony. Morgan agreed provided there would be complete religious freedom, self-government and a port of entry for direct control of trade. Gardoqui agreed and said Morgan could have 15 million acres. The year was 1788.

Morgan was both practical and a visionary. The capital, which he called "New" Madrid, was to be two miles wide and four miles long. Its streets were to be 120 feet wide, sidewalks 15 feet wide with a 12-acre lake with crystal pure water in the center, a tree-lined parkway and plenty of other beautifying foliage.

Although Burr hadn't appeared yet as an arch conspirator, General Wilkinson was already a slippery person. He had fought under Washington, then conspired against him. In 1787 he was in New Orleans swearing allegiance to Spain.

The Gardequi agreement had to the approved by Gov. Estvan Miro of the Louisiana territory and Miro was under Wilkinson's thumb. Wilkinson sensed a dangerous competitor in his plans to establish a new empire in the territory.

Miro reduced the acreage grants, insisted on allegiance of all

COL. GEORGE MORGAN   Credit: Washington County Historical Society

settlers in Morgan's colony to Spain and set forth other stipulations that so irritated Morgan that he soon left New Madrid for the family homestead, never returning to Missouri again.

February 8, 1969

BASEBALL CAME TO STATE
ALONG WITH EARLY SETTLERS

"Hey there, Mr. Kauffman, what's the score of the game?"

"It's 79 to 13, Cedric."

"I don't mean football, Mr. Kauffman; I mean baseball."

"That is baseball, Cedric."

That will not be the conversation when the Kansas City Royals play, but back in the last century this was the score between Jefferson City and Sedalia, and 45 runs were scored in one inning! The winner is not known.

The History of baseball in Missouri runs parallel with the general history of the state. Early Missourians had an interest in all types of sports.

Missourians just don't care when or where the game started, which is pretty much like Missourians once they've gotten the knack and interest of the game.

It is supposed to be a cross between two slow paced English games, cricket and rounders. Abner Doubleday, an American Army officer at Cooperstown, N. Y., probably in 1839, invented the game. Then, it was said that Alexander Cartwright of the Knickerbocker club invented it in 1845.

Even today there is so much disagreement on many topics in professional baseball that it will be no surprise that arguments began a long time ago. Consider these:

1. The game began back in the 16th century.

2. George Washington's men played the game at Valley Forge (undoubtedly using snowshoes for bases).

3. The Olympic Town Ball club at Philadelphia began playing in 1833.

4. The silk-stockinged Knickerbockers began playing in 1842.

5. The first organized teams began with the Knickerbockers in 1845.

So, on the national scale the main argument is between the supporters of Abner Doubelday and Alexander Cartwright and the first game between the New York Nine and the Knickerbockers—in 1846—

85

ended 23 to 1 in four innings, with the New York Nine the victors.

But Missourians didn't care. They played their own baseball.

The Springfield (Mo.) South West Union Press, August 11, 1866, wrote, "The game of baseball is both amusing and healthy, and we can see no reason why a club cannot be formed in this city and put into successful operation. It is a very popular game in the East, and for you that are so fond of aping Yankees should act."

Baseball already was in Missouri. On July 8, 1860, the Cyclones played the Morning Stars in St. Louis. The score was not recorded.

The score between Jefferson City and Sedalia, in all probaliity, hit some kind of record. Then there was the game between Marshfield and Carthage, regarded as a "close game," Marshfield winning, 43 to 39.

The Boonville Weekly Eagle, on May 23, 1868, wrote, "The young men of Boonville have formed a baseball club, and we now expect to have local items in abundance; broken fingers, sprained wrists and crippled legs will be all the go. Who will be the first victim? We are absolutely spoiling for a first-class item.

Seven days later the same newspaper, printed under the headline, "NURSES AIDES! THIS WAY!" the following story:

"The baseball club is under full steam and the young men talk of nothing else but the ins, the outs, catchers, pitchers, short stop, so far. No broken bones, but we anticipate a thrilling story soon."

Another "Close" game was played September 12, 1881, as reported by the Cameron (Mo.) Daily Vindicator. The game was between Cameron and Kidder and the reporter wrote, "Cameron bit off more than they could chaw, dug up more snakes than it could kill... Cameron 31, Kidder 51."

"The return game will be played at this place one week from next Saturday, but if both clubs don't play a better game than the above they ought to be run out of town! 51 to 31! Woo wee! Get out of the brush and hide, boys."

The gals liked baseball. Guess about the first ladies' day? In 1867, with the Knickerbockers.

Sportwriters now, and even in the future, who may wish to insert a little poetry into their reports, should read in the Sheldon (Mo.) Enterprise, June 24, 1910, about a girls' baseball game. The report is too long but the names of Willhemmina, Nelly and Clementina are mentioned and here is one verse:

"Twas Dorothea tossed the ball and had all kinds of speed;
Her outshoot was a beauty, and a thing of joy indeed.
The Models couldn't find her curves,
Or bluffed until they daren't,

But in the costume that she wore, her curves were all apparent."

The Bloomers beat the Models 23 to 1.

The records and unusual events in baseball include the following:

The first "champion" was Charles (Old Hoss) Radbourne, who pitched 72 games in 1884 for Providence, 38 in succession and won 60.

In those days, there were no pinch hitters. If a pitcher goofed he might replace a fielder instead of going to the showers.

The overarm delivery was barred until 1880. Catchers did not start wearing masks until 1880 and the regulation catcher's mitt didn't appear until 1869.

The Antelope club was formed in Kansas City in 1866 by D. S. Twitchell. It played the Hope club on a lot south of Fourteenth street and between McGee and Oak streets. The score is not known, but the Antelopes did defeat the Frontier club of Leavenworth, Kas., 47 to 27.

February 15, 1969

FRENCH PHYSICIAN BATTLED
SMALLPOX ON THE FRONTIER

History buffs are familiar with Dr. John Sappington, known for his quinine discovery, and Dr. Lewis Linn, who battled two Asiatic cholera epidemics but is better known for his record in the U. S. Senate, but virtually none has any acquaintance with Antoine Francois Saugrain de Vigne.

Saugrain supplied the thermometers, medicines and other scientific equipment for the Lewis and Clark expedition.

He was probably the first physician in Missouri to use vaccine for the prevention of smallpox and made it available to all.

He was one of 33 Missourians for whom Liberty ships were named in World War II.

Saugrain was born in France February 17, 1763, and went to St. Louis. He returned to France but in 1800 was back at St. Louis as the army post physician under Governor Delassus.

After the Louisiana purchase, he was appointed army surgeon at Ft. Bellefontaine and then began his experiments in medicine that led to the discovery of a vaccine that was successful in many cases of smallpox.

Whether he had any contact with Dr. Edward Jenner, a British physician, is a mystery, but the two were experimenting with the smallpox vaccine about the same time.

Jenner observed that persons exposed to cowpox, a mild disease of

89

cattle, became immune to smallpox. He innoculated a boy with cowpox virus and then later the smallpox germ and the boy was immune.

Saugrain sought to make no profit on his vaccine. And he offered it to other physicians provided they would not attempt to make a profit either.

He was regarded as the only trained physician in St. Louis around 1800. Dr. B. G. Farrar arrived in 1807 and Dr. J. M. Read in 1811.

Dr. Saugrain also used herbs in his prescriptions, inveighed against bloodletting to cure fevers and diseases and didn't think much of calomel as a cure-all.

When Lewis and Clark came up short of thermometers and barometers because there was no mercury, Saugrain prowled the town, and the homes of the rich, and took mercury from old silvered mirrors. He is said to have accompained Lewis and Clark but this is not true.

Saugrain soon became widely known in St. Louis. Before Rufus Easton was appointed the first postmaster of St. Louis in 1805 by Thomas Jefferson, the window sill of Dr. Saugrain's office was the "postoffice." Citizens called there and if Saugrain was present the window went up and the mail was handed out.

In his eagerness to promote more widespread use of his smallpox vaccine, Dr. Saugrain did something that the physicians of today cannot do by their own regulations: He advertised. In one St. Louis newspaper, May 26, 1809, the following was printed over his name:

"The undersigned has successfully communicated that inestimable preventive of the Small Pox to a number of the inhabitants of St. Louis and its vicinity, and from a sincere wish which he entertains more widely to disseminate this blessing he has taken this occasion to inform such physicians and other intelligent persons as reside beyond the limits of his accustomed practice that he will, with pleasure, on application, furnish them with the vaccine. Persons in indigent circumstances, paupers and Indians will be vaccinated and attended gratis, on application."

February 22, 1969

PIONEERING EFFORTS IN FULTON
AIDED THE AFFLICTED

Columbia is known in Missouri history as a fount of learning with the University of Missouri there, as well as Stephens and Christian Colleges. St. Louis is known around the world for its St. Louis and Washington Universities. William Jewell College in Liberty, the various state colleges and other institutions have marked Missouri as a leader in education in the last century.

In Fulton are Westminster college, William Woods and the Missouri School for the Deaf.

Perhaps, next to St. Louis, Fulton is paramount in helping those who seek education and those who are afflicted. The first hospital to help the mentally disturbed was established at Fulton in 1847, making it the oldest state mental hospital west of the Mississippi River. It was called an insane asylum. In recent years it has broadened its scope to include children and alcholics.

The Missouri School for the Deaf, established in 1851, was the first school of its kind west of the Mississippi river. It is generally agreed that the first education for the deaf began in 1839, the same year that the University of Missouri was started at Columbia. This help for the deaf and dumb began at Carondelet. The Missouri Legislature appropriated $2,000 and the Sisters of St. Joseph operated the school.

There were occasional appropriations until 1851 when the school for deaf children set up in Fulton. Forty acres of land were donated. County courts had to certify those between 10 and 30 years of age for admission and in November of 1851 the school term opened with one student.

Dr. William D. Kerr of Danville, Ky., a person with long experience in teaching the deaf, was brought to Missouri as the superintendent. He had some experince in teaching the blind.

In 1853, two years after the opening, 18 acres were added and a $28,000 building erected, and 19 years later more buildings were added.

The Union and Confederate armies took over the buildings during the war and Kerr took many of his students to homes in Audrain County.

The school was reopened near the end of the Civil war and Kerr resumed the post of superintendent. He retired February 28, 1889, and died May 24 of the same year.

Westminster College and the Missouri School for the Deaf celebrated their centennial together. Alben Barkley, then vice-president, officiated at the double centennial.

The Missouri School for the Blind was organized in 1850 and opened in 1851. The first superintendent was Eli Whalen who was himself blind. Dr. Kerr assisted in helping to establish the school in St. Louis.

The State hospital for the mentally ill has an intensive treatment building, a hospital with 86 medical and surgical beds for acute cases, many buildings for long-term patients and the Biggs Memorial building, a psychiatric unit for the criminally insane. More than 2,000 patients under 18 have been treated there and it has an approved postgraduate training course in psychiatry.

March 1, 1969

GERMAN IMMIGRANT BEGAN
POLITICAL CAREER IN MISSOURI

He had fled Germany after a revolt, France had kicked him out and he sat on a park bench in Hyde Park of London somewhat dejected and discouraged. He decided to go to that great new land of hope and opportunity and this thought crossed his mind:

"The ideals for which I have fought, I shall find there." And as he rubbed the cold from his hands he thought again, "That is a new world, a free world, a world of great ideas and aims."

And so he came to America, and his accomplishments in this country are many. Consider the major ones:

He played a great role in the nomination and election of Abraham Lincoln.

He edited several newspapers.

He was a U.S. senator.

He had an excellent Civil war record.

He was the first German-born immigrant appointed to the cabinet of the United States.

Carl Schurz was born 140 years ago last Sunday in Liblar, Germany.

He was impatient and impetuous and after the 1848 revolution fled to Switzerland. He belonged to a group of liberal intellectuals of the middle class. Prof. Gottfried Kinkel was his friend and counsel and Schurz aided in his escape from a German prison.

After France booted Schurz he went to London, wrote for awhile and taught languages and music. In 1852 he came to the United States with his bride of two months.

He and his 18-year-old bride remained in Philadelphia three years. Schurz was afloat in the great sea of American freedom and uncertain how to handle the rudder. In the meantime, he had been absorbing everything available on American politics and mastering the English language.

Wisconsin seemed to be a likely place, and Schurz went there in 1857. He received the Republican nomination for lieutenant governor and was defeated.

92

CARL SCHURZ

By then Schurz was beginning to find himself. He began to perceive that Lincoln had many ideas he liked. In 1858 he spoke for Lincoln in Lincoln's race against Stephen Douglas and two years later Schurz stumped the Middle West for Lincoln.

By that time he was a master of the English language. He spoke for the many thousands of Germans who had come to the United States after the 1848 revolt. He and his fellow countrymen wanted liberty and freedom, and, he asked, why shouldn't a black man enjoy the same?

Lincoln rewarded him by appointing Schurz minister to Spain. Schurz accepted and then returned to take part in the Civil war. He was at Chancellorsville, Bull Run, Chattanooga and Gettysburg, and came out of the war as a brigadier general.

After the war, President Andrew Johnson sent him into the South to study the Reconstruction problems.

Schurz, in 1867, became an editor of the St. Louis Westliche Post, a German newspaper which had tremendous influence among the Germans in the state.

Schurz rose to a power in Missouri politics and in 1869 the Missouri Legislature elected him U.S. senator. He became one of the country's most controversial political figures.

Schurz helped to elect Rutherford Hayes governor of Ohio and then to push him into the White House. Hayes rewarded Schurz by naming him Secretary of the Interior.

In 1881 he became editor of the New York Evening Post and resigned two years later after a clash with a colleague.

As Secretary of the Interior, Schurz worked for better treatment of the Indians, a merit system in his department and conservation of the nation's resources, which was tied in with a proposed development of a national park system.

There was no doubt where Schurz stood on any point. He attacked Grant's military record so vehemently that the editor of the St. Louis Globe Democrat protested that Schurz was hardly a second lieutenant. The editor revealed a letter from Lincoln in which the President wrote, "I have received yours about Gen. Carl Schurz. I appreciate him certainly as highly as you do, but you can never know until you have the trial how difficult it is to find a place for an officer of so high rank when there is no place seeking him."

Lincoln's subtlety apparently was not lost on the editor. Schurz's patriotism had not been attacked, but his zeal for military promotion had drawn snickers from enemies, nothing new in any war. But Lincoln was always well aware of the worth of the German immigrant.

March 8, 1969

A MISSOURIAN'S TREK TO OREGON PROFITABLE FOR COUNTRY

In the annals of exploring, the name of Wilson Price Hunt does not mean much, probably because there were other names that seemed to get more attention from historians.

The major goal of an expedition at the beginning of the last century, conceived and directed by John Jacob Astor, was to unite land and sea forces and establish a fur-trading empire larger than those of his rivals.

IT WAS NOT exactly a howling success, although it did open the way for fur trading to the Northwest. Among the expeditions accomplishments:

It was the first party of white men to travel what later became known as the Oregon trail.

The penetration provided a later basic claim by the United States to Oregon.

To the many Indian tribes, and the British, it proved that the nation could move men and equipment expeditiously from Missouri.

It was more than 30 years later that wagon trains began rumbling northwest to Oregon and the nation became embroiled in a dispute— "54-40 or Fight"—with England. The important information that Hunt and his group collected was valuable later to the government.

HUNT WAS BORN 186 years ago next Thursday in New Jersey and went to St. Louis in 1804 where he entered the general business arena, being interested specifically in fur trading.

Neither the expeditions of Lewis and Clark, nor of Wilson Hunt, were the first to penetrate the general area, but they were the first to do it successfully.

Jean Baptiste Trudeau, (also spelled Truteau), a school teacher, left St. Louis on June 7, 1794, with an expedition for the Northwest by way of the Missouri river, but lost almost all of his trading goods and equipment to Indians and wily frontier traders. He tried it again the next year with virtually the same result. A third expedition headed by James Mackey also failed.

A fourth headed by John Evans did go overland in 1796 and reached Mandan villages in the Dakotas.

BUT IT WAS Lewis and Clark who made the first successful expedition to the Northwest and Wilson Hunt was first to do it by a different route. Also, one was military, the other civilian-business.

The rush to establish fur-trading posts began after Lewis and Clark returned. Manuel Lisa and the Missouri Fur company had established posts in Sioux and Mandan territory by 1808.

In all probability Hunt and Lisa staged the first, and maybe only, race of its kind—to the Northwest.

His party consisted of 65 persons, mostly Missourians. Benjamin Jones, a Missourian, was his huntsman. Pierre Dorion, a half-breed interpreter, had worked for Lisa and owed him a whisky bill.

There also were three nephews of Alexander McNair, Missouri's first governor; Robert McClellan, widely known Missouri fur trader, and others.

NINETEEN DAYS after Hunt left St. Louis, Lisa began a race to overtake him and collect his debt from Dorion. The long race is believed to have ended at an Indian village on June 12, but whether Lisa exacted his debt from Dorion is not known. At least, Dorion stayed with the expedition because his wife on December 30 gave birth to their child, the first born on the Oregon trail.

Lewis and Clark had had trouble with the Blackfeet tribe along their river route, so Hunt bought horses and went overland or around the Blackfeet, to Fort Henry on the Snake river.

They embarked on the Columbia river early in 1812 and reached Astoria February 15. The men began gathering furs. Hunt sailed to Alaska to widen operations and upon his return several months later learned of the war between his nation and England. His partners had arranged to sell to the Northwest company, a rival British firm, and Hunt agreed in view of the war.

He dabbled in two or three business ventures upon his return to St. Louis and in 1817 bought land in St. Louis County upon which he erected a mill. In 1822 he was appointed postmaster, holding the post 18 years. He died April 13, 1842.

The information he and his men brought back from the expedition about the tribes and British machinations and intrigue in the Northwest was valuable to the government in the War of 1812 and afterward. There were 33 Liberty ships named for Missourians in World War II, and one was for Wilson Price Hunt.

March 15, 1968

JOE BOWERS

Dear John:

Because you are a plural symbol of thousands of young men who, while away at war, received letters from sweethearts at home saying they had changed their minds, I would like to join your organization.

My name is Joe Bowers and I was born in a log cabin on Salt river in Pike County, Missouri, in 1829. Although my "membership" is not based on war duty, I suffered your fate while mining gold in California during the gold rush.

SALLY! Ah! She was tall and stately, just 16 with heavenly blue eyes and coppery red hair that fell in glittering ringlets around her swan-like neck. We walked together, dreamed together, floated the streams of my Pike County home area. I asked for her hand.

At 16, she was too young to marry, she said, but she did promise to marry me after I returned from California, loaded with gold, and she sealed it with many kisses.

Capt. Abe McPike, a wealthy and respected citizen of our county, was organizing a train for California and hired me as a cattle driver. Then I became a bull-whip driver and finally aide to McPike. My brother Ike stayed behind.

I was happy. The captain liked me. I was in love and could not hide it. Frank Smith, a fellow traveler, hearing all of this, composed verses which a musician in the train set to song. Here are a few verses:

> My name is Joe Bowers
>> And I've got a brother Ike;
> I came from Old Missouri
>> And all the way from Pike.
> I'll tell you why I left there,
>> And why I came to roam,
> And leave my poor old mammy
>> So far away from home.
>
> I used to court a gal there—
>> Her name was Sally Black;
> I asked her if she'd marry me;
>> She said it was a whack.
> Says she to me, "Joe Bowers,

Before we hitch for life,
    You ought to get a little home
        To keep your little wife."

O Sally, dearest Sally
    O Sally for your sake,
I'll go to California
    And try to make a stake.
Says she to me, "Joe Bowers,
    You are the man to win;
Here's a kiss to bind the bargain"
    And she hove a dozen in.

OH YES, there were other verses. We got to California. I worked hard and saved my money. I felt it would not be long until I could return and marry Sally.

Then I got a letter from Ike. I guess Sally didn't have the nerve to write a "Dear John" letter herself, but it was along the theme that many "Dear Johns" have been receiving over thousands of years.

Yep! He wrote that Sally was married, and to a red-haired butcher and they had a red-haired baby!

I was heartbroken. Soon I encountered Frank Smith, He added a couple of verses:

At length I got a letter
    From my dear brother Ike;
It came from old Missouri,
    And all the way from Pike;
It brought to me the darndest news
    That ever you did hear—
My heart is almost bursting,
    So pray excuse this tear.

It said that Sal was false to me,
    Her love for me had fled;
She's got married to a butcher—
    And the butcher's hair was red;
And more than that the letter said
    It's enough to make me swear—
That Sally has a baby,
    And the baby has red hair!

I wandered for awhile around the Pacific area and those transcendent historians will have to tell you my burial place; I do not know myself.

But I wasn't forgotten. The Missouri Legislature passed a bill which Gov. Lon Stephens signed into law March 23, 1897, just 72 years ago tomorrow, and it stated:

"Whereas, the true-hearted and illustrious Joe Bowers, late of Pike, has done more than any thousand other men, living or dead, real or imaginary, to advertise the great state of Missouri, and her splendid people, causing our name and fame to be sung and rung in every clime, on every sea, in every land, and,

"Whereas, his soul-stirring ballad, beginning, 'My Name, it is Joe Bowers,' has served to rekindle patriotism and to foster paternal and filial devotion in the heart of every true Missourian at home and abroad, as well as to enlist for us the sympathy, interest and respect of all men and genuine worth the world over, and the admiration of all women whose admiration is worth having..."

I'll stop with that last line, which the "Dear Johns" the world over will quickly recognize. The Legislature appointed a commission to direct the collection of voluntary contributions to erect a "suitable monument" to me of the "best Missouri granite or limestone."

But maybe too much time had elapsed. The project was never finished. Perhaps it is for the best because it would have been my wish that the inscription not be to "Joe Bowers" but to DEAR JOHN.

March 22, 1969

THE MARAIS DES CYGNES MASSACRE

Almost everyone has heard of Quantrill's raid on Lawrence, Kas., in which 179 men and one boy were killed and the business district was razed.

At that time—1863—the war was well under way. There had been killings, snipings and border raids for more than eight years.

MISSOURIANS along the southern border had been raided and killed by many Kansans, most led by James Montgomery, a black-bearded ex-preacher from Ohio; Charles R. Jennison, a dandified former dentist from Wisconsin, and James Lane.

The Hamelton family had come up from the South to help make Kansas a slave state and settled in Linn County, Kansas.

Charles A. Hamelton, a handsome Georgian from a family of

100

THE MARAIS DES CYGNES MASSACRE

wealth and influence, was hot-headed and impetuous. He was the leader of the clan which did not distinguish itself for any acts of courage or bravery during the troublesome period.

Col. Lindsay Johnson, a widely-known free state Kansan, was challenged to a duel by a Hamelton, and under the dueling code Johnson could select his own weapon. He chose broadswords, knowing that his smaller and lighter opponent couldn't swing one very fast. The Hameltons called it off.

Sometime later they took on Lindsay Johnson and his two sons, Jefferson and William Johnson, in a shoot-out and fared badly.

THE FIREBRAND Hamelton and his brother, Alvin, and others decided Kansas was a little too hot and moved into Missouri, settling not far from West Point. But Charles Hamelton was determined the Kansas Jayhawkers would pay for their "misdeeds" and he drew up a list marked for slaughter.

On May 19, a bright and clear day, Hamelton and 32 well armed men struck the general Trading Post area. The men were boisterous, laughing, cursing and drinking whisky.

WITHIN a short time they had taken Patrick Ross; William Stillwell; the Rev. B. L. Reed; John F. Campbell; Amos Cross Hall; Austin Hall; William Colpetzer; William Hairgrove and his son, Asa Hairgrove; Charles Snyder and Michael Robinson. With one or two exceptions most of the men were known only for their allegiance to free statism and had not been violent against the slavery crowd.

One-fourth mile nothwest of Snider's blacksmith shop, Hamelton called a halt, began cursing the others and ordered them to line up.

William Hairgrove seemed to sense the impending tragedy and snapped, "Gentlemen, if you are going to shoot us, take good aim."

Hamelton prepared to give the order. W. B. (Fort Scott) Brockett raised his hand and said he would have nothing to do with such a senseless slaughter and turned and rode away.

Hamelton gave the second signal and the rifles cracked. Five were killed almost instantly five wounded seriously. One killer yelled, "They're not all dead," and a second volley was fired.

Austin Hall feigned death and crawled away as soon as the killers left. He ran to Snider's home for help. The five who were wounded eventually recovered.

Reed was one to recover, although shot twice. He wiggled a leg in the mass of bodies and blood and Hamelton yelled, "Kill that damned preacher." Many of the killers rifled the pockets of the dead and wounded.

Colpetzer, Campbell, Ross, Robinson and Stillwell were killed.

THE MASSACRE shocked the nation. Whittier immortalized it in a poem.

The killers melted away into the forested and brushy areas of the Missouri border just as Quantrill would do five years later.

March 29, 1969

CHARLES MARION RUSSELL

Charles Marion Russell could execute works of art in oil, water colors and charcoal, or almost anything handy that would make a mark, and he was equally adept in sculpturing, whether wax, clay or bronze.

His reputation was built chiefly on his expressions of the west— cowboys, Indians, buffalo herds and breathtaking scenery—just as Frederick Remington's was.

RUSSELL was born March 19, 1864, in St. Louis and educated in the public schools there. He showed an early precocity toward art in using wax, mud and soap to fashion animals.

He was happy when his parents moved to a farm where he could better exercise his growing talents, but a short time later they moved back to the city and the boy, only 15 years of age, packed up some worn brushes and paint and left for the west.

The boy found a job in Montana wrangling horses in the spring and herding beef in the fall. Jake Hunter, a widely-known hunter and trapper, who perceived Russell's artistic abilities, encouraged him to paint wherever and whenever he wished.

Russell always carried his brushes and paints with him on the range and after the day's work he'd dip into the woolen sack and bring out the materials. Sometimes he would do a pencil sketch long after the other cowhands were asleep.

RUSSELL was 23 when fame began to nudge him. His painting, "Waiting for a Chinook," got instant attention. A terrible Montana winter had destroyed a large part of the cattle business, cattle by the tens of thousands dying. He portrayed a steer, knee-deep in a drift, head down and soon to die, and the solitary coyote crouched in the distance. Then he did several illustrations for Emerson Hough's "Story of the Outlaw."

He illustrated Olin Dunbar Wheeler's book, "The Trail of Lewis and Clark," and Stewart Edward White's "Arizona Nights." His works soon were widely circulated in New York, Chicago, Los Angeles, San Francisco and London.

MANY of Russell's followers couldn't agree on whether his oils were better than the bronze works.

"The Buffalo Hunt" is regarded as one of his best bronzes. Others widely heralded are, "Where the Best of Riders Quit," which shows a rider being thrown off a rearing bronc, and "When the Sioux and Blackfeet Meet," depicting Indian braves in fierce battle, is a painting.

He died at Great Falls, Mont., Oct. 24, 1926.

There is a statue of him in the Statuary Hall of Fame in the Capitol in Washington.

April 5, 1969

GOV. LILBURN W. BOGGS

Almost any religious persecution by a public official, regardless of any extenuating or explanatory circumstances, usually dulls or blackens his general record, so it is not unusual that history recalls Lilburn W. Boggs, sixth governor of Missouri, as the one who gave the "extermination order" against the Mormons 131 years ago.

Otherwise, his record as governor and a public servant is far better than average. He served several terms in the Missouri Senate and was lieutenant governor, first clerk of Jackson County and an assistant factor at Fort Osage.

He served in the War of 1812, quickly called out Missouri regiments to fight the Seminoles in Florida and in the "Honey war" with Iowa called out Missouri troops.

Boggs was born December 14, 1792, near Lexington, Ky., went to St. Louis in 1816 and became cashier of the new Missouri bank, the president of which was Auguste Chouteau.

The bank counter became too monotonous for him and he went west, stopping in Old Franklin for a short time and then becoming an assistant to George Sibley at Fort Osage.

He had married the granddaughter of Daniel Boone. Jackson County was being organized. He owned a store in Independence, the county seat, and was appointed the first clerk of the county.

In 1826 he was elected to the state Senate and was reelected in 1830. Two years later he became lieutenant governor. In 1836, when Daniel Dunklin resigned, he became governor.

He proved to be a vote-getter. His own party, Democratic, declined to nominate him for governor, so he ran as a Benton Democrat and defeated the widely known and highly respected William H. Ashley.

LILBURN W. BOGGS

As governor he was somewhat liberal in his views and, having won despite the opposition of his old party, he was very independent in his appointments.

The capitol burned in 1837 and the Legislature appropriated $75,000 for a new one. Boggs insisted this was not enough. The lawmakers told him to jump in the river, but they didn't realize that he had final authority in approving construction bills. By 1840 the capitol had cost $200,000 as approved by Boggs, and the Legislature had to appropriate the additional money.

His enemies sought vainly to find some dishonesty on his part but he was able to account for every penny he had spent.

The governor also supported all public school measures, including the Geyer act, that laid the foundation for public education in Missouri, and bills to establish the University of Missouri.

The Mormons had begun to become a problem before Boggs became governor. They came from Ohio and settled first in Jackson County in 1831. Two years later they were expelled and they went to Clay County. In 1836 they left that area for Caldwell County, created by the Legislature as a home for the Mormons in the hope that this would settle the difficulties.

It did not, however. The Mormons were hard workers, anti-slavery, peaceful and closely united. They began to branch out in Carroll and Daviess Counties. This infuriated many Missourians. The situation became worse and by August, 1838, open fighting seemed imminent.

The climax occurred in October when a group of Mormons routed the state militia on Crooked river in Daviess County. A force of angry Missourians then swept down on Mormons at Haun's mill and massacred 17. The leaders managed to escape.

Governor Boggs made his monumental mistake October 27, 1838, by directing that the Mormons be treated as enemies of Missouri and either exterminated or driven from the state. The leaders were condemned by court martial to be shot.

Col. Alexander Doniphan, then a brigade commander in the state militia, said he would not permit the execution or "extermination" of any Mormon.

Public opinion seemed to calm down within weeks and history now regards Doniphan as the hero in the incident and Boggs as the "villain."

His term as governor over, Boggs was sitting in his front room at Independence reading one evening when a shotgun blast ripped through the window. He was near death for many weeks.

There were charges the Mormons were to blame. One leader was arrested and then a second person. Both were released, there being no evidence against them.

Boggs recovered and served a term in the state Senate, 1842-46. At the end of his term he went to Northern California and opened a store. He was soon appointed Alcalde, or Governor, for the area which extended over Sutter's fort and the Sacramento Valley, scene of the great gold discovery.

Boggs held the post until 1850. Having become a fairly wealthy man through selling supplies and merchandise to the gold miners, he retired to a farm in the Napa valley and died March 14, 1860.

April 12, 1969

ENTERTAINMENT IN ST. LOUIS

The play was entitled, "Honey Moon," and among the numerous actors and actresses billed were, "Mr. Smith," "Mr. Sol Smith," "Mr. S. Smith" and "Mr. S. F. Smith."

This brought a comment from a St. Louisan reading the poster, "There are a lot of Smiths in the play."

The four actors happened to be one, Solomon Franklin Smith, who played a major role in the development of the theater in St. Louis in the first half of the last century. His playing four parts in this particular play did not mean that there was a lack of thespians, just that Smith was a versatile man.

There wasn't much in formal entertainment in St. Louis around 1815. The population was only 2,000 from which there was insufficient support for dramatic productions. Also, there was the language difficulty—English and French.

Probably the first performance with any professional tinge occurred in January or February, 1818 when William Turner took his troupe to St. Louis from the East and performed in the courthouse and, reportedly, in the Green Tree tavern.

Alphonso Wetmore, a veteran of the War of 1812, wrote, "The Pedlar," a farce in three acts, which was produced around 1821 in a small structure on Main street between Olive and Locust.

James H. Caldwell took a troupe to St. Louis from New Orleans and performed there in 1826. Some historians give him precedence over Turner for turning out plays with a professional touch.

So, while there was a stirring among the devotees of the drama and the stagestuck thespians for almost a decade, the major impetus actually occurred when Solomon Smith arrived on the scene and later teamed up with Noah M. Ludlow.

110

Smith was born April 20, 1801, in Norwich, N.Y., had little education, worked briefly as a clerk in Albany and then as an apprentice printer in Louisville.

In 1820 he joined a troupe, went to Cincinnati and quit at the age of 23 to edit and publish a small newspaper.

But acting was in his blood and in 1823 he organized and managed a troupe that played the Mississippi river towns between New Orleans and St. Louis. In this group his versatility began to be revealed. He played several roles, one being "Sheepface" in "The Village Lawyer," but just what "Sheepface" did in the play is not fully known.

Ludlow was born in 1795 in New York, went to Kentucky as an actor in 1815 and then on to St. Louis four years later with a small stock company.

Smith and Ludlow knew each other for several years before they formed a partnership in 1835 that lasted 18 years and was terminated in a bitter dispute. However, they combined their talents to give St. Louis its first firmly established dramatic playhouse that produced many fine plays over the years. A few preceded them and other troupes and producers drifted in and out of St. Louis, but none matched their productions and abilities over a span of almost two decades.

Smith's versatility was extensive. He was an excellent actor when the part demanded quality performance. He was also a writer, journalist, lawyer and storyteller, and even preached briefly.

Ludlow also was a writer, associated with Wetmore, Joseph M. Field, Matthew C. Field, John S. Robb and Charles Keemle, editor of the Commercial Bulletin. They were loosely banded together as publishers and wrote many stories of "Western Life" published in the East.

Matthew Field liked to relate Sol Smith's own stories and even acted them out. He said Smith was a "born wag," and that at his funeral he would surely play a "droll trick" on his pallbearers.

There were many places used for plays in those early years. A blacksmith shop served as a playhouse for a while, then a revamped salt house. A new theater was built partly from public subscription.

Although Smith and Ludlow were the premier producers for many years, they encountered difficulties, especially in the late 1880s when economic troubles struck the nation. They booked lecturers, dancers and other nondramatic acts to take up the slack between legitimate productions.

They were among the first to realize the importance of music for some plays and the introduction of orchestral renditions was received with mixed reaction by the regular patrons of the theater.

Smith read law, passed the bar and about the time he and Ludlow disagreed he began his practice. He wrote three books, the first in 1845, entitled "The Theatrical Apprenticeship and Anecdotical Recollections of Sol Smith, Commedian, Attorney-at-Law, Etc." The second in 1854 and the last in 1868 had equally long titles.

Smith unsuccessfully sought the office of city recorder. When the Civil war started he was a strong Union supporter and was elected to the 1861 convention that voted against secession. He died February 14, 1869, at his home in St. Louis.

Ludlow lived until 1886. He apparently nursed his bitterness against Smith so thoroughly that his memoirs, "Dramatic Life As I Found It," published in 1880, never mentioned Smith's name.

April 19, 1969

DONIPHAN'S MISSOURI VOLUNTEERS

A great deal of emphasis has been placed on the study of wars and the military in recent years. Books by the hundreds have been written on the subject yet many of the so-called "official military studies" have failed to discuss in very much detail the role Missourians played in the nation's military history.

Of particular importance in this regard are the outstanding achievements of Col. Alexander Doniphan of Liberty, and his Missouri volunteers in the war with Mexico.

Those who have been volunteers in recent wars are well aware of the fact that "regulars," those professionally trained for warfare, sometimes look down on volunteers. This was in part the case concerning Colonel Doniphan and his Missouri volunteers.

They participated in a battle known as the "Battle of Sacramento," which took place about 15 miles north of Chihuahua, Mexico, on February 28, 1847.

It was a frosty Sunday morning when Doniphan with 856 men faced 4,228 Mexicans. under the command of five generals led by Gen. Garcia Conde, former Mexican minister of war. The Mexicans were strongly entrenched in 28 fortified redoubts with 16 cannons on an elevation overlooking "the miserable rabble from Missouri."

There could be no retreat for the Missourians. They had expected help from General Wool of the regular United States Army but he had failed to rendezvous with Doniphan.

The Missouri volunteers were a sad lot to be sure. They had to

112

COL. ALEXANDER DONIPHAN

furnish their own horses and weapons. Uniforms were out of the question. Their food was terrible. Many slept under wagons because they had no blankets. Their ammunition supply was short. They were lice-ridden, snake-bitten and in the position they were in, no doubt they wondered what the future held for them.

Scouts from Chihuahua reported the situation to the Mexican generals. Chihuahua officials decided to turn their expected victory into a holiday. Handcuffs and leg irons for the soon to-be-captured Missourians were prepared and it was decreed that if there were any survivors they would be driven and whipped to Mexico City in handcuffs and leg irons.

Officials of Chihuahua urged the townspeople to come out and watch the merciless slaughter.

Doniphan's scouts had also been busy. Learning of the Mexicans' plan, he told his men what the Mexicans had in store for them.

Doniphan and his staff methodically planned their strategy, and the miserable, poorly clad, poorly-weaponed force moved forward. High on the hill thousands of highly trained Mexican soldiers waited to pounce on them.

But there was one important signal about to be given.

Just before rifles cracked and cannons boomed, Doniphan thrust his fist into the air. The Missourians deflected to the right, crossed an unguarded arroyo and quickly gained a plateau that put them on a shooting level with the enemy. The movement was unexpected and took the Mexicans by surprise.

When the smoke cleared from the battlefield that day, 304 Mexicans had been killed, about 500 wounded and 70 captured. Four Missourians were killed and only a few had been wounded.

The Missourians' captured booty included a wagonload of handcuffs—ones the Mexicans had planned to use on captured Missourians for their death march to Mexico City.

Missourians participated in other battles as well. Brazito was the first and although the percentages were not as one-sided as in the Battle of Sacramento, victory was also theirs in this one.

During the entire Mexican war, Doniphan's Missouri volunteers marched almost 3,600 miles, occupied three capitols, four Mexican states, defeated two larger Mexican armies, negotiated treaties with several tribes and captured large quantities of supplies.

The entire march, conducted with small loss under adverse circumstances is one of the most famous expeditions in American history.

April 26, 1969

JOHN SMITH T.

In Missouri history there are many individuals whose names are tossed about with superficial familiarity but when the details of their lives are mentioned, without the name, not many can make the connection. Consider these major points of one man's career:

He was ostensibly mild-mannered, well-dressed and courteous.

He supposedly killed between 13 and 15 men in duels.

He ran for governor of Missouri, but got less than 2 per cent of the total vote.

His name? John Smith T. That is not an appellative error. He insisted on placing the "T" behind his name because there were so many "John T. Smiths" and just plain "John Smiths."

He was born in Virginia in 1770. He was educated at the William and Mary College at Williamsburg, Va., and spent some of his youth in Georgia. From Georgia he moved to Tennessee and then to Missouri sometime around 1804.

John Smith T seems to have had a knack for getting himself into trouble. He joined up with Burr and the notorious General Wilkinson. At various times in his career he served as a lieutenant colonel in the Missouri militia, judge of the Ste. Genevieve court of quarter and sessions and commissioner of rates. In almost all instances he was ousted from office for one reason or another.

In those days the codeduello carried a sort of sacrosanct background. Nobody talked. Many men were killed in duels. Only duels such as the Benton-Lucas encounter, on August 12, 1817, and others where the participants were nationally known received any publicity.

Even the killing of Lionel Browne is somewhat shrouded in secrecy. Through his affiliations with Burr and Wilkinson, Smith T had purchased lead mines and acreage in Southeastern Missouri. He was a fairly weathly man by 1815. Smith T was in the best of company with Burr. Burr had plans for a new nation. Wilkinson loitered in the background and Smith T planned to have a hand in starting a revolution that would free Mexico from Spain.

The killing of Browne on September 20, 1819, caused considerable discussion. The sentiment was against Smith T.

Just why Smith T could kill so many men and get away with it is not known. Neither is it known how he died in 1836.

In addition to removing Smith T from public office, Secretary

Bates also interfered with some of his questionable mining operations. The duelist sent a challenge to Bates, who declined, sending back the modern equivalent of "go fly a kite." Actually, Bates said he was just too busy, but Smith T wisely chose not to pursue his point.

Many men undoubtedly owed their lives then to the fact they would not accept Smith T's challenge. Col. James Rollins probably was one of these. The story is that Smith T invited Rollins to have a drink in a Jefferson City tavern. Rollins, who did not drink, declined. Smith T repeated the invitation. Rollins again declined, not knowing his host's identity.

Smith T is supposed to have placed his pistols on the bar and repeated the invitation, the bartender told Rollins who his host was and Rollins accepted. Rollins was not a coward but neither was he adept with the pistol.

Smith T was a small man and wouldn't have lasted long in a barroom brawl then with only his fists. His courage was also questionable because, as one writer said, "he traveled ate and slept" with his guns, including a rifle he called "Hark from the Tombs."

Smith T saw himself as one of the big leaders in Mexico. His lead mines would provide the ammunition for Mexico to wrest its independence from Spain.

The Mexican bubble burst and in 1821 that government granted Stephen Austin the right to colonize a part of the area which later became the state of Texas.

Smith T still had his wealth. He blustered his way around Southeastern Missouri for awhile, bought and controlled lead mines, even invested in Saline County land.

In 1832 he decided to run for governor of Missouri. There were four candidates: Daniel Dunklin, the winner, who received 9,121 votes; Dr. John Bull, who received 8,035 votes; Dr. S. C. Dorris, 386 votes and Smith T, 314 votes, which represented less than 2 per cent of the total. In Saline County where he owned extensive property, his total vote count was zero.

John Smith T died in 1836 at the home of Mr. Hale (who had been an old friend of the Smiths in Virginia), while on a trip to Hale's Point, Tenn., to establish a cotton plantation near Memphis. His body is believed to have been brought back to Jefferson County, Missouri, and buried there.

May 3, 1969

HENRY M. BRACKENRIDGE

Henry M. Brackenridge, who was born 183 years ago tomorrow in Pittsburgh, wrote extensively about Missouri following the Louisiana Purchase. Alexander Nicholas DeMenil, St. Louis author-critic, said in 1920 of him, "Although he published the majority of his books prior to July 19, 1820, he is virtually our first author."

Brackenridge's father, Hugh Henry Brackenridge, was an author and lawyer, so it was not unusual that the son would follow in these professions. When Henry was seven his father sent him westward to Ste. Genevieve, Mo., to learn the French language. He enrolled at a French school there and stayed in the home of Mons. and Madame Beauvais. In six months he spoke almost flawless French.

He returned home at the age of 10. In 1801 his father was appointed to the Pennsylvania Supreme court and the son served two years as his father's clerk in preparation for a career in law. He passed the bar, went to Baltimore and at 21 began his practice.

The three years in Ste. Genevieve had wedded the young man to the West and in 1810 he returned to Missouri. He wrote for the Missouri Gazette, dabbled in law and quickly learned to speak Spanish with the same fluency he had in French.

He studied in the extensive St. Louis libraries of Auguste Chouteau and Frederick Bates. Hearing of Pierre Tardiveau's library in New Madrid, Mo., with books in five languages, he journeyed there, being one of those "lucky" reporters who "just happened to be on the spot," witnessing the New Madrid earthquake.

He was an avid traveler and in 1811 accompanied Manuel Lisa in his historic, 1,400-mile trip up the Missouri river to establish fur-trading posts. From this trip came Brackenridge's book, "Journal of a Voyage up the Missouri River," "Views of Louisiana," a book about the upper Missouri, both published in 1814.

Although Brackenridge was highly intelligent and erudite, he was also able to communicate with the "common" man. While walking near a prison in St. Louis an Indian behind the iron gate beckoned to him. Brackenridge went over and talked to him. He learned that the Indian had been in jail for 18 months before being tried for killing his wife on the St. Louis streets.

This outraged Brackenridge's sense of fairness. He secured an immediate trial, arguing two major points: The Indian was not a citizen of the United States and, therefore, not subject to the white man's code of laws. Since he had not killed a white man he should be judged by his own people.

The Indian was freed.

Brackenridge practiced law in St. Louis and probably could have been an extremely successful lawyer there, but he preferred to travel and write.

"The territory of Missouri and the State of Louisiana," he said "are equal in extent to any three of the largest states, whatever may administer to the convenience or luxury of man; rich in minerals, fertile in soil and favorably situated for commerce and manufacture."

In 1815 he said of St. Louis: "St. Louis will probably become one of those great reservoirs of the valley between the Rocky Mountains and the Allegheny from whence merchandise will be distributed to an extensive country. It unites the advantages of three noble rivers, the Mississippi, Missouri and Illinois."

Some of the French and Spanish citizens were fearful of the transfer to the United States, after the Louisiana Purchase was announced, and Brackenridge commented, "And is it nothing to exchange the name of colonists, Creoles, for that of AMERICANS, for that of a citizen of an independent state, where they can aspire to the highest employments and honors?"

His advice to those who would write is also worth noting. "It has always appeared to me that the observations of travelers, if made with any tolerable degree of accuracy, should rank amongst the most useful productions and should, moreover, be entitled to great indulgence. In this kind of writing, the fidelity of truth is far to be preferred to the mere artifice or elegance of diction."

In 1817 Brackenridge was appointed secretary to the government commissioners to the South American Republics and a short time later wrote "A Voyage to South America" in two volumes.

He returned to Baltimore, practiced law briefly, served two terms in the Maryland Legislature and then returned to St. Louis. He journeyed down to New Orleans and on the way met Andrew Jackson, who had just been appointed governor of Florida. Jackson persuaded Brackenridge to become his secretary, negotiator and counselor. From 1821 to 1832 Brackenridge served as United States judge for the western district of Florida.

He returned to Pittsburgh and in 1834 published this book, "Recollections of Persons and Places in the West," now considered a valuable historical source.

In 1841 President Harrison appointed him to a commission to try and work out a treaty with Mexico and in 1844 he served one term in the Pennsylvania Legislature.

Sharing to some extent similar honors with Capt. Amos Stoddard and Henry Rowe Schoolcraft, Henry M. Brackenridge was the first and one of the greatest of the "chamber of commerce" writer-promoters for Missouri and the western empire in the decade after the Louisiana Purchase. He died January 18, 1871, in Pittsburgh.

May 10, 1969

MISSOURI PRESS ASSOCIATION

The Missouri Press association, founded 102 years ago today, has a tradition of service to the state.

It took the leadership in establishing the State Historical Society of Missouri which, from membership and other factors, is regarded as the No. 1 state historical society in the nation.

It helped to establish the first school of journalism in the world at the University of Missouri at Columbia.

The general orgnizational format of the association has been copied by more than a score of similar state associations throughout the nation.

The Civil war was just finished when the association was formed. In some communities brother hated brother. And there were newspapers that supported the Union cause and the Confederacy.

Although most Missouri editors now resolve their differences over a cocktail or at the rural-type picnic dinner, it wasn't so 100 years ago. There brawls, fistfights, cane whippings and even duels. Such charges and foul language as were commonly heard then would lead directly to the courtroom today, but those rock-ribbed, independent and courageous Missourians preferred to settle differences their own way.

Perhaps those violent differences produced an amalgam right after the Civil war that resulted in the association becoming so powerful. Not that brotherly love prevails now 100 per cent. It is more like the adage, "My cousin isn't perfect but you'd better not pick on him."

There are several dates on the association, but May 17, 1867, is the official one. Abel Rathbone Corbin of the Missouri Argus in St. Louis proposed in 1837 that a state organization be established, and many regional meetings were held for almost 20 years. William F. Switzler, editor of the Columbia Missouri Statesman, also was a leader in these meetings.

The 1867 meeting was in St. Louis and attracted editors from 38 newspapers in 31 counties. Jesse W. Barrett was the first president. His grandson, of the same name, was Missouri attorney general.

Barrett came from Pennsylvania, was educated for the ministry and was president of the Methodist seminary at Canton, Mo., for several years. In 1862 he founded the Canton Press and was editor for 24 years. It was one of the few newspapers founded during the Civil war that survived. Barrett's editorial motto was, "Pledged but to truth, to liberty and law, no favor swings us and no fear shall awe us."

The association was actually formed June 8, 1859, in the Missouri House of Representatives at Jefferson City. Switzler was elected president and G.C. Stedman of St. Louis Republican was elected secretary. This organization was short-lived because of the approaching war.

An attempt was made to revive the the association at a meeting in Macon on June 12, 1866 but it just didn't seem to catch on, so the 1867 meeting became the official one. The association then was called the Editors and Publishers Association of Missouri, later changed to the Missouri Press association.

N. J. Colman, editor of the Rural World of St. Louis, was the association's second president. He later became the first U.S. Secretary of Agriculture.

Colman may be given credit for the idea of a journalism school, although Dean Walter Williams actually founded it in 1908. Colman, on the University of Missouri Board of Curators, suggested that a "course of study" be offered in journalism in 1864. Barrett also backed him and it is believed that one or two courses, no more than slightly altered English courses, were offered.

It remained however, for the young Boonville editor, Williams, to later push the idea vigorously and found the journalism school.

In January, 1898, the Missouri Press association met at the Coates house in Kansas City and laid the foundation for establishment of the State Historical Society. Almost all of the members were history-minded and saw the probability of important Missouri history slipping away, or being forgotten, unless some kind of official organization was founded to preserve it.

For almost 20 years the association existed on "oratory, poetry and banquets," as Clint Denman of the Sikeston Herald once said. Then the meetings took on a more serious slant.

He might have had in mind the immortal Eugene Field who was a member of the association and at the meeting in Fredericktown, June 6, 1877, offered this bit of verse:

Gayly the morning sun looked down
  on the busy streets of Fredericktown.
Old Bill Jones came out of his store
  In his arms a two-gallon keg he bore.
This is the long expected day
  When the editor men come down this way.

May 17, 1969

BENJAMIN GRATZ BROWN

The old saying about a man jumping onto his horse and galloping off in all directions could certainly apply to B. Gratz Brown, Missouri's 20th Governor and also a U.S. Senator.

He was born Benjamin Gratz Brown 143 years ago Wednesday in Lexington, Ky., and was graduated from Yale University in 1847. He was admitted to the bar in Louisville and began practicing law in St. Louis in 1849.

It is doubtful if any Missourian became assoicated with so many political movements and organizations as Brown. He was a Whig, a Democrat, a Benton Democrat, a Repbublican, a Radical Republican and a Free Soil Democrat.

He helped to organize the Republican party in Missouri. He supported Abraham Lincoln at the 1860 convention after casting his first three ballots for Edward Bates. In 1872 he was the vice-presidential candidate for the Liberal Republican party running with Horace Greeley. He was an early campaigner for the abolition of slavery.

One historian has explained that the political "fluctuations" of Brown were due to the general instability of American politics from 1850 to 1870.

However, with the exception of three years, Brown held office continuously from 1852 to 1873 in the Missouri Legislature, the U.S. Senate or as Governor, and was generally regarded as a much better than average public servant.

As Governor he pushed through important changes in the taxation and revenue systems, repealed the poll taxes, unified the assessment and collection of railroad taxes and gave major impetus to the establishment of schools for Negroes.

He early began cultivating the German vote and was elected to three terms in the Missouri Legislature, beginning in 1852. In 1857 he

122

B. GRATZ BROWN

delivered a bitter speech against slavery that was not very popular. He insisted that slavery would be a deterrent to Missouri's economic progress.

In 1863 Missouri's pro-Southern U.S. Senator, Waldo P. Johnson, was expelled from the Senate and Brown served out his unexpired term.

In March of 1867, at the end of the term, he returned to his home at Ironton, Mo., and in 1870 was elected governor of Missouri on the Liberal Republican ticket by a heavy majority of 42,000 votes.

After his defeat for the vice-presidency, he went to Kirkwood, Mo., and established his law practice. He died December 13, 1885, after an illness brought about mainly by overwork on a railroad case.

Although Brown jumped around politically, nobody questioned his courage. When Gen. John Charles Fremont, in charge of the Missouri district at the start of the Civil war, somewhat arbitrarily issued his proclamation of emancipation, Brown rose to his defense and he and Frank Blair violently disagreed.

Brown was a feudist of the old order. He criticized Missouri's war-time governor, Hamilton Gamble, for being "too lenient" toward the rebels and said Lincoln was too slow in his move for emancipation.

He was editor of the Missouri Democrat from 1854 to 1858 and fired broadsides at the supporters of slavery and the South.

After returning from his senatorial term in 1867 he announced his political "retirement," but he could not accept the Draconian code with the odious test oath, and ran for governor. Brown was a fine speaker and phrase-maker and said of the test oath, "While you stand here to commemorate the dead, you rest beneath a charter of constitutional state government that is in itself only a bundle of disenfranchisements of black and white whose discriminations are founded upon the color of skin and the oaths of the vanquished."

He married Mary Hansome Gunn of Jefferson City and they had two sons and six daughters. What is now the Cole County Historical Museum was his home while the 3-story executive mansion across the street was being built. The mansion, which is still being used, is regarded as one of the most attractive buildings in the nation.

May 24, 1969

CHARLES HENRY HARDIN

St. Patrick is supposed to have driven the snakes out of Ireland, but his feat may not have been as great as Charles Henry Hardin, the

125

22nd governor of Missouri, who drove the grasshoppers and locusts out of Missouri.

Public men are sometimes known for an accomplishment probably not as governmentally basic as their general services in office, and this most aptly applies to Hardin.

He had held many offices and was elected governor and inaugurated January 12, 1875. He was a religious man, had founded the Hardin college for women at Mexico and performed other commendable public acts even before becoming governor.

(Note: In all reports then, and even to modern times, the words "grasshopper" and "locusts" are used interchangeably. Actually, they belong to the same family but the locust is simply a short-horned grasshopper, that is with a short antennae, and sometimes inclined to cover much longer distances. So the word "locust" will be used here.)

The 1875 devastation of Western Missouri by the locust was probably the worst in history. There had been a plague in 1821 but it could not compare with the one in 1875, because the insects in 1821 destroyed vegetation on usettled land.

The 1875 invasion is called the "Rocky Mountain" plague because it began in the Northwest. It actually began in 1874 with enormous and considerable destruction and the laying of eggs for the much bigger destructiveness the next year.

With the young locusts crawling along the ground and joined by fresh swarms, the 1875 invasion was unbelievable. At one time the swarm was 300 miles long and 100 miles wide, shutting out the sun and with a whirring of wings that probably sounded like today's jet planes.

Their devastation was in most of Western Missouri. Bushes and trees were denuded in a few minutes. The locusts ate the wool off the backs of sheep on the farmlands. It was as if a magic wand were waved over miles and miles of green countryside to suddenly see it become gray and brown with vegetation.

The locusts slithered along miles of railroad tracks causing the rails to become so slick and slimy the train crews had to clear the insects away. Corn and wheat fields were denuded. Many families left Western Missouri.

Kansas City organized a relief society and collected food and other necessary articles for the suffering families.

Governor Hardin, in the face of some jests and ridicule, issued his famous "Grasshopper Proclamation," asking the people to set aside June 3, 1875 as a day of prayer for the relief from the billions of locusts.

There were prayers in many parts of the state. Farmers stopped

GOVERNOR CHARLES HENRY HARDIN   Credit: State Historical Society of Mo.

momentarily from digging miles of trenches to pray. The crawling insects would fall into the trenches and great logs were pulled through them. Huge fires were set on mounds of insects, some mounds higher than the men. Stone rollers were pulled over the fields where the crawling insects were a foot deep.

Within a few days the scoffers stared in utter disbelief. A strong wind came out of the east and heavy rains began to fall. The winds carried many insects back toward the northwest, and Iowa got a good proportion. The rains washed millions away into choking streams and otherwise prevented those in the air from alighting.

By June 15 Missouri was free of the destructive swarms. With some restraint, Hardin commented on the event by saying there is "divine manifestation" in the power of prayer.

Prof. C. V. Riley, then one of Missouri's outstanding entomologists, estimated the loss to Missouri at 15 million dollars, this being mainly in crops.

But there wasn't a total loss. Missouri farmers learned much about locusts in a short time and fed them alive and roasted to their hogs and poultry. Roasted locusts were put away for later feeding to the stock.

There was some levity other than that directed at Hardin's action. Someone recalled that John the Baptist ate locusts and honey, and that several Indian tribes ate them. After pulling off the wings and legs, the locusts were fried in oil by the Indians, or roasted, or allowed to dry in the sun and then pounded into a meal for bread.

A Warrensburg newspaper reported a complete locust "dinner" by two men. First there was locust soup, then baked locusts, locust cakes made from a batter and finally the "dessert" of John the Baptist, locusts and honey. There wasn't enough confirmation in the story to prove any truth but it lightened the otherwise grim situation.

To those who professed nausea at the idea of eating locusts, the proponents pointed out the insects ate only green vegetation and were cleaner than pigs and poultry.

The situation also produced tests by chemists on locusts as fertilizer and locust oil, and launched chemical companies on the long trail of chemicals for destruction of the insects.

In addition to being a circuit attorney from 1848 to 1852, and serving very creditably in the Missouri House and Senate, Hardin was selected in 1855 as one of three men to revise and codify the Missouri statutes. Shortly afterward he said he would retire. But he did not.

As governor he reduced the state debt, cut state government expenses and hit at crime and lawlessness.

But ask students of Missouri history just what Hardin was noted for and in all probability the answer will be for driving the locusts out of Missouri in 1875.

May 31, 1969

SUSAN ELIZABETH BLOW

Today as an anniversary may be lost in the main on most of the United States, but those who teach kindergarten probably will remember it as the 126th birthday anniversary of the woman who opened the first public kindergarten in this nation and gave the movement tremendous impetus.

As the daughter of Henry T. Blow, a civic-minded industrialist and congressman, she had access to the highest social circles. But this didn't suit the young woman. She was a scholar and follower of Hegel and restlessly was seeking some way to justify her existence.

Then she became interested in the educational philosophy of Friedrich Froebel, who actually founded the kindergarten plan in Germany. In 1872 she discussed the idea with Dr. William Torrey Harris, superintendent of the St. Louis public schools and a nationally known scholar and educator.

He encouraged the young woman and she went to New York to study under Mrs. Maria Kraus-Boelte who was pioneering the Froebel methods in the city kindergartens.

She returned burning with enthusiasm. The farsighted Harris agreed to set aside a room in the Des Peres school at Carondelet and in September, 1873, Miss Blow opened the first public kindergarten in the United States.

She was the unpaid director, agreeing to work without a salary. Mary Timberlake was the only paid teacher and there were two unpaid apprentices, Cynthia Dozier and Sally Hawk.

Because this unusual class changed almost from day to day at the start, there are differences in the attendance figures. Harris said in his report to the school board that there were 30 boys and 38 girls.

Miss Blow's first report said there were 20 children the first day and "this quickly grew to 42." At the beginning of the second year in September, 1874, the enrollment began with 75 and a second room was added.

The basic philosophy of the kindergarten has changed little since Froebel, only the procedures and educational format, but it was evident that Miss Blow understood this philosophy when she said this in her first report:

130

SUSAN BLOW   Credit: State Historical Society of Mo.

"Personally, however, I feel that the strongest claim of the kindergarten is the happiness it produces. If we can create in children a love for work, we shall have no difficulty in making them persistently industrious; if we can make children love intellectual effort we shall prolong the habits of study beyond school years, and if we can ensure to all children every day four hours of pleasurable activity without excitement, we lay strong foundation for a calm, contented and cheerful disposition."

The spread of the kingergarten movement in America's public schools was assured. In 1877 Miss Blow spent a year in Europe and Germany further studying the general methods and when she returned the St. Louis school board placed her in charge of the first kindergarten training school.

Miss Blow began giving lectures in other cities and helping to establish kindergartens and then training schools for teachers. Educators went to St. Louis to study the classes there. She started classed for mothers whose children had started, or were about ready to start, to kindergarten, the forerunner to the "Parent-Teacher" movement.

The almost immediate success of the movement assured her immortality in the educational field, although now and then a detractor appears.

Mrs. Carl Schurz, wife of the man who became United States Senator from Missouri, opened a private kindergarten in Watertown, Wis., primarily for German children, before Schurz went to St. Louis. This was 1855 or 1856. Around 1860 Elizabeth Peabody opened a private kindergarten in Boston.

All responsible authorities agree that Miss Blow opened the first public kindergarten in this country and give her credit for the early development of the idea.

From 1894 Miss Blow wrote books, lectured and continued to study. In 1910, when the National Kindergarten union (teachers), met in St. Louis, the 67-year-old Susan Elizabeth Blow marched at the head of 600 teachers from all parts of the nation and received a tremendous ovation. She died in 1916 at Avon, N. Y., where she was associated with the graduate department of the New York Kindergarten association.

June 7, 1969

PHILIP FRANCIS RENAULT

Long before the first towns were established along the banks of the Mississippi river in what is now Illinois and Missouri, an enterprising Frenchman did extensive lead mining for more than 10 years.

He was Philip Francis Renault (the Anglicized version of Phillippe Francois), who was also the first white man to do any mining of consequence in Missouri.

Both De Soto and Coronado, mesmerized by the Indian stories of the abundance of gold on the new continent, had unsuccessfully sought the metal. De Soto and his men got as far as what is now Arkansas before he was killed.

The stories persisted, and a century and half later La Motte Cadillac and his men came to Missouri in search of gold and silver. They did not find it, but they are believed to have been the first white men to discover the rich lead deposits in the present Washington County area.

They mined some lead, about 1715, but were content with only scraping it from near the top of the ground. Shaft mining was entirely new and a major problem was getting the lead to France. They did not come to find lead, so they really didn't know what to do with it.

Cadillac returned to France and his stories about lead attracted the attention of Philip Renault, Sr., a widely known iron foundry owner and owner of iron mines. He proceeded to organize the Company of the West to go to the new land and mine the lead.

His son was placed in charge of the rather ambitious undertaking. The son left France about 1719 with 200 "artificers," meaning workmen, and some who understood mining. They also took all of the tools needed and even bricks for a smelting furnace with the Renault name on them.

He brought some Negro slaves to Missouri to work in the mines. Undoubtedly he is the first white man to introduce slavery into what is now Missouri.

The charter provisions of the Company of the West called for the European managers to furnish Renault with no fewer than 25 Negroes annually, and the general settlement was to gradually expand to 6,000 white persons and about 3,000 slaves.

Although Cadillac probably was the first white man to mine lead in Missouri, Renault undoubtedly was the first to (1) mine it extensively, (2) use the shaft methods, and (3) use a smelter.

Renault came up the Mississippi in 1723 from New Orleans and established his camp near Fort Chartres, near what is now Ste. Genevieve. It is believed he formally named it "Phillippe" from the family name.

Considerable time was required to set up the camp, then to explore the area.

Renault eventually received a land grant from his own government for a large area five miles northeast of what was Mine A Breton.

Renault worked hard. Within two years he and his men were bringing out 1,500 pounds of lead daily. The lead was smelted into "pigs" shaped somewhat like horse collars and shipped to New Orleans for further shipment to France.

Renault was a successful lead producer. He built a stone house for himself across the river in Illinois and he returned to France in 1842.

Although he introduced shaft mining., some thought that he had already mined all the lead. Records indicate some financial difficulties.

The miners, most of whom lived across the river near Kaskaskia, had become prosperous. The Indians, mainly the Fox tribes, and then the Kickapoo, Chickasaw and Osage, began to step up their depredations upon the scattered settlements of miners. Sometimes the miners were under siege for days within the mines.

Some of Renault's men returned to France with him. Some stayed, and undoubtedly a few of these provided the nucleus for the establishment of Ste. Genevieve. But Renault had pioneered the industry which, today, is a major one in Missouri, and this state for years has produced more lead than any other state.

June 14, 1969

EARLY ROAD NETWORK

Missouri has sometimes been known for good roads. It was 161 years ago yesterday when the Territory of Missouri Legislature enacted the first road law that called for a "waggon" road from St. Louis to Ste. Genevieve and then on to Cape Girardeau and New Madrid.

Meriwether Lewis, the territorial governor, and the two territorial judges, John B. C. Lucas and Otho Shrader, signed the act.

They appointed three commissioners to lay out the route and provide a map. The road became El Camino Real, or the King's Highway. It followed an old Indian trail that had been marked by the tribes about 1789, although part of it probably belonged to the mine owners who needed roads for the marketing of the lead.

The territorial Legislature passed another road law, or supplementary act, November 10, 1808, calling for a width of 25 feet and permanent supervisors.

As Missouri's population increased there were demands for more roads. The Boonslick trail from St. Charles to Franklin was a heavily traveled road before Missouri became a state, and soon was extended to Independence and the western settlements.

Citizens could pay their taxes, or part of them, by working on the roads, and usually in the late summer all able-bodied, taxpaying men held a "road bee" to repair the roads.

Missouri and the nation began building roads, if they could be called that, shortly after the end of the Revolutionary War.

In the 20 years following 1792 a total of 300 charters were granted for turnpikes and more than 4,500 miles of roads were constructed in this country.

Missouri's first transportation arteries were the rivers and Indian trails. The Indians were efficient road builders.

There originally were nine major Indian trails in Missouri. They included trails from the Osage villages to the Boonslick area and to St. Louis. Whether all the tribes followed the practice of the Osages is not known, but the Osages usually laid out three different kinds of trails. One was for hunting, the second for visiting with other tribes and general travel and the third for trading with other tribes and the white men.

The Osages took into account rivers and streams, general topography, watersheds, forested areas and the prevalence of game.

The Santa Fe trail, beginning in Franklin, was the longest road. Part of it was first traveled in 1804, but the first regular travel along all of the road—beginning in Missouri—began in 1822 when Capt. William Becknell of Franklin and several men made the trips in their own wagons, but it was not until 1849 that the first stagecoach trip was made. It took two weeks and the fare was $250.

The first roads were rough and bumpy, many times not level and quite often almost impassable because of mud. Charles Dickens in 1842 wrote of some of the roads and stagecoach travel:

"At one time we were flung together in a heap at the bottom of the coach; at another we were crushing our heads against the roof. Now one side was deep in the mire, and we were holding onto the other. The very slightest jolts with which the ponderous carriage fell from log to log was enough, it seemed, to dislocate all the bones in the human body."

Undoubtedly the first roads in Missouri were laid out, sometimes along Indian trails, in Southeast Missouri in the early 1700s to transport the lead to the Mississippi river for further transportation either to the Eastern states or to Europe.

They started at Mine la Motte, a major producer for more than a century, and went directly to the Mississippi River. Later there was a branch to Ste. Genevieve. This was called the "Three Notch road" because three notches on the trees provided the "guide posts."

The first public law 'which Meriwether Lewis, as territorial governor, signed shortly after the Louisiana Purchase, was the first legally designated road west of the Mississippi River.

The wave of turnpike construction began around 1830 and before the plank-road craze. Private corporations built the turnpikes with toll gates every five to ten miles. There were long poles with spikes on the end that halted the travelers at the toll gates.

In 1839 the St. Louis and St. Charles Turnpike company was formed. The proposed road was an ambitious undertaking—80 feet wide, 24 of it to be macadamized and with three toll gates. It was not completed until after the end of the Civil War.

By the middle of the century there was a fairly good network of roads in Missouri. Springfield was connected with St. Louis and there were roads across the entire state. Southeast Missiouri was well connected with many of the old towns along the Mississippi River.

June 21, 1969

RACE BETWEEN STEAMBOATS

All the superlatives may be used to describe a steamboat race on the Mississippi River that began 99 years ago Monday at New Orleans.

It was between the Robert E. Lee and the Natchez, and most of the United States and part of continental Europe were excited over the outcome. Undoubtedly it was the most famous steamboat race in American history by virtue of the 1,200-mile course, the experienced captains and the public's knowledge of steamboat racing.

Just who issued the challenge is not known, but there had been some good-natured rivalry between these two luxury boats and the able skippers for years. The race was as inevitable as a fight between two well-matched heavyweights.

The Lee, with Capt. John W. Cannon as skipper, left the New Orleans wharf about 5 o'clock the afternoon of June 30, 1870. Half of

THE HISTORIC MISSISSIPPI RIVER—STEAMBOAT RACE BETWEEN THE ROBERT E. LEE AND THE NATCHEZ
(from a currier and Ives print)

the New Orleans population had lined the river banks to cheer the departure.

Four minutes later the Natchez, with Capt. Thomas P. Leathers as skipper, slipped away and another tremendous roar went up from the crowd.

The Natchez cost $200,000 to build and the boats were similar in appointments—luxurious staterooms, double decks, thick rugs, gilded decorations, red plush upholstering and mahogany woodwork. The menus, with many French dishes, caused many an experienced gourmet trouble even arising from the table.

Otherwise, the two boats had some structural differences. The Lee was smaller but with a broader beam and large top hamper it appeared to be larger.

The Natchez was more graceful and had a sharper stem, which made her appear to slice through the water while the Lee seemed to shove through it.

Cannon meant to race and showed it by pre-race changes. He stripped the Lee to her spars, even removing parts of the guards abaft the wheelhouses to cut down wind resistance—probably the first "streamlining" of a water craft.

Cannon also loaded the fire bunkers with choice dry pine knots, select coal, resin and barrels of coal oil and even spoiled fat bacon to force the boiler fires.

In addition to being the first skipper to streamline his boat, at least for racing purposes, he also was the first to take on wood fuel while moving. He hired the Frank Paragaud, a smaller craft, to come alongside, and while the two craft were lashed together crews hastily tossed firewood to the Lee crewmen.

This brought on the only argument between the two skippers. Leathers contended that the Pargaud's engines gave an added boost to the Lee.

The supporters of the Natchez afterward contended that Leathers could have won if he had put more effort into the race and if a heavy fog hadn't held up the boat five hours. Leathers did take on several tons of freight and even made several stops to take on special passengers.

On July 1 the boats passed Vicksburg and thousands lined the banks. In fact, all along the river townspeople turned out to cheer their favorites.

There were several times that only minutes separated the two boats. After they passed the mouth of the Ohio River low water and fog forced them to proceed slowly.

This was when Cannon added daring to his ingenuity to sew up the victory. He pushed on slowly, but Leathers stopped for about five hours in a dense fog. He contended that the safety of his passengers and the luxury craft were more important than running onto a sand bar or into another boat.

The Lee pulled into St. Louis July 4 at 11:25 o'clock in the morning the Natchez arrived shortly before 5 o'clock that afternoon. The Lee had broken a 14-year record and her time of three days, 18 hours and 14 minutes stood as long as steamboats made the New Orleans-to-St. Louis run.

St. Louis staged a series of parties for both skippers. A flotilla of excursion steamers steamed out to officially escort the Lee to dock. Cannon and Leathers were royally entertained. They gave innumerable speeches and received medals from the City of St. Louis.

What youngsters now call "drag racing" was popular in the steamboat days. If two boats were fairly well matched, and one pulled up alongside the other, it was almost certain one skipper would yell and dare the other one to try and pass him. Sometimes two skippers would plan a race at one wharf to a certain town and the passengers of the two boats would bet on their favorite.

Almost all the planned races were on the Mississippi. The Missouri river channel and current were too tricky; the sand bars shifted too often.

The winning boat could carry a big broom lashed to the pilot house as evidence to all she was the "champion." The broom came down, of course, when the craft was beaten.

June 28, 1969

RAVENSWOOD

Tourists already are beating a path to one of the grand show places of Missouri—Ravenswood, which is 13 miles south of Boonville and loaded with antiques, stained-glass windows, Tiffany glass and almost everything to delight those who worship memorabilia and venerate the past.

The almost 2,000 acres of beautiful, rolling South-Central Missouri land is owned by Charles Willard Leonard, whose great-great-great-grandfather, Nathaniel Leonard, was minister of the First Church of Plymouth, Mass., from 1724 to 1761.

His son, the Rev. Abiel Leonard, was an Episcopalian minister and pastor of Woodstock church in Connecticut from 1763 to 1777. Abiel was a chaplain in the Revolutionary army and drew praise from General Washington.

A grandson, Abiel Leonard, studied law in New York and in 1819 he came west and settled in Missouri.

Abiel induced his brother, Nathaniel Leonard, to come to Missouri. He arrived in Missouri in 1824 and proceeded to his brother's farm near Franklin.

Abiel helped Nathaniel to buy 80 acres of land in Cooper County, and Nathaniel began to build Ravenswood into about 2,000 acres.

Abiel Leonard fought a duel with Taylor Berry on an island near New Madrid and killed Berry in a pistol duel. Leonard later regretted the action and refused to discuss it.

Leonard continued to build the estate, adding a few acres now and then, went into the mule business and in 1839 bought several purebred Shorthorn cattle, the first of the breed west of the Mississippi River.

Then he went on to build a herd that garnered international honors. His son, Charles Edward Leonard, born in 1839, attended Kemper Military Academy in Boonville, one of three generations to attend the academy, and was graduated from the University of Missouri in 1860 at the top of his class. He continued to build both Ravenswood and the Shorthorn herd and became an international leader in pushing the potentials of the Shorthorns.

The original house burned after the Civil War. Charles Edward Leonard married Miss Nadine Nelson of Boonville and they built the present Ravenswood mansion in 1880.

The present owner is Charles Willard Leonard, who looks after the estate and shows tourists through the house and around the grounds.

July 5, 1969

REV. TIMOTHY FLINT

"He is generally an amiable, virtuous man but with vices and barbarisms peculiar to his situation; his manners are rough . . . he is destitute of the forms and observances of religion, but sincere and hospitable to strangers."

That is a description of the average Missourian in the early 19th century, and was made by the Rev. Timothy Flint, who was a far better writer and reporter than he was a missionary.

Flint was one of a small group of men who came to Missouri after 1800 and became a chronicler of early Missouri. Strangely enough, none professed to be writers.

Flint was a Harvard-educated Presbyterian. John Mason Peck also was a frontier missionary. Henry Brackenridge was a Maryland lawyer and Amos Stoddard, the U. S. Army captain who formally and officially took over the Louisiana Purchase for his nation. Yet, these four, with several others, so accurately depicted early Missouri and Missourians that their writings were definitive textbooks for years.

Flint was perhaps the most unusual personality of the group. He was born 189 years ago yesterday in Massachusetts and shortly after being graduated from Harvard university was ordained a Congregational minister. The Connecticut Presbyterian Missionary society sought frontier preachers and Flint resigned his pulpit at Lunenburg, Mass., and came west as a minister.

He told of one community on a river where the pioneers were eager for religious help but almost every one had his own religion still operating.

"They wanted their religion but the Minister must permit them their poison," Flint lamented. He said the people regarded their "red-eye liquor" as medicine and usually spread a layer of black pepper on top before downing it raw.

He wrote that Ste. Genevieve, the state's oldest, continuous city, is populated by "amiable and polished people, evidencing the possession of a considerable degree of refinement."

Of St. Louis, he wrote, "St. Louis, as you approach it, shows like other French towns in this region, to much the greatest advantage at a distance. The French mode of building, and the white coat of lime applied to the mud or rough stone walls, gives them beauty at a distance."

After the Louisiana Purchase, and when Anglo-Saxon Americans began arriving in St. Louis after the War of 1812, the city got a "strong economic impulse," Flint said. "Before that the town was dirty and backward."

He liked St. Charles, where he conducted his ministry for awhile, and wrote that it reminded him somewhat of Albany, N. Y. Land values began to rise after the Anglo-Saxon immigration and agriculture boomed. The sometimes indolent French could never understand the nervous eagerness of the Americans.

The bright little town of Florissant bewitched Flint, who commented, "The quality and fertility of this place is indicated by the French name."

Flint deplored horse racing before the Sunday morning services and got the St. Charles grand jury to stop the playing of billiards on Sunday.

While a part of his moral crusade was basic, it did go to extremes now and then, especially when a Jackson, Mo., grand jury indicted a farmer for feeding his cattle on Sunday.

He was most vehement against the so-called "camp meeting," when the preacher worked his listeners into an emotional frenzy. Flint wrote about the "head jerking and holy toppling."

One of his best descriptions concerned dueling—"In the towns of the upper country on the Mississippi, and especially in St. Louis there is one species of barbarism that is but too common; I mean the horrid practice of dueling.

"But be it remembered, this is the barbarism only of that small class that denominate themselves 'The Gentlemen.' It cannot be a matter of astonishment that these are common here, when we recollect that the fierce and adventurous spirits are naturally attracted to these regions, and that it is a common proverb of the people, that when we cross the Mississippi, 'We travel beyond the Sabbath.' "

He and his wife opened a school for "lads and misses" in Jackson and after detailing the curses available the advertisement said about the pupils, "Their morals, their habits, their comfort and general improvement will be assiduously watched."

July 12, 1969

SHOOTING WAR IN CUBA

Missouri played the usual important role militarily in the Spanish-American war, and the 6th Missouri infantry saw service.

The 6th was the last to take the field. Orders came in August, 1898, to proceed to Jacksonville, Fla. A St. Louis newspaper reported at the time about the 6th regiment, "There is but one thing that stands in the way of striking camp this evening and that is the possibility that the tourist rail cars may not arrive in time. In that event the trip will be postponed until Thursday."

The article continued, "The contract for transporting the troops from Jefferson Barracks to Camp Jackson was awarded to the Missouri Pacific at $6.50 per capita and far below five other railroads."

At Jacksonville, the 6th was assigned to the 2nd brigade, 3rd division of the 7th Army corps. The camp was named "Cuba Libre." Col. Letcher Hardeman spent a lot of time drilling the troops and bringing them to a high point of efficiency.

145

SIXTH MO. REGIMENT

Credit: State Historical Society of Mo.

The 6th was moved several times, finally reaching Camp Marianno, not far from Havana. It took part in the occupation of the island.

Hardeman was placed in command of the 6th regiment. It was made up of companies from Brookfield, California, Doniphan, Carondelet, Kennett, St. Louis, Willow Springs, Bloomfield, St. Charles, Lutesville and De Soto.

The 6th was composed of 46 officers and 1,077 men. It was mustered into the service July 20, 1898, at Jefferson barracks.

The nation was woefully unprepared at the start of the war, with only 28,000 regular troops, part of which had to be stationed in the West to guard against Indian forays.

Missouri furnished 8,083 volunteers to the armed forces, plus about 3,000 men for the regular forces. Of course, there were hundreds in nonmilitary organizations.

Only four states—New York, Illinois, Ohio and North Dakota—gave more men than Missouri. The University of Missouri may have set a national record among all universities and colleges by sending one-fourth of its total enrollment into the military forces.

In addition to the 6th being one of the best regiments in the Army, there also were many individual heroes among Missourians.

The New York Herald offered $100 to the first American to plant the flag on Cuban soil, and Arthur L. Willard of Kirksville won the money, accomplishing the act at Diana City.

Frank Fulton of St. Louis became the first to plant the flag atop San Juan hill.

One of Admiral Dewey's crack gunners was A. L. Smith of Sedalia. Edward P. Stanton of St. Louis raised the first American flag over Manila.

Ensign Leigh C. Palmer of the USS New York, also a Missourian, conducted a reconnaissance of the land batteries at Santiago under heavy fire and was decorated.

Major Enoch Crowder of Edinburg, Mo., and Lt. John Henry "Gatling Gun" Parker of Tipton, Mo., played important roles.

At El Caney the courageous conduct of a young lieutenant caught the attention of his superiors.

The name? John J. Pershing.

July 19, 1969

ZEBULON PIKE

Zebulon Pike was a distinguished soldier, but he is undoubtedly best known as the man who "discovered" Pike's peak.

He is also the first American whose name was given to a Mississippi river steamboat.

The Zebulon M. Pike, usually referred to as the "Pike," first landed in 1817 at St. Louis wharf. It had made the trip from Louisville in six weeks.

The Pike was built at Henderson, Ky., and its first trip was to Louisville in 1815.

It had a walking beam and low-pressure engine. The cabin, on the main deck, had inside running boards.

When the current slowed a little, the crew could add a little extra propellant to the engine by mounting the running boards and pushing against the river bottom with long poles.

After the Pike made its first trip on the upper Mississippi from Louisville to St. Louis, regular 4-week trips were made with stops at Herculaneum, Ste. Genevieve, Cape Girardeau and other towns along the river.

Early issues of the St. Louis Gazette carried notices of the Pike's arrival and departure, the early notices being signed by the captain, Jacob Reed.

The Zebulon Pike and the Independence were the first two steamboats to move up to St. Louis. The latter was the first to get to Franklin.

After the Pike docked at St. Louis, river travel became more popular as the fear of it lessened.

The steamboats were fitted out with wall-to-wall carpeting, gilded dance lounges and all of the conveniences of the shore.

Among those who witnessed the arrival of the Pike in St. Louis were some Indians. When they saw the steamboat puffing up the river, sparks shooting into the sky and ugly smoke billowing from its stacks, they decided the white man's river travel was not for them.

July 26, 1969

CONFEDERATE GENERAL

In a general discussion of Missouri Confederate leaders in the Civil war, the names heard most often are Sterling Price, Jo Shelby, Jeff Thompson, Hiram Bledsoe and maybe one or two others, but one of the ablest and bravest generals has not received the attention he deserves.

He is William Yarnel Slack, born 153 years ago yesterday in Macon County, Kentucky. He was only three when the family moved to Boone County. He received a common-school education in Columbia, studied law there and was admitted to the bar in 1837.

He thought Columbia was getting a little crowded then so he moved to Chillicothe to establish his law office. He became one of the leading lawyers of Livingston County, and was elected to the Missouri House of Representatives in 1842, at the age of 26, and to the 1845 Constitutional convention.

At the outbreak of the war with Mexico, Slack organized a company in his general area and was elected captain by the men. The company joined Alexander Doniphan in the march to the Southwest. Slack and his company distinguished themselves in three battles, and, according to one report, Slack conducted himself with "coolness, courage and gallantry."

After the war he resumed the practice of law in Chillicothe. His record in the Mexican war, plus his Southern leanings, caused Gov. Claiborne Jackson to commission Slack a brigadier general of the Missouri Guard at the start of the Civil war and to place him in charge of the 4th military district, which included 11 counties.

He immediately organized the district. The 4th division under him was composed of 500 cavalrymen and 700 infantrymen. His courageous service to the South almost didn't occur because June 14, 1861, while he was organizing his district, 800 federal troops swooped down on Chillicothe and he and his family barely escaped. He never saw his home again.

Slack first distinguished himself in the Battle of Carthage, which the rebels won, but lost Franz Sigel's army. Slack's cavalry and Col. Richard Weightman's brigade bore the brunt of this attack for a part of the battle.

Following was the Battle of Wilson's Creek, in which Slack was dangerously wounded. He led about 1,000 men against 5,000 Yankees and finally was relieved by Louisiana troops and Weightman's brigade. Weightman was mortally wounded and Sterling Price suffered a minor wound. General Lyon, the brilliant Union leader, also was killed in this battle, one of the major conflicts of the war in Missouri.

Slack's wife, Mrs. Isabella Bower Slack, and the family physician Dr. William Keith, of Chillicothe, hastened to Springfield to nurse him back to health. They unsuccessfully sought to persuade him to rest on his laurels, but Col. James A. Mulligan surrendered to Price at Lexington the same day Slack rejoined his men.

ZEBULON PIKE   Credit: State Historical Society of Mo.

GENERAL WILLIAM Y. SLACK   Credit: State Historical Society of Mo.

The Battle of Pea Ridge, Ark., just below the Missouri border, March 7 and 8, 1862, might well rank as the major turning point because it kept Missouri in the Union for the duration of the conflict.

Gen. Samuel R. Curtis, a crusty and dour West Point graduate, whose salient military feature was that he loved to fight, regardless of the odds, had 10,500 men when Gen. Earl Van Dorn, also a West Point graduate, confronted him with 16,000 troops.

Price had organized his Missourians into two brigades commanded by Slack and Col. Henry Little, and they were regarded as among the best drilled and equipped of all Missourians.

Slack and Little moved forward to the right and two divisions under Gen. James R. Rains and Gen. Daniel M. Frost advanced to the left. They hammered hard at the Yankees and pushed them back. The rebels gained a hill and thus an advantage.

The battle raged throughout the day and then the tactical pieces Curtis had fashioned began to fall into place and the second morning the rout of the rebels was accomplished.

This was one of the most sanguinary battles of the war, especially from the loss of commanding officers. Slack was mortally wounded. Price suffered another wound. Gen. Ben McCulloch and Gen. James McIntosh of the Confederate army were killed.

In his official report Van Dorn wrote of Slack's "gallantly maintaining a continued and successful attack," and added, "He always endeared himself to his command by his bravery and great prudence and his name is embalmed in the hearts of the people of Missouri."

Slack lived several days after being wounded. The Confederate command at Richmond heard of his bravery and Jefferson Davis brevetted him brigadier general of the Confederate armies. (He had been brigadier general of the Missouri State Guard).

Slack, whose comrades such as Price, Shelly, Thompson, Bledsoe and others lived to see the end of the war and the aftermath, would have been pleased with the Confederate commission, but it arrived after he died.

He was only 45 years old. He was buried in the Confederate cemetery at Fayetteville Ark., and after the war a monument was erected honoring him and other Southern soldiers who fell at Pea Ridge near Bentonville, Ark.

Aug. 2, 1969

HOW GOOD WERE THE "GOOD OLD DAYS"?

No, there was no Vietnam then, no surtax and high taxes, no rioting, not much worrying about tomorrow or whether junior would do a little drag racing with the team of mules.

Those were the "good old days" so many pine for today, perhaps, and as tensions in the world grow, many may wish for those days of the pioneer 150 years ago, more or less.

And what were those "good old days," at least in Missouri?

The pioneers came into Missouri in their wagons, selected their land and settled. After tethering the livestock, the men brought out the ax, ring mauls, wedges and gluts and cut down trees and split rails to build an enclosure for the livestock.

They always stopped at a nearby stream for water to quench the thirst of man and beast and to provide a cool cache for meat, butter and milk. The corn crib sort of sprouted. Then it was time to provide quarters for humans.

The barn and the smokehouse seemed to spring from the soil, but "house raisings" were different. Neighbors, not like yours next door, but who lived miles away, came to help with this important task. And they got acquainted and stayed a couple of days until the house was up and the land cleared.

The rifle brought in deer, turkey, quail, dove, pheasant, snipe and other meat. The streams abounded with fish. Ginseng weeds were gathered, maple trees tapped, the courser followed the honey bee to the tree.

And soon they raised corn and beans and many other vegetables, hogs, horses, cattle and chickens and maybe sheep for meat and clothing.

There were many specialists then, too, but the "fence rider" was always in demand. He knew how to make a solid fence that would keep in the stock and keep out the marauding wild animals. White oaks made the best rails, walnut and wild cherry were next. White oak seemed to last longer and better withstood the weather.

An experienced rail-maker could hack into a tree and determine if it would split into rails satisfactorily. He became the expert carpenter of the community. The going wage then was 75 cents for 100 rails ten feet long, and 85 cents for 100 rails 12 feet long. It required considerable work to turn out 100 in a day.

But they seemed to have fun in those good old days, perhaps because work was not something to be avoided—building, planting, plowing, hoeing, milking, killing gray squirrels, blackbirds, wolves and other varmints; the inescapable weeding, husking and shelling of corn, rolling logs, treading out and cleaning wheat, slaughtering hogs and hanging the shanks in the smokehouse, harvesting the walnuts and boiling out the hulls to color pants and coats.

There was nothing thrown away then, except the squeal of the pig. Corn shucks were laid out in the barn lofts and weighted with poles. Later they were woven into horse collars, sewed into chair bottoms, shredded and mixed with feathers for bed ticking, tied onto sticks for brooms, used for sausage casing and put into the bottoms of boots in the winter.

They worked hard in those good old days, maybe because they always had faith in the future. There were house raisings and house warmings, sap collecting, sugaring-offs, corn shucking and plowing contests, quilting bees, bonnet shows, cooking contests, dressmaking shows and shooting matches.

There was always plenty of venison and wild turkey, mush, pone, johnnycake, and hoecakes cornbread, chicken and beef, sorghum and the sweetening, pumpkins, potatoes and potpie. It was always easy to pop something into the spider and set it right over the fireplace coals.

They enjoyed the holidays, too, perhaps a bit differently than today. On Independence Day the band played "Jefferson's March," "Washington's March," and "The Soldier's Return," and many others.

Then they listened to long speeches while the tantalizing odors of barbecued venison, pork, beef and mutton floated over the meeting, and they watched kettles of burgoo hung over the fire and sniffed the aroma of freshly-baked bread.

They danced to "The Sailor's Hornpipe." "Great Tater in the Sandy Land," "Old Dan Tucker." and other tunes that "swung them."

"Divorce" was a seldom heard word in those pioneering days. In addition to giving birth almost once a year, the women did all the housework and cooking, cared for the sheep, chickens and other animals, did the washing, knitting, spinning and weaving, made the blankets and clothing for the family, made the soap and candles and helped with the planting and harvesting.

It was impossible to get on the train, or plane, and go home to mother. The husband and father realized that if she managed to do anything akin to this, he'd have to "break in" another wife for the 12- to 15- hour day schedule, or hire a woman, and this would be too costly.

So they just learned to live together and continue raising children, having little time to argue about unimportant matters.

At the apothecary in town there was castor oil, camphor, sulphur, Dr. Lee's Bilious Pills, snake root and Turlington's Balm of Life, but no tranquilizers, sleeping pills or nerve medicine.

Those were the conditions which the pioneers, who built this state and nation, had to endure in the "good old days," which Longfellow called "the irrevocable past."

How fortunate the present civilization does not have to endure those conditions.

Aug. 9, 1969

BATTLE OF LONE JACK

Today is the 107th anniversary of the battle of Lone Jack—in which almost all the combatants on both sides were Missourians.

There are several other interesting aspects of the battle:

The unintentional rifle shot by a stumbling Confederate soldier may have altered the eventual outcome of the engagement.

The Union cannons on the square changed hands several times.

Although the Rebels won the battle they continued to lose the war in Missouri.

On August 14, 1862, Maj. Emory S. Foster and a force of more than 800 men set out from Lexington for Lone Jack, where they arrived about 9 o'clock the night of August 15. Col. Fitz Henry Warren and about 1,500 men were marching up from Clinton to reinforce Foster, who moved into Lone Jack and stationed his battery of two cannons in the town square across from the Cave hotel.

There were plenty of Rebels around. Col. J. Ward Cockrell was bivouacked near Lone Jack with 1,500 men. Rebel scouts knew about Foster's force and then learned that 1,500 Kansans were being moved up from Fort Scott.

Col. Upton. Hays was camped with his detachment on the Harbaugh farm 12 miles northwest of Lone Jack and Col. John Coffee, another rebel leader, had 800 men camped one mile south of Lone Jack.

Foster, knowing he had fewer men, apparently hoped to hold out until Warren and the Kansans, and possibly other troops, could help him.

Cockrell and Hays conferred and decided on a surprise attack at sunrise the next morning before reinforcing Union forces could arrive.

Extra ammunition was doled out that night to the Rebels, and plans were carefully detailed by the commanders. Shortly before dawn the Confederates moved forward stealthily, rifles cocked for action.

Then one of the rebels stumbled and his rifle went off. Foster's pickets, instructed to expect a surprise attack, sounded the alarm and the battle began before the Confederates could launch their charge.

The Rebels rushed the square and Foster's men poured a heavy fire from the cannons. His sharpshooters from the Cave hotel windows also took a toll.

Four Rebels charged across the square and captured the cannons. A few minutes later the Union troops regained control of them.

Against a rain of bullets, the Rebels regained the battery, but couldn't hold it against a vicious countercharge by the Yankees.

There were now so many bodies around the cannons it was doubtful if the Rebels could retake it, but they did with an attack by Hays and his men.

Foster than led a wild charge of yelling Union troops and regained the battery.

Meanwhile, there was considerable cavalry and infantry fighting in and around the square.

The bloody conflict had not been decided by 10 o'clock, but Foster's smaller force was slowly being whipped by the 3,000 Rebels. Foster was wounded. Then Coffee moved on the Union's left flank and Foster's scouts reported a column of Quantrill's guerrillas under William H. Gregg was approaching the town.

Capt. Milton H. Brawner, who took over after Foster was wounded, realized the capture and further slaughter would occur and retreated to Camp Powell near Lexington.

There have been various estimates of the number killed and wounded in the battle, but the accepted figure is about 200 killed and 400 wounded. There were many officers killed on each side.

Families from around the area, both Union and Confederate, drove into Lone Jack to claim a body or take the wounded home. There was insufficient identification on many of those killed. Those bodies were buried in long trenches east of the square.

In the cemetery today there is an obelisk 10 feet high to mark the graves of the Confederates and a short distance away a stone column about 7 feet high stands guard over the Yankees.

The lone jack oak, that gave the town its name and witnessed the sanguinary conflict, is no longer there.

August 16, 1969

JESSE JAMES

THE JAMES BOYS

It is always a sort of "literary open season" on the James boys—Jesse and Frank—and almost any book these days on the robbers and killers will arouse some interest and sell some copies.

This almost certain reaction, based on books of the past, is expected to apply to one recently written by relatives who say that it really wasn't Jesse who was killed by that "dirty little coward" in St. Joseph, that the real Jesse James lived to be more than 100 at Granbury, Tex., as J. Frank Dalton. They allege that a "saddle tramp" was killed in Jesse's place.

They also insist that Frank really never surrendered to Governor Crittenden but that he fled to Wayton, Ark., assumed the alias of "Joe Vaughn," married and fathered nine children.

The authors of "This Was Frank James," are Sara Elizabeth Snow, 79 years old, Farmersville, Calif., who claims to be one of the nine children Frank fathered in Arkansas; Columbus Vaughn, a Knoxville, La., schoolteacher and nephew of Sarah Snow, and Lester Snow, a cousin of Sarah Snow. Vaughn's father is William Nelson Vaughn, now 77, who lives in Wayton, Ark.

The late Homer Croy who wrote "Jesse James Was My Neighbor," (Croy's home was in Maryville) always performed his research chores with meticulous accuracy and always agreed with the facts as they have been written.

William A. Settle, Jr., who wrote "Jesse James Was His Name," which is regarded as one of the best on this subject, also did exhaustive research and accepted the facts.

Fred L. Lee, a member of The Star's staff, who has written articles about the family, says he ran down the information about Frank James's burial and that he is buried at a privately owned cemetery in Independence. Calvin B. Manon of the Associated Press staff here, who also has written a great deal about the James family, points out that the body was on display at the Sidenfaden funeral home in St. Joseph, then taken to Kearney and that hundreds, maybe thousands, saw it, including many who knew Jesse James personally.

There are 450 catalogue cards on Jesse James at the State Historical Society Library in Columbia. Dr. Richard Browniee, director, said that no one card has any information leading to a substantiation of the claims made in the new book.

LONE JACK CEMETERY

After Jesse was killed, Frank feared for his life, too, because the big reward was out for both of them. A newspaper reporter became an intermediary and arranged for Frank's surrender in Jefferson City to Governor Crittenden. The reporter knew Frank well by sight.

Charles Philip Johnson, one of Missouri's great criminal lawyers of that era, made plea at Frank James's trial in 1883 that the courtroom spectators applauded loud and long and the jury acquitted him.

A brick building on a corner in Liberty was the scene of the first daylight bank robbery by Jesse James and his gang. Four years ago Jack Wymore, Liberty businessman, bought the building and set up a museum. It is now loaded with James family memorabilia.

"I have talked with hundreds of persons the past four years, including descendants of relatives who knew Jesse and Frank personally and not one contradicts the facts as we know them," Wymore said.

Mrs. Marina Erhard, 1229 West Seventy-second street, said that her grandfather, Dr. A. B. Hereford, a physician removed the bullet from Jesse James's body and that Hereford had no doubt about the identity.

Both the World Book Encyclopedia and the Encyclopedia International give the accepted version of the deaths of the brothers. Cole Younger served a sentence for the Northfield, Minn., bank robbery and was pardoned in 1903. He and Frank James teamed up for wild west shows and exhibitions and thousands saw Frank.

August 23, 1969

GRANT'S WIFE

The world lives on love and the readers on love stories, so the adage goes, and although there have been many so-called "great" love stories written, one of the most touchingly beautiful still hasn't been "discovered."

Even mentioning the name of the fair-skinned, attractive and vivacious young woman may not stir any recollection among the writers.

Julia Dent. No response.

But how about Mrs. Ulysses S. Grant?

Undoubtedly the military achievements of Grant and his rise to the presidency have eclipsed the lifetime and perhaps routine procedures of Julia Dent Grant, but the entire history of the nation

169

ULYSSES S. GRANT

might have been changed had it not been for her unfailing love for Grant, her patience in seeing him through the roughest part of his life and a steadfast belief in his future greatness.

Fresh from West Point in 1843, Grant was stationed at Jefferson Barracks in St. Louis. Not far from the barracks was the home of Frederick T. Dent, also a West Point graduate and Grant's roomate the last year. So it was inevitable that Grant would be invited to Dent's home where he met Julia, then 17.

Grant was subtle in his memoirs when he wrote, "As I found the family congenial, my visits became frequent."

Early in 1844 Grant's regiment was ordered to the Mexican border in view of the impending trouble. Before leaving he asked Julia to marry him. She agreed, but also agreed to keep the engagement a secret.

He returned in 1845 and Colonel Dent, Julia's father, agreed to the marriage, although he wasn't entirely happy with his future son-in-law. There just wasn't the dash and debonair personality Dent thought should exist for his daughter's husband.

Colonel Dent operated a 1,000 acre plantation, with slaves, near St. Louis, where Julia was born, and he had Southern leanings.

Grant returned to his command in Mexico and distinguished himself, in several battles. He was one of the first in Molina del Rey, and at Chapultepec he scaled the castle walls with several others and captured some Mexican officers.

Grant wrote Julia almost every day while he was in Mexico and this carried over into the Civil War, regardless of how hard-pressed he was in a campaign.

St. Louis did not give much attention to the wedding August 22, 1848, at the town house of Colonel Dent's at Fourth and Cerre streets. Neither Julia nor the young lieutenant wanted a society wedding, and their wishes were followed by Julia's parents.

After the wedding Grant elected to stay in the army because of the uncertainties of civilian life. He was moved around considerably and one of his posts was at Fort Vancouver, Ore. He could not support a family on either a lieutenant's or captain's salary, so Julia and the growing family stayed at home, some of the time with Grant's family.

He became depressed and heartsick for his family. There was nothing to test his talents and his introversion did not help. The bottle did. He began drinking too much and at Fort Humboldt, Cal., in 1854 his commanding officer ordered him to reform or resign. He chose the latter.

The next six years tested the patience of Julia Grant. Her husband was the most abject and miserable failure possible. He tried selling real estate but met with little success.

He peddled cord wood. Grant's father-in-law gave the couple several acres, and Grant, with the help of friends, erected a home. But the soil was poor and Grant's farming venture failed. He later referred to this endeavor as "Hardscrabble."

The St. Louis city engineering post was open at $125 a month. Grant applied but was turned down on a 3 to 2 vote by the court. However, it was learned later that the vote was influenced by the Southern leanings of Colonel Dent.

He obtained a job in the United States customs house but lost it. His brothers opened a leather goods store in Galena, Ill., where Grant worked for a short time.

Grant finally obtained a command and that almost ineffable mystery whereby one person can transfer confidence to another appeared to produce a coalescence.

With a shrug that she had done her bit by seeing Grant through those six years, Julia might have stayed securely at home. But she didn't. In an interview shortly before her death, she said, "I was never far away from headquarters and always kept myself informed of the movements of the army. My husband wrote to me almost daily."

In Ishbel Ross's biography of Julia Dent Grant, published in 1959, she wrote of the two, "Her faith in him was like a charm throughout his life. His love for her was a shield against destruction."

August 30, 1969

WILLIAM BECKNELL

Some men of public renown—such as explorers, military leaders and statesmen—who have soared to lofty heights, are memorialized by monuments, markers and other physical evidence of their attainments.

Undoubtedly the "champion" in this specialized category would be William Becknell, known as the "Father of the Santa Fe trail," who might tally many hundreds of markers in four states.

Becknell was born in Amherst County, Virginia, and came to Missouri in 1816 following service in the War of 1812. He also had a reputation as a tough Indian-fighter.

According to Mrs. Dorothy Caldwell, associate editor of the quarterly publication of the State Historical Society of Missouri, he became a partner with James and Jesse Morrison, at Boon's Lick Salt works across the river from Arrow Rock.

In the summer of 1821, four auspicious events occurred that

changed the entire future of the United States, Mexico, Spain and the North American continent:

(1) Missouri officially became a state, (2) Mexico won its independence from Spain, (3) Stephen Austin started for San Antonio to lay plans for the colonization of what is now Texas and (4) Becknell started for Santa Fe.

Spain had refused to permit trade between Santa Fe and the United States but Mexico was eager to do so and it was understood that if and when independence was obtained the gates would be opened.

Becknell had a letter placed in the Franklin, Mo., Intelligencer on June 25 announcing that he would lead an expedition to the West "for the purpose of catching wild horses" and that "trading goods" would be taken. Those interested would meet August 5 at the home of Ezekiel Williams, five miles north of Franklin. Williams was a Missouri Fur company mountain man who had settled in Franklin in 1817.

About 17 attended, plans were laid and Becknell was elected captain. Just how many went on this first trip is not known. Josiah Gregg, chronicler of the trail, said that only four went, but he wrote about it a quarter-of-a-century afterward and his statement cannot be substantiated. Two or three other writers have estimated that "over 20" accompanied Becknell.

Becknell speaks of the "group" or the "company" in his first journal. On the second trek he does give the number—21 men. But it is certain Becknell made the first trek with "several" men.

The group left 148 years ago Monday on a trek that opened the Santa Fe trail and would mean tremendous economic and financial benefit to the United States and Mexico generally and Missouri in particular.

They camped the first night six miles west of Franklin and then forged on to Fort Osage where they bought medicines and supplies. They crossed into what is now Kansas and then followed the Arknasas river.

Becknell's own journals are somewhat descriptive.

"It is a circumstance of surprise to us," he wrote, "that we have seen no Indians, or fresh signs of them, although we have traversed their most frequented hunting ground."

Every such expedition always had some discouragement, and Becknell noted, "Having been now traveling about 50 days, our diet being altogether different from what we had been accustomed to, and unexpected hardships and obstacles occurring almost daily, our company is mot discouraged."

WILLIAM BECKNELL MONUMENT

Photo credit: E. W. Bowers

On November 13, near San Miguel, they met some Spanish soldiers who were cordial and friendly, clear evidence that relations had changed since Mexican independence.

Becknell, who could speak some French, hired an interpreter, who spoke French and Spanish, and on November 15, he wrote, "we arrived at Santa Fe and were received with apparent pleasure and joy."

He then described his meeting with the Mexican governor, who was "courteous and friendly" and who expressed a hope for cordial relations with the United States and for mutual trade.

The governor might even welcome American emigration to his country. In all probability couriers had already brought news of the momentous meeting between Stephen Austin and Mexican government officials in San Antonio.

Although Becknell and his men traveled to Santa Fe on horses (no wagons), the door had been opened, the trip was a tremendous success. He wrote in his journal, "Those who visit the country for the purpose of vending merchandise will do well to take goods of excellent quality and unfaded colors. An idea prevails among the people there, which is certainly a very just one, that the goods hitherto imported into their country were the remains of old stock and sometimes damaged.

"A very great advance is obtained on goods, and the trade is very profitable. Money and mules are plentiful, and they do not hesitate to pay the price demanded for an article if it suits their purpose or their fancy.

"An excellent road may be made from Fort Osage to Santa Fe. Few places would require much labor to make them passable."

September 6, 1969

JOHN SAPPINGTON MARMADUKE

There were many duels in Missouri and almost all of them with tragic consequences. The cold-blooded John Smith T may be the only killer (12 to 15 victims) who seemed not to worry about his victims, but the famous duels usually involved participants of high standing and others who suffered the pangs of remorse.

The Benton-Lucas duel was one of the most notable in Missouri. Sen. Thomas Hart Benton, the "grand old Roman," the mellifluous orator and supreme egotist, was so remorseful in slaying Charles H. Lucas, a prominent lawyer, that he ordered all of his records destroyed before he died.

The Marmaduke-Walker duel, on September 6, 1863, virtually closed Missouri's part in a half-century of dueling. Dueling had lost prestige before the Civil war. None occurred in the Union army during the war but several were fought in Confederate ranks.

John S. Marmaduke and Marsh Walker commanded cavalry divisions in the abortive Confederate attack at Helena, Ark., July 4, 1863. Marmaduke first complained that his inability to seize his objective stemmed from Walker's failure to press the attack on his left flank. Marmaduke sent orders twice to Walker to move on the flank, but Walker did not comply.

Nettled, Marmaduke pulled his men out and left Walker to defend himself. Walker and his division barely escaped a federal noose.

Walker later contended that he did try to protect Marmaduke's flank and had to fight hard to shake loose after Marmaduke left him. Lt. Gen. T. H. Holmes, over both men, was inclined to side with Marmaduke.

Gen. Sterling Price succeeded Holmes and in further skirmishing near Little Rock, Walker purposely did not support Marmaduke who almost was captured.

The Missourian's dander was up. He sought twice unsuccessfully to confer with Walker. Then he asked to be removed from Walker's command or he threatened to resign from the Confederate army.

Walker regarded this as a slap in the face. He also was irked by some derogatory comments by Marmaduke about Walker's courage at the Reed's bridge battle.

Notes were exchanged by the two men. Then came the duel.

The seconds were Capt. John C. Moore for Marmaduke and Col. Robert H. Crockett, grandson of the immortal Davy, for Walker.

Everyone met a few miles below Little Rock on the north side of the Arkansas river near the LeFevre plantation.

Crockett and Moore paced off the ground about daylight. Each had an 1851 Navy Colt revolver. Crockett flipped a coin for the choice of position and command.

Marmaduke won!

And so the paces...one, two, three, four...

And the command, FIRE!

Both missed. After a pause of one second, Marmaduke fired again. The ball struck Walker in the left side and he fell backward. The first to reach him was Marmaduke. The ball had passed through Walker's right kidney and lodged in the spine.

Marmaduke ordered Moore to use his horse-drawn ambulance to take Walker into Little Rock. Crockett held Walker's head in his lap during the ride.

The bitterness among Walker's men did not lessen. In a military charge on an Arkansas City September 10, two days after Walker was buried, Col. Archibald S. Dobbin, who took over Walker's division, refused to advance on Marmaduke's orders. Marmaduke arrested Dobbin but Price later released him.

No charges ever were preferred against Marmaduke who regretted the incident the remainder of his life. He was in the Battle of Westport and was captured and imprisoned at Ft. Warren, Mass., until the end of the war.

John Sappington Marmaduke, the bachelor son of Meredith Miles Marmaduke, became governor of Missouri. The Civil war general was elected in 1884 and inaugurated Janurary 12, 1885. He died in office December 28, 1887, about one year before the expiration of his term.

Marmaduke's record as governor was about average. He showed courage against the railroads in the first strike that occurred in his administration. He handled it effectively, then sponsored a bill for regulation. The bill was defeated in the Legislature. Marmaduke called a special session and warned the lawmakers they would be in special sessions continuously until they passed his bill. It passed.

September 13, 1969

MANUEL LISA

I go a great distance while some are considering whether they will start today or tomorrow.

The philosophy by which successful men attain their goals is seldom so succinctly expressed as it was by Manuel Lisa, the champion of a tough band of fur traders, who also served Missouri and the nation well in the first two decades of the last century.

Lisa, of Spanish descent, was born 197 years ago September 8 in New Orleans. Little is known of his childhood but at 18 he arrived at New Madrid, Mo., stayed briefly and then went on to St. Louis.

Lisa made a contribution of $1,000 to Spain and helped build a flour mill, and in return in 1802 Spain gave him a monopoly in the fur trade with the Osage tribe. Lisa lost the Osage monopoly to the Chouteaus after the Louisiana Purchase in 1803.

Lisa had ideas and was willing to work hard. His first major fur expedition probably was in the spring of 1807 with George Drouillard who had been with Lewis and Clark. Until then the fur traders would

181

MANUEL LISA

visit the tribes and buy the furs. Lisa decided that a string of forts, also called trading posts, was a better answer.

The trading post at the mouth of the Big Horn in 1807 probably was the first. Others followed. He established trading posts in what is now North and South Dakota, Nebraska, Colorado and other states in the western Rocky Mountain area.

Lisa worked hard and he realized early that one had to learn how to get along with the Indians to be successful in the fur buying business. Many other white traders wouldn't try to understand or get along with the Indians, and as a result many died.

On his first trip up the Missouri River with 45 men and 13 barges and keel boats in 1807, he met his baptism with the Arikara tribe. The tribe was more in an intimidating than a killing mood, but Lisa let the warriors know his positon. He knew that lesson No. 1 with troublesome Indians was not to show fear or alarm, and No. 2 was to mount an immediate show of force.

Lisa ordered this best sharpshooters ready and directed his men to load the swivel guns on the keelboats. The Arikaras stepped back and Lisa had won one of the most important confrontations of his career.

After that he was the friend of all tribes in the Missouri river area, except possibly the Black Feet. In his career he made 12 to 13 expeditions up the Missouri. He always loaded his keel boats with trinkets, seeds, tools, plows and colorful scarves for the squaws. He showed the Indians how to plant the seeds and harvest the crops, and how to handle the plow. He always had plenty of tobacco, and as he told Gen. William Clark, when Lisa resigned as Indian agent:

"A poor $500, as a sub-agent's salary does not buy the tobacco which I annually give to those who call me Father."

Lisa helped to plot and establish the Oregon trail. He also was one of the organizers of the Missouri Fur company in 1809. William Clark, of Lewis and Clark fame, was president and a director. Lisa was general manager and commandant of the trading expeditions. The organizing capital was between $40,000 and $50,000.

No fur trader worked harder than Lisa. For 12 years he headed the expeditions, and was gone almost 10 months of the year. No one worked harder at befriending the Indians, unless it was "Chief Red Head," as the Indians fondly referred to their friend, William Clark.

In those 12 years Lisa usually brought back furs valued at $30,000 each time. He traveled 26,000 miles.

With success like this, it was natural that competitors would be jealous. That was when, in his resignation to William Clark, he said, "I go a great distance while some are considering whether they will start today or tomorrow.

He had served his nation well and one other comment in his letter to Clark is worth noting:

"I have suffered enough in person and property under how to appreciate the one under which I I now live."

Lisa probably had the best spy system among the tribes that ever existed. A year before the war of 1812 he told officials that the British with money and other attractions were trying to win the tribes over in the West.

The War department did not exactly ignore this important information and General Clark appointed Lisa a captian in the Missouri militia so he would have some official status.

And so, Captain Lisa went back among his friends, the many tribes of the Missouri river valley reaching into the Pacific Northwest and persuaded almost all of them not to join the British in the War of 1812.

After the end of that conflict, Manuel Lisa led 43 tribal leaders from the Northwest into St. Louis where they signed treaties of friendship with the United States.

Lisa signed many petitions to Congress that sought statehood for Missouri. He built one of the first brick houses in St. Louis and was a civic leader there.

Henry Brackenridge, the traveler and historian who accurately described Missouri and its people at the start of the last century, accompanied Lisa on his third trip in 1811 to the Northwest. Of Lisa, Brackenridge wrote:

"A person better qualified for this arduous undertaking could not have been chosen. Mr. Lisa is not surpassed by anyone in the requisite experience in Indian trade and manners, and has few equals in perseverance and indefatigable industry. Ardent, bold and enterprising, when any undertaking is begun, no dangers or sufferings are sufficient to overcome his mind. I believe there are few men so completely master of that secret of doing much in a short space of time."

Manuel Lisa's first wife, Polly Charles, died in 1817, and he married Mrs. Mary Hempstead Keeney. Lisa died August 12, 1820, at his home near St. Louis and is buried in Bellefontaine cemetery.

September 20, 1969

IRISH WILDERNESS

Who now will build up these waste places? Who now will lead back the scattered settlers to their humbled but ruined homes? Who now will rekindle for them the light of faith or preach the word of God to them in their little chapel beneath the pines in the forest?

Those were the words of Father John Joseph Hogan as he beheld the war-devastated ruins of the Irish settlement he established in Southeastern Missouri before the Civil war.

This area is known today as the Irish Wilderness.

It is a land of legend and romance, of druidic mystery and misty leprechauns where the tree-shrouded hollows echoed the dreams of hope-filled and imaginative Irish more than a century ago.

It was in 1858 when a small wagon train crawled along the green ridges and beneath the tall shortleaf pines being led by Father Hogan who had beheld the rainbow along the tributaries of the Current and Eleven Point rivers.

With him were Sullivans, O' Briens, McNamaras, and Pat and Tom Griffin and many others who had left the old sod, mainly after the potato famine, for the bright, new and promising land across the sea.

There were 40 families. Father Hogan had served in a St. Louis mission in 1854-55. He began to worry about the few marriages of the Irish lads and lassies. The Irish youths, unable to find work in the cities, or on the farms competing with slave labor, usually joined railroad construction gangs moving from place to place, and out of matrimonial contract.

His mission was moved to Chillicothe and he began exploring the Missouri land for his colony. His travels took him to Southeast Missouri. He gathered his flock and they settled along Ten-Mile creek in 1858. They soon learned this land had been taken so they moved about 40 miles to the west.

Some of the land was tillable. The pine forests rose skyward like thousands of sentinels. There were oaks and other hardwoods, lush pastures for grazing. Game was plentiful for food, clothing and shoes, the streams teemed with fish.

The patron saint could not have planned it any better himself! Homestead land was 12½ cents an acre and the land soon produced many crops.

War was the first enemy of the settlement. Ripley County seemed to suffer the worst, being overrun by both Federal and Confederate troops. The chapel at Pine was destroyed as were most of the houses. The small town of Doniphan was burned by Union troops, and whatever one army failed to destroy in the general area, the other did.

187

Father Hogan's colony virtually disappeared during the Civil war. Many of the Irish joined the Union forces but some went over the South.

Patrick Griffin and his wife managed to stay but almost starved. Two or three other families trickled back after the war. Patrick's son, Billy Griffin, who had fought with the Rebels, returned with his war bride. But the Hogan settlement, as it was known before the war, never was to be the same.

The pines, the oaks, poplars, walnut and maple trees grew anew after being partly denuded by the war and years later the second enemy moved against the forest primeval. Hundreds of thousands of acres were stripped by lumber operations from 1890 to 1900, little railroad lines chugged up and down the hills and through the "hollers," the world's largest mill was built at Grandin, 16-foot pine logs went swirling down the Eleven Point and Current rivers and the angry whine of a hundred saws hit into the poetic stillness of the wilderness.

Twice betrayed by man, but like the indestructible race for which it was named, the Irish Wilderness slowly healed again. And, once more, it was not a match for the greed of mankind. Two decades later the hillsides resounded with the crashing of giant trees to be turned into charcoal for the big smelters of a large iron company.

This time the strange word, "conservation", was heard and mankind rushed to the defense of the Irish Wilderness. It now is within the Fristoe unit of the Mark Twain National forest and is a part of the Current, Eleven Point and Jack's Fork river areas, rich in natural beauty and mellowed with the vicissitudes of age, the only true wilderness in Missouri.

September 27, 1969

ETHELBERT TALBOT

A clergyman on the frontier didn't have it any easier than any other person. Consider the remarkable life of one and his accomplishments:

He founded the St. James academy in Macon, Mo., which later became a military academy.

Ordered to the west by his church, he became a bronco-busting bishop, built 38 churches, a cathedral at Laramie, Wyo., a hospital and several schools within 10 years.

He converted thousands of cattlemen, miners, laborers and Indians.

188

He became a close friend of Chief Washakie, and other tribal leaders, and was regarded as a "brother" by the Shoshones and Arapahoes.

He rose to bishop of the Protestant Episcopal church of America.

His name probably won't ring a bell even among history enthusiasts but he was Ethelbert Talbot, born in Fayette, Mo., October 9, 1848, who studied at Central college there and was graduated from Dartmouth college and the General Theological seminary in New York. He received an LLD from the University of Missouri in 1877.

He was ordained November 4, 1873, and became rector of St. James church in Macon. He founded the academy in 1875. At the church's general convention in Chicago in 1886, the missionary district of Wyoming and Idaho was created and he was named its first bishop. He considered the matter several months, decided to decline and then was swayed to accept by a teacher at the seminary.

Bishop Talbot's book, "My People of The Plains," is a classic on the trials and tribulations of a minister in the western area at the time. Rather then a dry and fusty account, it contains humorous aspects, incidents and people.

He tells of arriving in Cheyenne. No one met him at the stage but a man, noting that Talbot was a clergyman, offered him a lift.

"Now, Bishop," the man said," I have two broncos. One bucks pretty hard and the other bucks kind o' mild. Which do you want?"

"Suppose you let me have one that bucks kind of mild," the clergyman replied.

He arrived at the boarding house without mishap but it wasn't long when he could ride any bucking bronco.

Bishop Talbot's unorthodox missionary tactics and his broad-minded attitudes won him rapid approval from Chief Washakie, other Indians and the tough, whisky-drinking, gambling miners and the cattlemen.

His first unusual move was to go into the saloons and ask the customers to attend church. He wrote of his first such experience when the bartender said: "Why, Bishop, I am proud to know you. What will you have?"

Talbot replied he wanted nothing to drink, only to meet the boys in the gambling room. The bartender obliged.

"Boys," the bartender called out, "hold up the game. Put up the chips just a minute. This is the bishop and he wants to be introduced."

Talbot said they nodded couteously then he began: "Excuse me, gentlemen, I do not wish to interfere with your pleasure or your amuse-

BISHOP TALBOT

Credit: State Historical Society of Mo.

ment. I have just come in to pay my respects to you. I am the bishop and am going to hold services in the dance hall tomorrow morning and evening, and I shall be very glad to see you there."

Talbot "invaded" six other saloons and to his surprise many showed up.

Another preacher who had seen the bishop coming out of one saloon made a clucking sound.

Talbot replied what if it was necessary to go into saloons to save souls and lives for Christ, he doubted very much if the Lord worried.

Later he gave the formula for his popularity over the years with drunks, gamblers, bartenders and others by saying:

"The successful man of God in the mining camp need not lose his dignity or self respect, but it is of vital importance that he be a man among men and, above all possess the capacity of loving men, and with the aid of that gift know how to reach their hearts."

So, the bishop made conversions and if he failed at that he made friends.

One Sunday night, Harry, a friend, offered to drive Bishop Talbot to a service. On the way the horses became mired. Harry applied the whip silently but the horses wouldn't move. Finally Harry explained:

"Well, Bishop, I ask it just once. You see these horses are used to my style of talking to 'em. I know it's a bad habit, and I know it's wrong, but will you please give me a dispensation, just this one time? If you will I'll get you there."

The bishop smiled, nodded and said, "Fire away."

Harry then ripped out a string of well-chosen imprecations and the horses moved out of the mudhole.

Bishop Talbot also expressed his philosophy of "his" people this way:

"The cowboy or the miner has sometimes but little religion to talk about, but he usually responds nobly to an appeal to his unselfishness or generosity or courage. Let some misfortune befall a brother man, and see how quickly he will come to the rescue. Judged by many of the outward or conventional standards. I admit he falls far short, but when you put him to the test of real fraternity, and measure him by the spirit of disinterested service to his fellow man, he will often surprise you."

The Bishop also became a bitter critic of the government's policy on the Indians. He called the "reservation program" anti-Christian and said the reason Indians did not advance was because they were shunted onto the reservations and forgotten.

In 1897 Bishop Talbot accepted a postion as bishop of the Central Pennsylvania diocese. Delegations of white men and Indians urged him to stay.

From 1924 to 1926 he was presiding bishop of the national church and he died in 1928.

Oct. 4, 1969.

GENERAL STERLING PRICE

Gen. Sterling Price suffered his "Achilles' heel" at Pilot Knob.

Now and then top military commanders make their monumental error against a vastly inferior force, and this was Price's grand mistake.

It was September, 1864, and Missouri still belonged to the Union despite many skirmishes and battles.

Those who viewed the war with any sense of realism knew that by July, 1864, the end was not far away. But there were several die-hards who saw it differently. They merely misinterpreted General Grant's strategy of leaving the western flank exposed in order to turn everything against General Lee. Price believed Grant had made a mistake and he and other Confederate leaders planned a giant push up from Arkansas, take St. Louis and then move across the state to capture Kansas City. The strategy seemed sound. The Confederacy then would control the western flank and Grant would have to release some of his men to try and retake the western area. In addition, the Department of Missouri was commanded by Gen. William S. Rosecrans, in whom Grant had little confidence.

The Confederate leaders bought the plan although some thought Price was not the man to lead the invasion. He had shared the dubious victories at Lexington and Wilson's creek as well as the defeats at Pea Ridge and Little Rock.

But the plan moved forward. Gen. Joe Shelby, Missouri's great cavalry leader, headed one division; Gen. John S. Marmaduke, later to be governor of Missouri, headed a second, and James F. Fagan, an Arkansas politician with little military knowledge, headed the third.

There were 12,000 troops, although some historians have added one or two thousand more; also 14 pieces of artillery.

The march from Arkansas into Missouri resembled a circus parade, especially after spies and scouts reported there was no Union force to stop either swing to St. Louis or across the state to Kansas City.

Price had a brass band that played "The Yellow Rose of Texas," "Dixie," "Listen to the Mocking Bird," and other tunes. Some of the officers brought their Negro servants. Good food and champagne were plentiful. War was just simply wonderful!

194

But the army moved. Price, despite the lighter touches, was aware that sooner or later the line of march would be known to the North, and September 21 the first courier brought word that transports loaded with Union troops were moving up the river.

The North now moved. Grant was consulted. Several thousand men moved down from St. Louis standing in the way of any attack by the Confederates.

At this point there was monumental indecision by the officers on both sides. Rosecrans hardly knew where Price's army was but begged for reinforcements. On the Confederate side, Shelby wanted to take St. Louis, Marmaduke wanted to move toward Kansas City and Fagan scarcely knew where he was.

Rosecrans ordered a district commander, Gen. Thomas Ewing, and his assistant, Col. Thomas C. Fletcher, later to be governor, to Pilot Knob.

In view of the indecision among his commanders, Price made up his and their minds, St. Louis seemed a bit risky and Price decided that to sweep Missouri at long last into the Confederacy would be the juciest plum.

And, Missourians on both sides had no love for General Ewing who had issued the hated Order No. 11 following Quantrill's raid on Lawrence, Kas. Tom Ewing's courage never had been criticized, only his judgment in issuing No. 11, and at Pilot Knob his courage met the supreme test successfully.

Ewing yelled to Col. David Murphy, "All right, let'em have it." Eleven cannons spewed death and destruction. Marksmen took a deadly toll. Murphy's men sweat and swabbed and shot with accuracy, sometimes almost at point-blank range. But the rebels came on, almost like the charge of the light brigade. Union sharpshooters fired and handed the hot guns backward while they grabbed others as the guns were reloaded.

Colonel Murphy, his face livid with rage, jumped onto a parapet, cursed the rebels and dared them to "come on and be killed," Ewing pulled Murphy down.

The break occurred at 30 yards. Price's thin line wavered, then broke and the rebels fell back. In 20 minutes Price had lost more than 1,000 officers and men, the greatest carnage in the shortest time of the Civil war. Ewing had lost 200.

The sun dropped, the rain fell, the wounded screamed. Near midnight Ewing's men stoked camp fires, muffled the wheels of field guns, spiked others and began a successful retreat. The morale of Price and his men was shattered and it probably contributed to his ignominious defeat at the battle of Westport the following month.

Oct. 11, 1969

NATHAN BOONE

The biological yardstick sometimes referred to as the so-called laws of genetics can never be certain to any degree of accuracy in attempting to forecast a brilliant son from a brilliant father.

In fact, history has many examples of sons, basking in the reflected glow of great fathers, falling flat and being failures.

This is not so with the Daniel Boone family. So let's pinpoint these accomplishments of Nathan Boone, youngest son of Daniel:

He played an important role in the War of 1812.

He was a member of the 1820 Missouri Constitution convention.

He fought with distinction in the Black Hawk war.

His general military career covered 31 years and many wars.

Actually, this scroll of accomplishments might well apply to Daniel Boone who lived to witness many of Nathan's achievements.

Meriwether Lewis and William Clark had spotted the Ft. Osage bulff on their historic trip as a possible military base to begin the expansion of the West. After they returned, the recommendation was carried out and Nathan Boone was one of the leaders in the building of the fort and in the treaty negotiations.

James Boone, the oldest son of Daniel and Rebecca Bryan Boone, was killed by Indians. Daniel Morgan Boone was the second son.

Nathan, the youngest, was born in Kentucky in 1781, and when he was 18 he and his 16 year old bride came to Missouri. Clark and Lewis recognized the qualities of leadership in young Nathan Boone who had absorbed a lot of his father's tact and abilities in dealing with Indians.

The British showed less understanding of the western pioneers in the War of 1812 than in the Revolutionary war when George Rogers Clark, brother of William Clark, and his men defeated British-led tribes at the gates of St. Louis.

In the War of 1812, Nathan Boone and others assembled several companies of Missouri Rangers. The men had to furnish their own clothing, food, weapons and horses and received $1 a day. The Rangers were well-trained, tough, hard-riding and excellent marksmen.

NATHAN BOONE

One newspaper commented, "The new company of Rangers now doing duty in the district of St. Charles is perhaps as fine a body of hardy woodsmen as ever took the field." Another paper observed later, "Perhaps no company in the United States promises to be more efficient than this, commanded by Capt. Nathan Boone, of high merit and composed of young, active and enterprising men."

Nathan was experienced in unorthodox Indian fighting as he was in the British antiquated rule of the book. Knowing the tribes would do what their British officers told them to do, as they did against George Rogers Clark, Nathan Boone decided to be unorthodox.

The established military rules called for the Missouri Rangers to cross the Mississippi at St. Louis and move northward along the east bank.

But Nathan Boone and his men took the tough route. They swam their horses up the river at night, clutching rifles and ammunition above their heads, made predawn attacks while the British waited and watched southward. Demoralization resulted and the Missourians pursued the tribes to the Great Lakes, established an army of occupation on the continent and then pow-wowed with about 40 tribes, winning them to the American side.

Nathan Boone, in addition to serving in the Black Hawk war, also was in several western campaigns against the Indians. He retired to his Greene County home in 1853 after an illustrious career and died there in 1856.

Rebecca Boone had died in 1813 and Daniel lived part of the time on the farm near Marthasville and then alternately with Daniel Morgan and Nathan Boone. The latter built a 2½ story stone house near Defiance, Mo., and his father, having little else to do, hand-carved the seven walnut fireplace mantels in an intricate sunburst detail.

Nathan Boone moved to Greene County in 1837 and built a home there. The following year the War department ordered him to Ft. Wayne, established in 1832.

Nathan Boone, in addition to helping build Ft. Osage, also helped or directed the building of many military installations mainly in Missouri and Iowa. There is a Boone County and a Boone river in Iowa, not named for Daniel but for Nathan.

October 18, 1969

FORTS

Two major military forts and reservations that played the big roles in helping to settle the West in the last century were Jefferson barracks' at St. Louis and Ft. Leavenworth, Kas.

The Jefferson barracks site was first occupied in Missouri July 10, 1826, by four companies under Capt. Stephen W. Kearny, and it was formally named on October 23 of that year for Thomas Jefferson who had died July 4, 1826. Ft. Leavenworth was established the following year.

In 1829 four companies of the sixth U.S. infantry were transferred to Ft. Leavenworth to guard the Santa Fe wagon trains as far as the international boundary at the Arkansas River. Maj. Bennett Riley was commander of this expedition and Ft. Riley, Kas., was later named for him. For his "valuable efforts" in protecting the travelers, the Missouri Legislature presented him with an ornate sword in a special ceremony. He was the last military governor of the Territory of California being succeeded by Peter Burnett, a Missourian, the first elected California governor.

In the Black Hawk War, Lt. Jefferson Davis was assigned to bring the captured chief and his braves to Jefferson barracks which he did with such tact and diplomacy that Black Hawk said many nice things about the young man who would later be President of the Confederacy.

A large part of the troops recruited for the Mexican war were outfitted and trained at the barracks and it expanded almost every year, seeming, as one writer stated, "to rise from the Mississippi River and swell across the beautiful bluffs covered with oak and hickory."

The list of the nation's outstanding military men, who served the post at one time or another, and many more than once, is a long one—Riley, Davis and Henry Atkinson in the early days, later Zachary Taylor, Robert E. Lee, George A. Custer, William T. Sherman, John C. Fremont, Kearny, and many others.

Ulysses S. Grant made three visits to Jefferson barracks all under far different circumstances. The first was in 1843 when he was fresh from West Point. The second in 1856 when he delivered vegetables to the fort from his farm nearby. The third was as President of the United States.

Many Missourians were trained at Jefferson barracks. There are many sets of figures to show the importance of the post over the years. One official figure is 250,000 from 1906 to 1921. It has been garrisoned by infantry, cavalry and artillery troops, ordnance, air corps and other military units.

Jefferson barracks replaced Ft. Bellefontaine which was established near St. Louis in 1805.

During the feverish recruitment-training periods of World War II, it housed as many as 40,000 men at a time. In 1950 when a 130-acre site in the northeast corner of the post was dedicated as the Jefferson Barracks Historical park, the main address was made by Maj. Gen. U. S. Grant III.

The park now has the trappings of a large antique center. The stables, erected in 1851, now houses fine saddles, harness, grooming equipment and other cavalry memorabilia. There are photostatic murals on the general history of the installation, some in the powder magazine built in 1854, and several other structures have been restored. More than $100,000 has been spent for these projects. But there are little remains of the first barracks erected 140 years ago.

October 25, 1969

BLUEBOOK

An Irishman born in County Cork launched the first Missouri Manual, or "Bluebook," but it was not until 91 years later—this year—that the cover was changed to green.

Michael K. McGrath's "Almanac" of 160 pages with advertisements of patent medicine eventually grew into the Official Manual of Missouri.

The 1969-70 book was officially released yesterday in Jefferson City by another Irishman, James C. Kirkpatrick, secretary of state. The current volume has 1,530 pages and is illustrated with 1,200 photographs.

The first book dates to 1878 when McGrath was secretary of state. McGrath was born in Ireland, in 1833 and came to America in 1851. He held several jobs in the East and moved in 1857 to St. Louis where he obtained a job as a clerk in the office of recorder of deeds. He read law and was admitted to the bar and held several other positions before being elected secretary of state in 1874.

McGrath's first publication was called "The State Almanac and Official Directory of Missouri." It became known as "McGrath's Almanac." It was a private enterprise for which he charged 25 cents. In addition to advertising it carried election tables, names of county and state officers and odd tidbits about the state government.

McGrath lost money even though the record issue carried advertising for beer and champagne. He published three more editions and in 1889 was succeeded by Alexander A. Lesueur who was elected secretary of state in 1888. .

THE COVERS OF THE SECOND MANUAL PUBLISHED BY A. A. LESUEUR AND THAT OF THE 1969-1970 MANUAL ARE SHOWN HERE.

The "Almanac" had been growing but Lesueur soon realized he could not finance publication, even with the help of friends who had aided McGrath.

Maj. Thomas Park, father of the late Gov. Guy B. Park, Lesueur's chief clerk, suggested that a regular state appropriation be made to finance publication. Park helped to draft the necessary legislation.

Lesueur published the first "Official Manual of Missouri" in 1889-90. There were no pictures or illustrations but the 1893-94 edition carried maps of the senatorial districts.

Lesueur's third editon was a ponderous 464 pages with maps, platforms of the two major parties, and a postal directory. The 1895-96 edition attracted considerable attention, the Jefferson City Tribune commenting, "It has attracted general attention for its completeness and usefulness" and that "each biennial publication has been an improvement on its predecessor."

And the legislature astounded almost everyone in calling for 10,000 copies to be printed, twice the number of the preceding publication. The present publication is 40,000 copies.

In the 1891-92 edition a stiff blue binding was placed on the publication and it became known as the "Missouri Bluebook," although officially it was and still is "The Official Manual of the State of Missouri."

Kirkpartick, a Windsor, Mo., newspaper publisher who is serving his second term as secretary of state, made some major changes in the publication format of the 1967-68 book. The columns were rearranged for easier reading, 25 Missouri scenes in full color used and the cover was decorated in a full-color reproduction of the Missouri seal.

The present publication is no longer blue. Kirkpatrick, who has used green stationery and a green ball-point pen for years, has given the new "Bluebook" a green tinge on the binding. It also has 30 color photographs. It is dedicated to Thomas Hart Benton, Kansas City artist.

The manual will be distributed to state senators, representatives, county officials, newspapers, radio and television stations, school libraries and the various state departments.

November 4, 1969

SARPY FAMILY

The showcase of history in connection with development of the fur trade in the West during the beginning of the last century is studded with such names as Manuel Lisa, the Chouteaus, Wilson Hunt, William Henry Ashley and many others, but now and then a new name appears.

Sarpy! the name hasn't received a lot of attention from those who wrote the development of the fur business but the Sarpy family made major contributions in this endeavor.

In those days entire families entered into the general industry— such as the Chouteaus, the Sublettes, the Bents, the Walkers, the Ribidouxs and others.

Peter A. Sarpy, born in St. Louis November 3, 1805, became one of the giants in the industry although his father and brothers played major roles.

When Peter Sarpy was about 18—and many who became outstanding fur traders in those days began in their teens—he became a clerk for John P. Cabanne, an agent for the Missouri and American Fur companies at Council Bluffs, Ia. He was sent to a trading post at Bellevue, Neb., a major site because it commanded both the Missouri and the Platte Rivers.

Peter Sarpy soon built up a large business at the fort between the whites and the Indians and got along well with the Indians. He married Nicomi, the daughter of an Indian chief.

Sarphy's reputation grew. He directed the arrest of a spying party and received the title of "colonel." He established a post store at St. Mary, Neb., and founded the St. Mary Gazette. He helped to lay out the town of Bellevue, which had been only a trading post, and the town of Decatur, Neb. In 1862 he moved to Plattsmouth, Neb., and lived there until his death in 1865.

Peter Sarpy became one of the most respected men and trading post operators in the Nebraska area. In 1842 he built a river ship for General Fremont. He was called "White Chief" by the Indians who realized they could get an honest deal from him in fur selling and trading.

One historian referred to Sarpy as a "courageous agent for the American and Missouri Fur companies and probably the first white resident in Nebraska."

Peter Sarpy, in addition to being regarded as trustworthy and honest by both whites and Indians, possessed many personal characteristics that attracted others. He was short of stature, handsome, with a magnetic personality and a master of several languages and many Indian dialects.

When Brigham Young decided to go west he asked Peter Sarpy for assistance. Sarpy, because of his knowledge of Indian customs, guided Young and the Mormons through the dangerous areas.

He played a significant role in negotiating treaties with the Omaha and Oto tribes and in 1855 when several tribes went on the warpath in the Nebraska area, two regiments were raised and he was appointed quartermaster general.

He established ferries over the Missouri, Elkhorn and Loup Rivers and a steamboat ferry service between St. Mary, towns in Iowa and Bellevue.

The Sarpy family, as the many other leading fur traders, built trading posts across the north-central part of the Mid-West.

His father was Gregory Sarpy who is credited with pioneering the navigation of the Missouri River northward with Manuel Lisa. In 1802 Lisa, Gregory Sarpy, Francis M. Benoit and Charles Sanguinet formed an association.

John Sarpy, a brother of Peter, was killed in a powder explosion at the Ogalallah Indian trading post.

Gregory Sarpy had a close call when he was floating down the Mississippi River with considerable money aboard. That was December 15, 1811, the occasion of the New Madrid earthquake. Gregory had tied up for the night at Island No. 94 and then learned several men were on a nearby island waiting to rob him. During the night he slipped down the river. By the next morning the island and the robbers had disappeared in the earthquake.

Fort John on the Laramie River and Fort Sarpy on the Yellowstone were established by and named for the family. The latter was the last of the Crow Indian trading posts built in 1843.

Peter Sarpy has not had the historical recognition of other fur traders in the early part of the last century, but he and his family with widespread interests in several companies and over an 8-state area helped prevent many tribes from joining the British before and after the War of 1812.

November 8, 1969

JEAN LAFITTE

After the battle of New Orleans, Andrew Jackson, in his official report about a certain military company, stated:

"Captain Dominique and Beluche, lately commanding privateers, with part of their crews, were stationed at Batteries Three and Four.

The general cannot avoid giving his warm approbation of the manner in which these gentlemen have uniformly conducted themselves while under his command and the gallantry with which they redeemed the pledge they gave at the opening of the campaign to defend their country. The brothers Lafitte have exhibited the same courage and fidelity, and the general promises that the government shall be duly appraised of their conduct."

Another part of the report which General Jackson wrote at dawn January 8, 1815, said, "the Baratarians seem little worried and sipped coffee," and when the battle began he noted, watching Dominuqe, the expert artillerist, "I wish I had 50 such guns on this line with 500 devils as these fellows behind them."

General Jackson's report refers to the two expert artillerymen of Lafitte who, with his 1,000 men, played a major role in the battle of New Orleans, and may have altered American history because had not Jackson won the battle, even if it was two weeks after the end of the war, he might not have become President.

There was, and still is, considerable information about Jean Lafitte before the War of 1812 and during the conflict, but it is not easy to answer this question: Did Jean Lafitte go to St. Louis, using the name of "John Lafflin" and live there for almost a quarter century?

There are gaps in Lafitte's biography but his part in the battle of New Orleans is military history. He was born in either France or Port-au-Prince in 1782, reared by his maternal grandmother who fled the Spanish inquisition. Jean got some of his hatred of the Spanish here and the fact that he was imprisoned on an English ship.

But he later became powerful and raided only Spanish and British ships. The young republic charged he raided and robbed in American waters. He answered that he had a license from the Republic of Cartagena to raid any ship not a friend of Cartagena.

He lived in one of the best houses of New Orleans, was well dressed and charming of character, knew all of the bankers, and with his two brothers kept books similar to any establishment. He was friendly with Governor Claiborne, John R. Grymes, the district attorney; Edward Livingston, who was Claiborne's assistant. Lafitte attended the major social events. He was about 6 feet 2 inches tall with hazel eyes, dark hair and with all of the hand-kissing manners of that day.

On the business side, he insisted that all booty, or loot be brought into headquarters. Sometimes he advertised that such merchandise was for sale. He and his brothers ladled out the rewards on an almost military basis.

JEAN LAFITTE

He was the supreme commander of his band, an excellent pistol shot and swordsman. Only British and Spanish ships would be raided. Gambi, a lieutenant, attacked an American merchantman. Lafitte called a council, Gambi sent a man to kill Lafitte, who in turn killed the would-be assassin. Another ambitious lieutenant, seeking to steal a tray of watches, challenged Lafitte and only got a kick in his pants.

Lafitte was neither surly nor arrogant. The United States government, irked at Lafitte's failure to pay duty, ordered his arrest and Governor Claiborne posted a $500 reward for Lafitte's arrest. Laffite walked down the streets of what is now the French Quarter and tacked up a post of $1,500 for Claiborne's arrest. Not too much later the two clicked coffee cups together at the Cabildo and the Exchange Coffee house.

There is considerable doubt, despite tourist fancy, that Jackson and Lafitte ever got together in what is now called the Old Absinthe House, but they obviously got together somewhere.

The War of 1812 was languishing for England. One last stab might gain New Orleans and then a move up the Mississippi to seal off the western axis of the young republic.

Maj. Gen. Sir Edward Pakenham, charged by London with getting that beachhead at New Orleans, offered Lafitte $30,000 with a captain's commission in the British Navy. (One source states $50,000.)

Whether Lafitte gave an answer is not known, but it is known he went to Jackson, offered his men and almost guaranteed they could defeat the British force alone.

General Jackson asked Lafitte what he wanted in return. Only pardons for himself, his brothers and his men. Jackson agreed.

So, the 1,000 Baratarians, with Lafitte in command, plus the expert artillerists and 7,500 pistol flints that Lafitte tossed in for good measure, joined the Jackson forces.

Lafitte rode and moved among his men during the 20 minute battle that rivaled San Jacinto for its shortness and decisiveness. Pakenham was killed and more than 2,000 of his officers and men while the Americans and Baratarians lost seven killed and six wounded. The victor numbered about 5,000 men while the British had 14,000.

Lafitte had met many Missourians before and after the battle. Many, liking "Old Hickory," had ridden south to join his forces. The lead shot used in the battle had been produced in the shot tower near Herculaneum. John Mullanphy of St. Louis, a cotton broker, had furnished bales for breastworks.

Because of these Missouri contacts, it is not improbable that Lafitte decided to settle in Missouri. He realized he could not carry on his privateering ventures much longer in the Caribbean although he tried for a few years after war's end.

Several years ago Mrs. Madeleine Kent wrote a book, "The Corsair," based on papers brought to the Cuban consulate in New Orleans by Jean Andrechyne Lafitte, a great-grandson. She had chemical tests made of the paper and comparisons with Lafitte's handwriting and concluded they were genuine.

The letters and papers, some presumably written by Lafitte, related that he married a New Orleans girl and they moved to St. Louis. He became a partner in a gunpowder factory using the name of "John Lafflin."

November 15, 1969

CARRY NATION

Two persons of widely different morals and character, who regarded themselves as Missourians for a part of their lives, were most unwelcome in Kansas late in the last century.

One was Clarke Quantrill, the guerrilla leader and killer who led the raid on Lawrence, Kas., during the Civil War.

The other was a prim and sometime grim little woman who handled a hatchet like Babe Ruth swung a baseball bat.

She was Carry Nation, the fiery temperance leader who was born 123 years ago next Tuesday in Garrard County, Kentucky, and came to Missouri at the age of 9 with her parents, settling in Cass County just south of Kansas City in what is now Belton.

Her father was George Moore, a fairly prosperous stockman and farmer who moved the family to Texas, lost some money and then returned to Cass County.

Carry was not quite 21 years old when she married Dr. Charles Gloyd, a young physician who liked to drink. They separated after several months and he died of alcoholism six months later.

She attended what is now Central Missouri State College at Warrensburg for one year, obtained a teaching certificate, and then taught four years in the Holden schools.

In 1874 she married David Nation, 19 years her senior, a lawyer, minister and a one-time newspaper editor. Nation was one of the defense lawyers in the trail of Leonidas Hornsby who was charged with killing Old Drum, the dog immortalized by the other lawyer, George Graham Vest, who represented Charles Burden, Drum's owner.

212

Carry had become religious in her 30's, and also began nursing a delayed bitter hatred for liquor. David Nation was henpecked and entered the ministry at his wife's not so subtle suggestion. He preached at Holton and Medicine Lodge, Kas., but finally asserted himself and returned to the law.

It was in Medicine Lodge where she decided on a campaign against demon rum. At first she sang and prayed in front of the saloons but accomplished little.

In her memoirs she said that June 6, 1900, she had a vision from God who directed her to take "something" in her hands and throw at the saloons.

She wrapped bricks and stones in paper, drove to Kiowa near the Oklahoma border and wrecked three saloons the next day. The officials did not wish to prosecute her and face the embarrassment of failing to enforce the laws against saloons. Nothing was done.

Carry began experimenting with weapons. Bricks and stones were lost after one toss. She tied an iron bar to her husband's cane. Then she found a hatchet.

She scored some minor victories and then stormed into the elegant Carey hotel bar in Wichita December 26, 1900. The sight of liquor and a nude painting of Cleopatra over the bar incensed the crusader.

Carry not only wrecked the bar but used her rod and cane on the painting of John Noble, the well-known artist.

For the first time she went to jail. She was released January 12, 1901, wrecked two more saloons and later showed her disdain for Kansas legislators by wrecking the Senate saloon in Topeka.

She was put in jail again, refused to post a $2,000 bond and was released several days later. Sometime during that year, David Nation, who had been on a few of the early wreckings divorced Carrie, charging desertion.

Her campaign began to get attention of other women, most of whom had alcholic husbands. She wrecked other saloons in Kansas, went on a lecture tour in the east, visited Yale and Harvard Universities and sought to reform the drinking students but received only ridicule.

The public found it hard to believe the rather plainly dressed woman with graying hair tied in a knot at the nape of her neck and mild of manner could generate so much destructive energy with a hatchet.

At some saloons drunks would form a ring and prevent her from entering and if close enough she would heave the hatchet through the window. More than one bartender drew a gun when she sought to enter.

CARRY NATION

She frequently feared for her life but never admitted it except to two newspaper reporters who gave her protection in Hope, Kas.

Carry laughed rather heartily and walked away. Otherwise, she covered her real feelings with an icy exterior.

To a friend she wrote about being jailed, "I do not mind these things. Only one thing disturbs me—will I have the seat of the woman who did the best she could? I get tired of the world, tired of seeing its struggles and sorrows. I wake up in the night and cry because He stays away so long."

Early in her crusade, when she had accumulated sufficient money, she paid about $20,000 for a 23-room house in Kansas City, Kansas, where refugees from drunken husbands and fathers could find haven and protection.

The severe physical and emotional demands made upon her in the strenuous 10-year campaign finally forced her to a hospital in Leavenworth where she died June 9, 1911.

In 1924 a group of her friends and supporters erected a granite monument at her grave in the Belton cemetery.

November 22, 1969

MISSOURI GOVERNORS

Those who like quiz shows and are sharp with the answers on Missouri governors might like to try these:

Who was the only president pro tem of the Senate to become governor of Missouri in one direct leap?

What two men were governors of Missouri within 16 months but not in the normal order of succession?

Who was the first governor to commit suicide in office?

Who was the only one-legged governor of the state?

Which governor rode his horse into the executive mansion and allowed the animal to eat off the fireplace mantel?

This probably could go on indefinitedly but these are some of the more unusual aspects of a few of our governors? Here are the answers:

Abraham J. Williams, president pro tem of the Senate, became third governor of Missouri. Gov. Frederick Bates, the second governor, died August 4, 1825. Normally he would have been succeeded by the lieutenant governor, Benjamin H. Reeves, but Reeves already had resigned to become commissioner of a survey party to chart the road from Ft. Osage to Santa Fe, N. M. So Williams became governor, serving only 5½ months. He never lived in the executive mansion.

217

As to question No. 2, Bates had been in office only about eight months when he died. Abraham Williams succeeded him and served 5½ months until a special election had been held and the winner, John Miller, could take office.

Thomas Reynolds, Missouri's 7th governor, shot and killed himself February 9, 1844 in his office at the executive mansion, about 10 months before the expiration of his term. He had been a popular and constructive governor but was in ill health. He left a note saying the "slanders and abuse" of his political enemies were too much for him.

To those of you who like to wager, beware of the name Thomas Reynolds, because Thomas Caute Reynolds, who became the Confederate governor of Missouri following Claiborne Jackson's death in 1862, also is believed to have committed suicide. In 1887 his body was found at the bottom of an elevator shaft in a federal building in St. Louis and a note found saying that he had been melancholy and his life was a burden to him.

As far as it is known, the two Reynoldses were not related.

Gov. Albert P. Morehouse, the 26th governor, succeeded to the top post when Gov. John S. Marmaduke died. Morehouse was lieutenant governor. He finished out the term, about one year, and then retired to his farm. In September, 1891, he suffered heat prostration and a ruptured blood vessel in his brain. Fearing insanity, he took his own life.

Frederick Bates, the second elected governor and the first to die in office, was the only territorial governor to become an elected governor. In 1807 he became acting territorial governor until Meriwether Lewis could arrive to take the office. In 1809 he was acting governor a second time when Lewis died on the way to Washington. Bates had been in office less than a year as elected governor when he died of pleurisy.

For the avid bettor, Bates actually was acting governor three times. In the first two terms he was acting governor of the Territory of Louisiana of which Missouri was a part. When in 1812 the area officially became the Territory of Missouri, Bates again was acting governor from December 1812, to July 1813.

Abraham Williams was the one-legged governor. He was born with but one leg. A native of Virginia, Williams grew up in Boone County, Missouri, was a bachelor, shoemaker, farmer and tobacco grower. He is buried in a Columbia cemetery.

Robert M. Stewart, another bachelor governor who served from 1857 to 1861, also was a horse fancier. Once in the frivolous wake of a drinking session Stewart decided that his horse had just as much right to eat in the executive mansion as he did.

So Stewart rode the horse into the residence and allowed it to eat off a mantel.

Although this was a rather unusual incident, some historians point to Stewart's good record in office. Stewart was an unconditional Union man, but said Southerners had a right to take their slaves into Kansas. In his final message to the Legislature he became much stronger for the Union.

November 29, 1969

S. HAWKEN

Hollywood and television writers have done reams and stories about the "gun that won the West" and in almost all instances only two names appear—Colt and Winchester.

Whether they ever heard of the name Hawken is not known but it never has appeared in any of the productions; perhaps it is because Colt and Winchester had better public relations and those names still live today.

But the Hawken rifle "won the West" for 70 years or more before any other rifle. These facts speak for themselves:

Jim Bridger would have nothing except a Hawken and his rifle now is enshrined in the Montana Historical Society.

Kit Carson also was partial to a Hawken. He paid $60 for one of the first turned out and it is now in the Colorado State Museum.

Gen. William Henry Ashley liked the rifle so well that he ordered many for his expeditions.

Gen. John C. Fremont, after testing one, also ordered Hawkens for his several expeditions.

Sherley (Old Bill) Williams, one of the greatest of mountain men and scouts, was stubborn about changing from the flintlock to the Hawken caplock and afterward regarded "Old Fletchem," as he called the Hawken, as the world's best rifle.

Charles E. Hanson, Jr., who wrote a book about the rifles of the last century, "The Plains Rifle," said "Out of all this might be drawn a picture of the ideal Plains rifle in the mountain man. It would be about .53 caliber, have a heavy barrel around 36 inches long and be full-stocked in plain dark-maple. Actually this hits the Hawken of 1825-30 pretty close."

Several pages later he said, "Styles gradually changed. The average Hawken was about .53 caliber, bored with a slow twist to take charges

219

SAMUEL "HAWKEN AND RIFLE"   Credit: Missouri Historical Society of St. Louis, Mo.

of from 150 to 215 grains of gunpowder. This combination of slow twist and soft iron barrel was the big secret of the Hawken rifle's accuracy. It permitted heavy charges and attendant flat trajectory without undue recoil."

Henry Hawkins was a gunsmith in Pennsylvania in the 1720's and later went to Schenectady, N. Y. His son, Henry Hawkins, was a gunsmith at Hagerstown, Md., and is believed to have worked at Harpers Ferry. Jacob, his first son was born in 1786 and Samuel, the second, in 1792.

Jacob Hawken came to St. Louis in 1820, and opened a gun shop on Main street. Samuel Hawken came to St. Louis in 1822. (The two here changed the spelling from Hawkins to Hawkens and research doesn't reveal the reason. In most instances the "s" was dropped. Most of the rifles simply carry "J. Hawken" or "S. Hawken."

Rifle experts then argued that a longer barrel was necessary for mountain hunting. The Hawken brothers, however, seemed to realize that there would be much more traffic over the Plains, by wagon trains and against Indians, and that a shorter rifle would better serve the purpose. So, they cut the length of the barrel several inches.

The first Hawken had an octagonal barrel about 36 inches long, shot a .32-caliber ball, had a front sight with a steel knife edge and a rear of Rocky mount buckhorn. It had double hair triggers and a cheek rest on the stock. The locks were bar type.

The buffalo hunters, Pony Express riders and whites fighting Indians could handle the shorter rifle much easier, and this even permitted some of the experts to cradle the rifle against the shoulder and arm and fire with it while using a pistol with the other hand.

The Hawkens built their first rifles on the Army 1814 Flintlock, varying the barrel from 32 to 38 inches long and the ball up to .53 caliber.

Jacob moved to 21 Laurel street (now Washington) in St. Louis about 1820 and two years later was joined by his brother, Samuel. The flintlock had been in use about 200 years and to switch to the unusual caplock or percussion type, was an innovation, and Old Bill Williams was one of the first to see the advantage.

The Hawken rifle proved to be the most accurate, and while all competing weapons also were hand-made, the Hawken brothers took those special pains and skills to turn out the best.

The American Fur company and competing firms, frontiersmen, trappers and scouts and some military units, along with plain Joe Doakes, the family man, bought Hawken rifles. While the brothers, and their assistants, could not keep up with the demand, they never sacrificed precision workmanship for a growing demand.

Jacob Hawken died in the St. Louis cholera epidemic of 1849. Samuel Hawken roved a bit, to Independence, Iowa and Denver, and then back to St. Louis.

In the St. Louis Weekly Missouri Democrat of September 16, 1859, he published a vivid account of the gold rush to Colorado. He opened a gun shop in Denver and stayed about one year.

Samuel seemed more civic-minded than Jacob. Gil Chouteau chided Samuel about the need for a downtown fire fighting unit in St. Louis and Hawken organized one. He not only made many runs to fires but later was honored by the city for his interest and participation. He gave a swiftly working reel cart which the citizens christened the "Sam Hawken."

There are two unsolved points in the Hawken story. One is that most of the rifles bore the name, S. Hawken, although Jacob was turning them out in St. Louis several years before Samuel joined him. Samuel seemed to be more inventive and it is probable that Jacob, devoid of any family jealousy, simply let S. Hawken be stamped on the rifle.

In 1847 Samuel Colt, 33-year-old gun tinkerer, who knew about the Hawken, reportedly wrote Samuel Hawken a letter. There is no trace of the correspondence but it is believed he wanted to interest Hawken in the automatic firing mechanism he had invented.

Samuel Hawken retired to his farm 11 miles west of St. Louis after the Civil war and died in 1884. He was 92 and outlived all of the scouts, frontiersmen, trappers and others who used his rifle.

December 6, 1969

STATE BAR ASSOCIATION

Missouri can boast of many achievements in the last century, including the formation of many strong professional, patriotic and social organizations.

One is the Missouri Bar Association formed in Kansas City December 29, 1880, by 112 lawyers who came from 58 counties and St. Louis.

Until the railroads there was little opportunity for the lawyers to get acquainted around the state. They were limited to the circuits in which they practiced.

Strangely enough, fraternization was not the primary reason to organize. J. H. Drucker, writing in the Missouri Bar Journal, said "A major reason to form the Missouri association was to try and help the state Supreme Court to catch up with its docket. It was more than 1,500 cases behind and it took four years to get a decision."

The organization was formed but the high court remained far behind in turning out decision for many years. Twelve states formed bar associations before Missouri. Mississippi was the oldest; its bar assoication was formed in 1825.

Willard P. Hall was the first president. He was born at Harpers Ferry, Va., May 9, 1820, came to Missouri 20 years later, settled first in Randolph County and then moved to St. Joseph in 1843.

Hall joined Col. Alexander Doniphan's expedition to Mexico, abandoning his campaign for Congress. He drafted the civil code for the vast territory of the Southwest that stood for 45 years. While there he was elected to Congress.

He served three terms, resumed his law practice in St. Joseph and when Gov. Claiborne Jackson and his pro-slavery administration fled Missouri at the start of the Civil war, Hall was elected lieutenant-governor behind Hamilton Gamble. When Gamble died from injuries suffered in a fall on the icy Capitol steps, January, 1864, Hall became governor.

Hall was regarded as one of Missouri's greatest lawyers and a colleague once said of him, "He was always entirely respectful to the court, no matter what might be his opinion of the capacity of the judge."

Hall was ill at the time of his election as first president of the Missouri Bar Association and did not preside at any meetings. He died November 3, 1882, in St. Joseph.

In the early organization there were four classes of memberships—honorary, affiliated, regular and individual members. The distinction between the last two is not recorded.

John C. Gage, father of John B. Gage, a former mayor of Kansas City, was admitted to the Missouri bar in 1869 and became the fourth president of the state association in 1883. John C. Gage was regarded as one of the outstanding lawyers in Western Missouri and took a major role in helping to build and develop Kansas City.

In 1944 the Missouri Supreme Court ordered the "voluntary" bar association changed into an integrated bar and known as simply "The Missouri Bar." Under this arrangement, every Missouri lawyer practicing in Missouri must join the new organization.

WILLARD PREBEL HALL

At that time there were about 5,000 lawyers in Missouri, half of whom belonged to the voluntary organization. Now there are about 8,000 lawyers in the state and all belong to the Missouri Bar.

The Missouri association is regarded nationally as one of the best. Through the efforts of Henry Hitchcock of St. Louis, the second president, and his colleagues, Congress was induced to pass a law creating the United States Circuit Court of Appeals, thereby relieving the high court of an overburdened docket.

The Missouri association also took the leadership in getting the nonpartisan court plan passed, establishing the Missouri Supreme Court Commission and the Courts of Appeal at Kansas City and St. Louis, and in 1890 increasing the number of judges of the high state court. The latter was the original goal of the bar when it was formed 10 years earlier.

Through the years the Missouri Bar gradually has raised the standards of the legal profession in the state and been an alert watchdog on its own members.

The Missouri Bar, with its predecessor "association," has furnished five presidents to the American Bar Association, a justice to the U. S. Supreme Court, numerous judges to other federal courts, governors, congressmen and United States senators of Missouri. It has grown in authority, stature and accomplishments over the 89 years of its existence.

December 13, 1969

PIONEER WELCOME

"Light and tie, Mister—the latch string out."

It would be almost impossible for historians to agree on what the pat salutation was that a pioneer might direct at the stranger-traveler more than 100 years ago but the above would suffice, just in case the newcomer was a horse.

There were many others. The idiom and the idiosyncrasies of those pioneers are well known today, and our knowledge of them is usually an amalgam of hospitality, courage, industry and quietly inborn confidence in the ability to withstand the vicissitudes of the frontier.

The traveler always was welcome although there might be a few questions asked around the fireplace.

The stranger usually got the mattress with the softest corn husks, or even chicken feathers, and he knew when it was time to bid a courteous good-night to his host and hostess—that was when the owls began hooting and the whippoorwills ceased.

There were many amenities then. The seasoned traveler, although a stranger to his benefactors, gave thanks the next morning and departed. The mark of crudity and a lack of knowledge of frontier hospitality was an offer to pay for food and lodging.

Many a pioneer has replied to such a proffer, "You are welcome at all times but we are not running a tavern."

There were taverns then, of course, but the experienced traveler soon learned to avoid some of them whose money-hungry operators tried to sleep three in a bed and several on the floor. There were bugs, odors, snoring and a variety of other noises to prevent any possibility of rest.

The frontier language was salty. A shrewish wife was referred to as "half alligator and half snapping turtle."

If the "old settler" thought someone was lying, he would say that the man was from "Ol Kaintuck," "Carlin" or "Ol Vaginny." The second referred to South Carolina.

When two men, possibly strangers, squared off for a fist fight and an onlooker attached some professional or social importance to one of them, the comment was, "A governor is no more than any other man in a fight."

Everybody worked hard and many played hard. Some pioneers had their own stills. What was wrong with that? Any differant than slaughtering your own beef or pork? It was cheaper than paying 50 cents for a gallon from St. Louis.

Almost every community had a different term for the beverage. "Blue Ruin" was one in Central Missouri. Then a fancy Dan from Virginia began calling it "Old Monongahela," which was all right for the first several "sips," but watch the pronunciation after that.

Almost every stranger, unless he wore the cloth of the clergy, usually had a chance to "draw on the jug" before supper.

The young women of that day, as fashion-conscious as those today, bedeviled the storekeepers as to the date when the new bonnets and dresses would arrive from Philadelphia.

Sunday was a day of church-going and prayer, also for swapping horses and shooting for the beef. There was more horse swapping on Sunday than any other day.

Preachers usually were community leaders. Many criticized dancing, especially on Sunday in Southeast Missouri around Ste.

Genevieve. The stock reply was that if fiddling and dancing cleared Tom Jefferson's mind, then it was good enough for others.

Although the ministry moved almost continuously against drinking, it seemed sometimes to be a losing battle. In 1834, the Rev. William Horn was asked to make a survey of the distilleries in Missouri, located 38 and learned that half of them were operated by preachers or persons who professed to be men of the cloth.

There was plenty of land 150 years ago. Some in and around central Missouri sold for $1.50 an acre. It wasn't unusual for a squatter who had not filed a claim to fire off a blunderbuss at night, scream "Indians" and chase away some close squatters, thus getting the land the others had sought to claim and buy.

There was considerable gambling then, and the "deadman's" hand consisted of 2 black aces, two black eights and any fifth card.

The women vied for status through candle dipping in addition to bonnet and quilt contests. Those who could fuse and combine attractive vegetable dyes into a candle usually won the prize.

There are many who contend that the basic hospitality Missouri pioneers showed for travelers and strangers exists today, that generations of changes in customs have not erased that greeting that may occur between two persons, whether in Saskatoon or St. Louis, when one reaches out a hand and says, "I'm from Missouri," the modern rendering of "Light and tie, Mister; the latchstring's out."

December 20, 1969

FATHER DeSMET

Sitting Bull said—and he spoke loudly—that any white man who came upon the reservation and to his tent would be killed.

And so a white man arrived, dismounted casually and walked into Sitting Bull's tent, and the two embraced and feasted together and called each other "brother."

The white man was Father Pierre-Jean DeSmet, "Chief Black Robe" of the Jesuits who had tremendous influence among all of the tribes west of the Mississippi River.

In the 19th century there were many scouts, pathfinders, fur traders and military men who had the confidence of the Indian tribes. Several years ago John Upton Terrell wrote "Black Robe" a book that spelled out so well the influence DeSmet had with the tribes.

231

He was born in Belgium January 30, 1801, came to America and entered the Jesuit novitiate at Whitemarsh, Md. in 1821. Two years later he went to St. Louis and became professor of English and procurator at what is now St. Louis University.

In 1838 Father DeSmet traveled up the Missouri River to establish the Potawatomi mission at Council Bluffs, Ia. and bring about a peace treaty between the Sioux and the Potawatomis. It was here that his reputation as "Chief Black Robe," the white man, began as one who could bring about peace between the tribes.

For 30 years DeSmet probably was the most influential white man in the vast wilderness of the new nation, respected and revered by all tribes including the Black Feet who were the most troublesome.

Father DeSmet, 5 feet 7 inches tall, had no fear of Indians. He went among them as a missionary, a doctor and a peacemaker.

In July 1864, thousands of Sioux and whites on the banks of the Missouri River at Ft. Berthold watched the man row his boat across the river. There were no guards or companions, no bugles or ruffles of drums.

Father DeSmet stepped ashore, tied up his boat and received a royal reception. He brought greetings from President Lincoln and sought in the days of feasting that occurred to assure the Indians that Mr. Lincoln was their friend. It was intended to be a peacemaking mission and lasted several days.

In 1846 he had been successful on a peace mission with the Black Feet and had quelled many other smaller difficulties.

Perhaps in 1868 he achieved a major victory. He was 67 years old and rode 250 miles on a fast trip to meet with Sitting Bull, Two Bears, Black Moon and Four Horns. He successfully negotiated peace but a few years later the battle with Custer occurred. This was in 1876, three years after DeSmet died. There are some historians who believe the priest might have prevented the Custer battle because of his close friendship with Sitting Bull and many other tribal leaders.

Father DeSmet's historical importance is along the peacemaking route. Yet, he walked tight-rope on the medical side between the missionary-medical and the Indian medicine man.

"I visited the Indians in their wigwams as a missionary, and if they were disposed to listen to me, or as a physicain to see their sick, I did my best," he said.

Father DeSmet's prayers were not always understood. The Crows carried off the daughter of a Sioux tribal chief and the chief ordered war. DeSmet asked to intervene with prayer. Within a short time the daughter came into the Sioux reservation.

FATHER DE SMET

Father DeSmet might have become a multi-millionaire. He discovered gold in the Alder gulch of Montana in large quantities. He worried about it and did nothing. Others became wealthy.

Father DeSmet's greatest victory probably occurred in 1868 when the Sioux were moving. Alone, and on his horse, he met 500 of the tribe's bravest. Scalps dangled from all saddles. Blood was on almost all hands. It wasn't far to Powder River.

Father DeSmet took a slender pole and attached an emblem. On one side was the name "Jesus Christ," and on the other an image of the Virgin Mary.

This strange flag stopped the Sioux. They did not comprehend it but they knew "Chief Black Robe." When Father DeSmet died in 1873 this unusual flag, or banner, was hoisted with the American flag.

December 27, 1969

WILLIAM HENRY HATCH

In all probability if someone mentioned the "Hatch Act," you would somewhat automatically think of the congressional act sponsored by Sen. Carl Hatch of New Mexico 30 years ago that had to do with the political activities of federal employees.

But the farmers of Missouri, this nation and, perhaps, the world are far better off today because of a different "Hatch Act."

Let us pinpoint the major accomplishments of this Missourian, William Henry Hatch:

The original act he pushed through Congress, earned him the title of "Father of the agricultural experiment stations" in the United States.

He fathered or championed about 50 other bills to generally improve agriculture in this nation, including the first oleomargarine bill, one to control the spread of infectious and contagious diseases among domestic animals, another that would give cabinet rank to the then "commissioner of agriculture" and still another to help tobacco growers in relieving them of a license to grow the weed.

Hatch was born in Georgetown, Ky., September 11, 1833, read law and after being admitted to the bar of that state in 1854, came to Missouri and settled at Hannibal.

He became one of the outstanding lawyers of Missouri and in 1878, won his first race for Congress. He was re-elected for seven successive terms.

WILLIAM HENERY HATCH

Although Hatch practiced law for a livelihood he loved farming. He and Norman J. Colman, another Missourian, teamed up to advance the agricultural industry of the world more than any other two men.

Colman was Commissioner of Agriculture for the government and on July 5, 1885, he called a conference at Washington of all administrators or deans of colleges of agriculture in the nation.

There were many matters to be discussed but the major one was to try to get federal funds to establish experiment stations at the colleges. Sitting in on this conference was Hatch.

One bill had been introduced, but it never got to first base. Then Hatch got behind another bill. Colman worked on it and the two, with a few others, filed off the corners and made it more acceptable to members of Congress.

J. G. Carlisle and C. F. Crisp, House Democratic leaders, were quite friendly with Hatch, and the Hatch act passed through the House and Senate. President Cleveland signed it.

Hatch soon became known as Mr. Agriculture in Congress. His advice and counsel was sought on almost all legislation pertaining to agriculture.

He sponsored the bill giving cabinet rank to the commissioner of agriculture and the Hatch-Colman team won this, too. Colman became the first Secretary of Agriculture in the cabinet.

During Hatch's years in Congress, the nation was an agrarian country and inching into an industrial-agricultural amalgam. When he introduced the bill on oleomargarine the scoffers said the Missourian had finally met his Waterloo. But Hatch bowed his head bull-like and rode the bill through Congress. He was referred to afterward as Bull Butter Hatch.

Another Hatch bill created the Bureau of Animal Industry within the Department of Agriculture. There were many others, but the major achievement included the tie-in between the government and the colleges of agriculture on experiment stations. This provided a national network of interchange of information on improvements to agriculture.

After eight successive terms in Congress, Hatch was defeated in 1894. He accepted the presidency of the National Dairy Union and led a winning battle to get a law passed to tax filled cheese.

Then he came back to his "Strawberry Hill" farm near Hannibal and began raising Jersey cattle, Southdown sheep and Kentucky trotting horses.

Hatch died December 23, 1896, at his farm. A daughter, Sarah Rhodes Hatch, lived on the farm until 1923, when she willed it to the state. It became the Hatch Dairy Experiment station, operated jointly by the University of Missouri College of Agriculture and the U.S. Department of Agriculture.

A statue was dedicated to him in the Hannibal city park in 1915, and one of the residential halls on the University of Missouri campus at Columbia is named for him.

January 3, 1970

HERCULANEUM

The similarity of names among many Missouri cities and those in other lands—such as Carthage, Warsaw, Cuba and many others—never was more pronounced than in the case of Herculaneum, Mo.

It is one of the oldest towns in Missouri and has risen again as a bustling community.

When Moses Austin and Samuel Hammond founded the town in 1808, Herculaneum, south of Naples, Italy, was under from 50 to 100 feet of lava ashes from Mt. Vesuvius. Pompeii was a bustling commercial city and Herculaneum, named after Hercules, was a charming and pleasant residential city in 79 A. D. when Vesuvius erupted and buried them both. Herculaneum, Italy, and Herculaneum, Mo., had some similarities, both being good harbor cities.

Moses Austin came to Missouri at the turn of the century from Virginia. He was interested in mining and heard about the promising lead ore deposits. He soon began to prosper in mining, but he and his partner, John Rice Jones, wanted a river front city for shipping the ore to New Orleans and Europe.

Samuel Hammond had been civil commander of the Missouri part of the Louisiana Purchase, shortly after the papers were signed, and succeeded Capt. Amos Stoddard. The area was then a district to a territory and Gen. James Wilkinson became territorial governor.

He became a partner with Moses Austin although more on the real estate business level than mining. In order to cut down the overland transportation costs of lead ore, they bought land and founded Herculaneum. Austin is regarded as the authority for naming the town after the one in Italy because, as one historian wrote, "the edges of the limestone strata are worn away so as to resemble seats in the amphitheater of the ancient Herculaneum."

Frontier Missourians used a lot of lead shot in those days for hunting, defense and fighting Indians. Shortly after Austin and

240

Hammond founded Herculaneum, John Nicholas Maclot built a shot tower and on Nov. 16, 1789 advertised in the St. Louis Gazette that he was able to supply the best shot in the west.

The tower was at the top of an overhanging cliff. Workmen melted the lead there and then it was poured into receptacles of water below. The shot hardened on the way down and was cooled by the water. Workmen than dipped out the shot and polished and glazed them. Several thousands pounds could be processed daily. Cannon-size shot needed a drop of 140 feet, rifle shot about 90 feet.

Within a year or two Moses Austin erected a shot tower and by 1819 there were three in that area. A large amount of the shot for American forces in the War of 1812 came from the Herculaneum, Potosi area and Maclot went to New Orleans to be certain Andrew Jackson's artillerymen, and those of Jean Lafitte, knew how to handle it properly.

In 1811, Henry Brackenridge, the tourist and writer, wrote about Herculaneum with 20 houses, 200 persons, the shot towers, a store one blacksmith shop "an excellent hatter" and "the situation is extremely romantic." The scenic view of the river and lands in all directions was attractive.

That same year the first post office was established and Charles A. Austin, a son of Moses and brother of Stephen Austin, "the father of Texas," became the first postmaster.

Jefferson County officially was established in 1818 and Herculaneum became the county seat. Henry Schoolcraft, another wandering writer, wrote that year about "the 40 houses, three stores, postoffice, courthouse, school, three shot towers, mills and distillery." The last word, singular, is Schoolcraft's own and some historians wondered about it because for many years Herculaneum had a reputation for distilleries almost equal to that of shipping lead ore.

One writer reported that in 1818 there were 25 distilleries within the town in a 35-mile radius. New towns then often provided plenty to drink in order to attract the new arrivals. A jug in the cabin was almost as important as food, sometimes more important. Whisky then—and times haven't changed too much—was supposed to have certain curative qualities. One so-called prescription that had the "kill or cure" label was a big slug of whisky sprinkled with black pepper!

About 1832 a fight developed in Jefferson County over the location of the county seat and it was moved from Herculaneum to Monticello, the name of which changed a short time later to Hillsboro.

January 10, 1970

ANDREW DRUMM

A man who became many times a millionaire and pioneered the herding of cattle from the Southwest to the Kansas City markets still is mostly just a name to native Kansas Citians.

He is Andrew Drumm, best known for founding the Andrew Drumm Institute here to help deserving boys.

Yet, he had many accomplishments which have received scant attention in some of our historical presentations. Here are just a few:

*He was one of the original '49ers, going from the East to San Francisco where he mined gold for almost 20 years in El Dorado County, California. He made some money in this enterprise.

*He then went into the cattle business and owned or leased ranches in Texas, Oklahoma, Kansas, California, Missouri, New Mexico and Arizona.

*At peak times he owned 40,000 head of cattle and branded as many as 7,500 annually.

*For years he was the largest payer of individual taxes in Kansas City.

*He also became the biggest hog raiser in California and would drive as many as 2,500 at a time into the farming country near Sacramento and fatten them on barley.

Drumm was born February 6, 1828, in Muskingum County, Ohio. His paternal ancestors came from Virginia and his mother's family was from Pennsylvania.

Drumm apparently was destined to be both a wanderer and money-maker but he had been reared on a solid family discipline. Even when he became famous and wealthy Drumm always would go back to Ohio at least every two years to visit his parents and family.

After a visit in 1870 to Ohio he went to Texas and began buying and selling cattle.

As a man of vision and action, he foresaw the possiblilties of driving cattle up from the Southwest to Abilene and other Kansas railroad lines for transportation eastward.

"We used to trail cattle up from Texas and double our money on them," he explained years later. "We did not mind the distance. The range was free and there were no fences, so their feed cost us little. By the time we got them to the Kansas City market they were fat. Cattle in those days never knew the taste of corn."

242

DR. ANDREW DRUMM   Photo credit: Kansas City Star

He noted the heavy and nutritious grasses in the Cherokee strip area of Oklahoma and the Flint Hills of Kansas. Within a short time the Cherokee nation demanded a rental fee from the cattlemen. Some refused to pay but Drumm was one of the leaders in organizing in 1883 the Cherokee Strip Live Stock association in Caldwell, Kas. It negotiated a lease with the Cherokee nation for five years, paying $100,000 annually and 2½ cents an acre annually.

The lease was not renewed after five years because controversy had developed between the cattlemen, the federal govenment and the Cherokees.

Drumm's general faith in mankind, so demonstrated in the establishment of the institute here, was evident in his cattle days.

A friend came to him to borrow money to buy a ranch.

"What's the price, Tom?" Drumm asked.

He was told it was $85,000 and Drumm replied, "All right, Tom, you go out and buy it. I'll let you have the money." He asked for neither collateral nor notes in such transactions and there are no records that he ever lost money. He is reported to have lent cattlemen 8 to 10 million dollars during his career.

Although he had been a cattle buyer many years in Kansas City, it was in 1897 when he formed Drumm Commission company of Kansas City. It became one of the most extensive businesses of its kind in the Mid-West and Southwest, doing business with stockyards in both St. Louis and Chicago. He had other interests including several banks.

Drumm always was called "Major Drumm," but said he never knew how it started because he had had no military duty. During the trail days it was common to attach a military title to the large and extensive cattle barons.

Drumm's estate at the time of his death April 14, 1919, was estimated at 2 million dollars. He created a trust for the Andrew Drumm Institute which is located on 370 acres in the southeast part of Independence.

His plan was to provide the equivalent of a high school education, with the emphasis on agriculture, to boys of good character, preferably from Jackson County. Orphaned and neglected boys are accepted but no delinquents. There are more than 50 boys there now. About 200 have been graduated in the 40 years of the institution.

THE JONES FAMILY

The Jones boys (and girls) probably won a mythical championship of some sort in the last century in helping to settle the Middle West, Southwest and Far West.

JOHN RICE JONES

The history of colonization, discovery and settlement reveals many family teams, or brother teams, dominating the task of pushing back the frontiers in the 19th century.

To tick off a few, there is the Boone family, including sons who almost outshone their illustrious father; the five Sublette brothers and the Sarpy family that roamed over the West setting up a large network of trading posts; the Robidoux brothers, one of whom founded St. Joseph, Mo.; the Walker brothers, one of whom became the first sheriff of Jackson County, the five Bent brothers, one of whom was the first territorial governor of New Mexico, and many others.

But the Jones family, with the father, John Rice Jones, leading the group, mgiht well be judged the winner. He and his five sons and two daughters played important roles in various capacities in Missouri Illinois, Texas, Iowa, Michigan and Wisconsin.

John Rice Jones was born in Wales February 10, 1759. He was educated at Oxford, practiced law in London and then came to the United States. He settled in Pennsylvania and then began wandering west. He served with George Rogers Clark's army near Louisville at the end of the Revolutionary war and then went to Indiana territory where he became the first English-speaking lawyer.

Francis Breton had discovered rich lead deposits before the turn of the century in Missouri, got a land grant from Spain and opened Mine a Breton.

Moses Austin in Virginia heard about the deposits and left there in December, 1796, for Missouri, arriving first at Ste. Genevieve. Jones also had arrived in Missouri and he and Austin, after seeing the possibilities around Mine a Breton, formed a partnership.

Jones served in the Missouri territorial assembly in 1814 and when Washington County was organized about the same time he contributed 10 acres and Austin gave 40 acres to establish the town of Potosi which would be the county seat. Both men helped found the Potosi academy and Jones was a trustee.

Jones was one of the leaders in urging Congress to grant full statehood to the territory of Missouri and in 1820 he was elected a delegate from Washington County to the first Constitutional convention.

Although historians may differ on a name here and there it is generally agreed that the outstanding delegates to the convention in addition to Jones were David Barton, Edward Bates, Henry Dodge, Duff Green, John D. Cook, Jonathan Smith Findlay and one to two others.

It was a young and aggressive convention. The average age was about 38 but Jones at 61 was an outstanding delegate. He was wealthy from mining and land holdings, regarded as the best educated man in the convention, fluent in six languages and he had an amazing knowledge of Greek and Roman history.

The erudite Jones did have some political ambition but could not compete against several others. Barton and Benton ran ahead of him for the United States senatorial elections. Governor McNair, the first chief executive, appointed Jones to the state's first Supreme court where he served ably until his death in St. Louis, February 1, 1824. Among three judges, he was the "great dissenter."

Rice Jones, his eldest son, had become a lawyer in Kaskaskia and served in the lower house of the Indiana territory. He was a leader in attempting to establish what is now the state of Illinois out of Indiana territory.

John Rice Jones II, another son, grew up in Missouri with Stephen Austin, and went to Texas to help his boyhood friend achieve freedom from Mexico. He also became the first postmaster general of the Republic of Texas.

Two other sons, Augustus Fisher Jones and Miers Fisher Jones, also went to Texas to help Stephen Austin. Miers Jones had served two terms in the Missouri Assembly before going to Texas.

And George Wallace Jones, son No. 5, held some minor offices in Missouri, fought in the Black Hawk war, then served as a congressional delegate in the Territory of Michigan, held a similar post in the Territory of Wisconsin and became one of the first two United States senators from Iowa.

Harriet Jones married John Scott who was a congressman for the Territory of Missouri and after statehood served three terms in Congress.

Elizabeth Jones married Andrew Scott, a Missouri lawyer, who became a federal judge in Arkansas. The Scotts were brothers.

LIBERTY ARSENAL

Many years before the start of the Civil War, Liberty, Mo., was an important and strategic post.

The general Liberty area was inhabited by those of southern sympathies and just exactly what was stored in the Union arsenal there could not be a secret for long.

For Missouri and Kansas, the Civil War began almost 10 years before the official rebellion, although the height of this did not occur until about 1855. This was known as the "border warfare." between the two states. Those in Missouri who believed in slavery, wished to ascertain that Kansas, when it attained statehood, would be on the slavery side. There, also, were nonslavery supporters in Missouri, who wanted Kansas to be free.

The Liberty arsenal, on 10 acres of land three miles south of Liberty, was completed in 1839. Maj. Ebenezer Price raided it December 4, 1855, he and his men found a quantity of arms and ammunition.

Major Price and his 100 men took over the Liberty arsenal bloodlessly and detained Maj. Luther Leonard in command. They took over three cannons, 55 rifles, 100 pistols, 20 Colt revolvers, 67 sabers and various ammunition.

Price and his men started for Kansas Ctiy and Lawrence. Their flag was purple with a white star in the center. But they didn't get far. Lassitude seemed to be the worst enemy. Jefferson Davis was Secretary of War and took no action against the men. They returned and a troop of the 1st U.S. Cavalry from Ft. Leavenworth looked on while they returned the "borrowed" materials of war.

During the next several years the Liberty arsenal was maintained. As the clouds of war became blacker, it was obvious that the arsenal might play a very important part in case of Civil War.

The arsenal, built for protection against the Indians, was called the "Missouri Depot" in the official records. It consisted of a 3-story building, strongly constructed with storage rooms for the guns, a squad room and an assembly hall.

War came. Shots were fired at Ft. Sumter.

The proslavery, and pro-Southern, persons in and around Liberty, decided that the arsenal must be taken in order to prevent the distribution of weapons to Kansas and other pro-Union areas.

But who would do it this time? Henry Routt volunteered. He was a tall and handsome man, with dark wavy hair, a sweeping moustache and finely combed beard. He was the first probate judge of Clay County.

And so came the second raid on the arsenal. It was bloodless just as the first. Maj. Nathaniel Grant was the post storekeeper and taking a leisurely breakfast April 20, 1861.

Routt led his 200 men up the hill to the arsenal. Grant, with only two assistants, did not resist, It was a "friendly" surrender. Grant made a speech and read the War Department secession laws and regulations. Some historians report he even got some applause, whether cynical or real.

Routt had a better haul than Price; 1,180 muskets, 243 rifles, 923 pistols, 120 carbines, 29 swords, three 6-pounder brass cannons, five caissons, two battery wagons and considerable other weapons.

Everything seemed to disappear and it was reported that most of the weapons ended up in the homes and cellars of pro-Southern persons in and around Liberty.

This bloodless raid was the first armed action nationally after the Sumter attack and it occurred in Missouri the "Child of the Storm "

There were many incongruities about the two raids. In 1855 the U.S. secretary of War was Jefferson Davis, later to be President of the Confederacy, and the raiding officer was Major Price, not related to Sterling Price, who would be Missouri's military leader for the Confederacy.

And in the second raid, the commandant at the Liberty Arsenal would be a Grant, not related to U. S. Grant, a transplanted Missourian who won the war, changed the western concept of warfare and became President of the United States.

After the raid Judge Routt did not attempt to flee. Federal troops arrested him. He was taken to St. Louis, charged with treason, convicted and sentenced to death. One of President Lincoln's earliest acts of mercy was to pardon Judge Routt. He returned to Clay County and after the end of the war resumed practice of law.

January 31, 1970

ARROW ROCK

Whoa! Whoa! "We're tying up here tonight for some of that golden fried chicken, that old country ham with red-eye gravy, corn pudding and green beans, sticky buns and some of that long sweetening for the biscuits and then if you're hungry tomorrow we'll start out with venison and turkey, oyster dressing and a little fatback."

About 140 years ago you would have gotten all of that food at Arrow Rock tavern, and more, and even today you can get many of the items.

In 57 years the Arrow Rock tavern and the vicinity have become a tourist attraction. Arrow Rock is on M41 between Marshall and Boonville.

The Missouri chapter of the Daughters of the American Revolution has been instrumental in the restoration and rebuilding of Arrow Rock landmarks.

D. A. R. members decided it was time to quit just talking about how grandfather and great-grandfather fought in the Revolution and

TAVERN AT ARROW ROCK

decided that the restoration of Arrow Rock tavern and area might best reflect the deeds of their ancestors.

The women went to the Missouri Legislature about 1920 and got a $5,000 appropriation to buy the tavern. They went back and got $6,000 more to help in the restoration. Then the Missouri D. A. R. raised $16,000 and induced the late Hugh Stephens to undertake a general leadership of the project.

The D. A. R. pushed more and an endowment fund of $13,000 was established for help in the maintenance. Eleven years ago the D. A. R. spent $5,050 to purchase other properties in the tavern block and the Missouri park board added $2,750.

The D. A. R. has contributed about $34,000 but Mrs. Robert E. Cullers of Trenton, chairman of the Arrow Rock board of managers, which acts for the Missouri D. A. R., says, "the total is much more and we do not know how much without a careful check of our minutes over the last 60 years. Some members gave directly to the tavern many years ago and there were innumerable contributions of antiques, household items linens and relics of inestimable value."

The Missouri park board has spent thousands of dollars in helping the D. A. R. restore many of the old buildings, Dr. John Hall home, state D. A. R. headquarters in addition to the tavern. The Friends of Arrow Rock, a nonprofit organization, acquired five buildings in six years including the 100-year-old John P. Stites gun shop, the old Christian church, Odd Fellows hall, the old Saline County Herald and the 1-story courthouse.

George Caleb Bingham built his home there more than 130 years ago and it has been restored. It was dedicated two years ago by Mrs. Warren Hearnes, wife of Missouri's governor. Arrow Rock is now a national shrine.

The Lyceum, a summer theater group, has set up shop in the old Baptist church and over the years the crowds have increased.

The blacksmith shop still operates and there is a trading post, a postoffice, loom factory, 1-cubicle jail, two old homes loaded with antiques, the restored girls' seminary and many other attractions.

Arrow Rock is not on the tourist beaten path but more than 100,000 persons have visited it since the restoration. There are no neon signs, the country stores have their cracker boxes and many call the town "Missouri's Williamsburg."

Almost 200 years ago Arrow Rock became an outpost of commerce and civilization. It stood upon the Santa Fe trail and was the crossing point of Indian trails north, south, east and west. It was long an Indian rendezvous and the braves got their flint points for their arrows in the vicinity.

It was visited by early French explorers and Lewis and Clark noted the excellent geographical and strategic location. Judge Joseph Huston, who came from Virginia, foresaw the importance of the outpost and began construction of the tavern in 1832, using walnut and oak from nearby forests.

Slaves prepared the bricks. There are seven fireplaces in the tavern and the doors are called "Christian doors" because of the cross at the top and open Bible design at the bottom.

Tavern visitors included Kit Carson, Nathan Boone and other trappers and scouts, Bingham, Claiborne Jackson, the Marmadukes, Dr. John Sappington of quinine fame, Thomas Hart Benton and others.

The tavern has many rooms filled with period furniture, antiques and Missouri memorabilia.

And while it doesn't have venison, bear meat, wild turkey and similar offerings served 130 years ago, the tavern today offers Missouri specialties such as country ham, red eye gravy, fried chicken and hot biscuits.

The Missouri D. A. R. first began locating the old trails and placing markers on them, especially the Santa Fe trail westward. Arrow Rock was a starting point for many years and about 50 years ago the women saw the great historic possibilities in its restoration.

Just as the original Arrow Rock was a monument to Missouri's early pioneers, so the restored Arrow Rock is a monument to the Missouri D. A. R.

February 7, 1970

THE OZARKS' LURE

If you're looking for quiet, peace and serenity in this world of tension, try the "Aux Arcs!"

And what is that? It is that strip of hilly and mountainous country mainly along the southern part of Missouri that also laps over into two other states.

You know the area as the Ozarks.

The French Canadians normally abbreviated names and called the Arkansas mountains the Aux Arcs. Most historians, as well as the United States Geographic society, generally accept this version, that "Ozarks" is an Anglicized version of the French "Aux Arcs."

254

Explorers in the 16th, 17th and 18th centuries, who went through the region, attached no names to it, but in the 19th century, when there were many more explorers and writers roaming the areas, both the French and Anglicized versions began to be used. Official maps in 1821 and 1822 carried the name Ozarks.

The original settlers were mainly of Anglo-Saxon stock, although there were some Germanic pioneers.

The Shannon County Historical Review recently commented, "In spite of its awkward frontier name, Jacks Fork is the poet's river. All that does not contribute has been pruned away. All is concentrated, quintessential. All is at hand. There is not the stream AND the shore. There is only the one interest undivided. The river is personal, trusting, chatty. It romps like a Mozart concerto with learned grace, with heady melody, with consummate, conquering charm."

There is a humor in this quiet land that cannot be found anywhere else in the world.

If you're crossing a river, don't turn your chewing tobacco over in your mouth, is one familiar saying.

Uncle True recently told how flush the Current River is with fish.

"These Current River Fish are scared of thunder," he said. "And when it thunders, they'll come, thousands of them down the river. And, of course, when they come to the bend in the river where my house sets they're going so fast they just can't make the curve, and so they naturally slide right out of the river onto my front yard. I'm just naturally getting tired of shoveling all those big heavy fish back into the river where they belong. You'd think the government might bank the curves of the river a little so the fish could make it around the bend."

There are other stories. One native was asked if his hogs were "fattening up." The native replied that they got so fat they got stuck between the hills and he had to "thin 'em down" before they could move around.

There are thousands of sayings and superstitions in the area such as: The tree toad sings just before it rains. Snake rattlers inside a violin will improve the tone. It is bad luck to take a hoe in the house.

Some of the land is rocky and unproductive in places. The people regard the fish and game as theirs and take only what they need for sustenance. They lament with deep and righteous anger the rape of the forests and pollution of the streams by tourists and "other foreigners."

But many of the city folks, the tourists and "other foreigners" continue to go to the Aux Arcs because they have found the peace and contentment the big cities have destroyed.

February 14, 1970

ANDREW STILL

DR. ANDREW STILL

The lanky man, handsome and with a finely combed beard, masked the sadness in his face and turned away from the four graves in a Baldwin, Kas. cemetery.

These four victims probably were martyrs to the formation of a new school of physicians, of a different technique of doctoring the human body.

The man who walked with a measured step and tragic face from that cemetery that day more than 100 years ago kept asking himself, "What is wrong with medicine and the medical profession?"

He was Dr. Andrew Still, himself a medical practitioner, who became the founder of osteopathy which now has spread over the world and in recent years has come to be recognized by the scientific community.

The graves contained the bodies of his wife, who had died from cholera and his three young daughters who had died in a meningitis epidemic despite heroic efforts by Still, his father, also a doctor, and many other physicians.

Whether he founded osteopathy because of the deaths of his family, or because he was simply dissatisfied with the regular procedural practices, is not known for sure. Retrospect is a cruel evaluator and certainly the medical practice then offered little. The main killers were cholera, malaria, yellow fever, meningitis, smallpox, typhus and dysentery.

The treatments consisted of bleeding, calomel, purges and drugs, a variety of nostrums and even what later became a form of hypnotism.

Andrew Still was born in Virginia in 1828, went to Tennessee with his family and then to Macon County, Mo. His father was a Methodist preacher as well as a regular medical practitioner, and it is doubtful that any one family ever contributed so much to so many people.

Father and son were doctors. The father had four brothers who were doctors, and three other sons, along with Andrew, who were doctors. There were several cousins and nephews who were doctors, and Andrew Still's sons and grandsons have carried on the practice as physicians. Andrew Still obtained his training at the old Kansas City Medical college.

In 1837 in Macon, Mo., where the family lived, young Andrew loved to roam the countryside. Birds, flowers and animals attracted the boy and the skinning of squirrels brought him into contact with muscles, nerves and veins as well as the general bone structure.

He discovered that the skeleton and its supporting muscles and ligaments were subject to certain mechanical laws and therefore the objects of stresses and strains and within his philosophy was the concept that man among his many other attributes, was a mechanism subject to mechanistic law.

In his autobiography, Still told about one of his discoveries when he was 10 years old. He had a headache, made a pillow of his father's rope plow line and laid on it. He went to sleep and when he awakened the headache was gone. Pressure did it and years later he began to make a serious aspect of this discovery.

Because the family was opposed to slavery, it moved to Kansas. Andrew was elected to the Kansas Territorial Legislature on the Free State ticket in 1857. Father and son ministered to the Shawnee Indians as well as to whites.

Andrew and his two brothers gave land at Baldwin for the establishment of Baker University and Andrew supervised the construction of the first building. The Civil war came and Andrew joined the Union army, fought in the battle of Westport and was mustered out as a major.

After the death of his family in 1864, Andrew Still began asking himself those questions. He began a rigorous study of all aspects of medicine. He made scientific laboratory studies utilizing all the books he could obtain. He obtained the skeletons of Indians and made minute studies.

Andrew Still later wrote that on June 22, 1874, the idea of osteopathy came to him, "Like a burst of sunshine the whole truth dawned on me that I was gradually approaching a science by study, research and observation that would be a great benefit to the world."

It was then he began to suffer the ridicule which many great men experience who possess and try to put daring ideas into practice. Baker University and Baldwin didn't take to this "nut," called a "crazy crank" by children on the street. His brothers turned against him and ministers prayed for his soul. So Andrew Still went first to Macon and then to Kirksville where the family had lived.

In addition, he was denounced by the medical profession, expelled from his own church, impeached by the Missouri Masonic order and generally derided. He lost many patients but gained new ones and became so enthusiastic with his new-found healing art that he founded the first College of Osteopathy at Kirksville in 1894.

Andrew Still was not to be denied. He clung stubbornly to the Hippocratic oath and his own ideas of osteopathy. He traveled around Missouri, bore ridicule from many quarters, listened to denunciations from all sides and in 1892 obtained from the Missouri Legislature a charter permitting him to teach osteopathy.

Shortly afterward he held his first class of 18 students at the newly found "American School of Osteopathy." Unlike some visionaries, he lived to see the ramshackle building and ridiculed profession grow into a great institution and an accepted science.

Andrew Still not only was a pioneer and "rebel" in regular medicine but in his ideas of whom should study and practice osteopathy insisted that the schools be open to Negroes. He also pleaded for woman suffrage.

Today in the United States there are five private colleges of osteopathy that annually graduate 500 physicians. Another osteopathic college in Michigan is affiliated with the state university.

Feb. 21, 1970

BOONVILLE'S THESPIAN HALL

Thespian Hall in Boonville, Mo., exerted great social and cultural influence in the half of the 19th century—no doubt about that.

The 113-year-old structure, with its facade of stately columns, has survived wars, abandonment, neglect, weather and even the nickelodeon. And while residents of Boonville today may be somewhat oblivious of its rich past they rush to its defense when the suggestion is made that it be torn down.

In 1838 about 60 business and professional men of Boonville formed the Thespian society and began performances in a log-hewn building on bluffs overlooking the Missouri river. Eight years later the society moved to a vacant general store building and in 1854 to the upper floor of the courthouse.

The society then bought a lot for $500 and expanded its activities. More than heavy dramatic productions were presented. For example, the Polyhymnia, a musical society of Boonville, presented a program May 31, 1859, directed by Nikolaus Haerle.

The Boonville library, Reading room and Thespian society were incorporated, in order to expand the base of persons who might contribute to a building. The group raised $10,000 and the hall was built at a cost of $16,000.

The Thespians sold stock to make up the deficit and the hall was opened officially July 4, 1857, with a gala public event and dance.

In succeeding years, the hall felt the tears and heard the laughter of actors and actresses, celebrities, public figures, political leaders, listened to the anguished cries of the Civil war wounded, stood stoically

261

THESPIAN HALL

Boonville

silent when abandonment came and then again felt the pulse of people who seemed finally to recognize an old friend.

In 1901 the end appeared certain but the owners agreed to a remodeling. This included an enlarged stage, opera boxes, steam heat, oil paintings and even painted cherubs on the ceiling. It was reopened October 5, 1901 as Stephens Opera house with a play, "The Minister's Son."

The names of those who performed first before gas footlights and then electric lights are many—James J. Corbett, Edna May, who starred as a Salvation Army lassie with her classic line, "I told them to follow Jesus but they always follow me"; De Wolf Hopper, Marguerite Clark, Emma Abbott, Frank James and Cole Younger, Bill Corum and others.

Boonville was an outpost when settled in 1810 by Hannah Cole, the widow, and her several children.

The prairies were not settled. Boonville began to fill up with pioneers, bullwhackers, riverboatmen. The people did not think too well of actors and followers of the theater. But the Thespians persisted and had a major public relations job to perform especially when one of the players from a touring St. Louis company landed in the Boonville jail.

The Thespian leaders realized that if the hall survived it must become a community center as well as dramatic theater, and it became the center of community activity for many years. Masked balls, concerts, athletic drills and gymnastic performances, community singing, recitations, wrestling, boxing and other events occurred nightly.

Elston J. Melton, the Boonville newspaper publisher and author of several books, wrote one about the hall 13 years ago and it captured the almost humanistic aspects of the structure when he wrote, "The foundations of Thespian hall were laid in the hearts of pioneer merchants and professional men two decades before the building took form. And, for a century since its dedication the building has revealed much of the character of the people who built it and succeeding generations who used it. It is significant as an index of the life of the community, the early West and of later generations.

"The transition of drama and much of the political life are revealed in the story of a building that continues to serve well as the focal center of recreation in a community that has produced many noted men and women, some natives, others who located and developed here, and still others who in years of schooling felt the impact of Boonville on their later lives. Thespian hall, a temple to make believe has helped many dreams come true."

Feb. 28, 1970

WESTON

The Missouri river and the growing western wilderness were the main factors leading to the establishment of Weston, just north of Kansas City but today it is mainly known for its tobacco and whisky production, attractive antebellum homes, antiques and historical lore.

Lewis and Clark noted the beauty of the Weston site and spent a day and a night there cutting a new mast from a sycamore tree for their keelboat.

Joseph Moore, a discharged soldier, reportedly bought the site from an Indian trader for a barrel of whisky and Moore operated a trading post near the site of the McCormick distillery.

Moore hired Tom Weston first sergeant of company D, 1st dragons, to plat the site for him. Weston was stationed at Ft. Leavenworth. The town was named for him.

Weston was in the heart of the Platte purchase which involved 2 million acres of land bought from several Indian tribes for $7,500 plus livestock and farm equipment.

The land was beautiful and scenic. Bayard Taylor, the writer, who came through the territory about the time it was platted, called it "the Eden of the American continent."

A Liberty newspaper reported in 1839 of the real estate sellers:

"The proprietors are prepared to dispose of lots in Weston to persons who may desire situations in a growing town in the most fertile and beautiful region of the Western country. All who desire a situation on the Missouri river at a permanent point, in a healthy country, unequaled for the fertility of its soil, fine timber and water, are invited to visit the town of Weston."

Much has been written about Weston over the years and many attempts made to describe it adequately. That was accomplished last year by Mrs. B. J. Bless, jr., of the Weston Chronicle in her "Weston—Queen of the Platte Purchase."

Mrs. Bless, who doesn't mind talking about her age (she is 80) and is a working editor-reporter-author, was named "Missouri Woman of the Year" in 1969 by the Missouri Press Women. Her description of Weston:

"In this fragmentation of Weston's past, sometimes glorious, sometimes desolate, there is a pattern of today weaving itself into a future that will eclipse all her past and her present.

"The same foresight that sent our pioneers into a dense and dangerous wilderness, the same valor which endured its challenges, the same selflessness which built their schools and chruches, farms and town are here today. Not always in the same channels, but always here."

266

Weston was the first city in the Platte purchase with large hemp and tobacco warehouse, the first large distillery west of the Mississippi, first to have macadamized roads, a telegraph line to St. Louis and the first city west of St. Louis to have a gas works.

It also had the first newspaper in the area, the Platte Eagle established in 1842 in Platte City but moved the same year to Weston.

The first tobacco crop was harvested in 1840 and since then Weston has been a principal tobacco producer is the Middle west. The 7-million-dollar annual crop goes through the only tobacco warehouses west of the Mississippi.

The first settlers came from Kentucky, Tennessee and Virginia. Ben Holladay and his cousin, Bela M. Hughes, were among the early developers. Holladay married one of the town beauties, Notley Ann Calvert, only 16 years old, by abducting her. (Her family opposed the marriage because of the age difference). But it had a happy ending and Holladay built a house costing $36,000. By today's standards it is estimated it would cost $200,000.

Dave Holladay, Ben Holladay's brother, came for a visit and learned that bourbon whisky was being made out of limestone spring water and that it seemed to have a better taste. He hired a St. Louis chemist to test the water and opened his distillery in 1856. It is now McCormick Distilling company which is the oldest operating distillery in the United States. The company has beautified the grounds and buildings and about 10,000 persons visit it annually.

As a man once said, "My wife visited the wonderful old homes and the antique shops and I visited the distillery and we had a perfect day."

There is some dispute about the first white child born in the county. Leander Wells, son of Mr. and Mrs. John B. Wells, is believed to have been the first.

Wells became one of Weston's first wealthy men. He had a government contract to ferry wood across the river to Ft. Leavenworth, operated an inn frequented by heavy spenders and supposedly owned the largest barn in Missouri—three stories high.

Weston's population was 300 in 1839 and 2,000 by 1850. As in many Missouri cities and communities, the Civil war divided the citizens. Many Weston settlers brought their slaves with them, but the settlers weren't all for the South.

Silas M. Gordon, a Confederate guerrilla, raided Weston once or twice and defied Union soldiers to catch him. He almost captured Jim Lane of Kansas.

John Brown was a jail prisoner in Weston briefly but it was before he attained fame.

Over the centuries disastrous fires have struck the town, cholera in 1850 took a heavy toll, the Civil war brought death to many of its young men.

March 7, 1970

DREAM OF REPUBLIC

If fate, which nudges history, had had its way Missourians might not be living under the flag of the United States.

The supposition sparks one of the most interesting chapters of intrigue in the nations's history.

Consider these unusual developments:

Gen. James Wilkinson, territorial governor of Louisiana (which included Missouri) was one of the greatest connivers of American history, a colleague of Aaron Burr.

He first served with Benedict Arnold in Quebec, then with Washington at Trenton and Priceton and by 1777 had risen to brigadier general. He tried intrigue and was forced to resign when he took part in the Conway Cabal.

In 1804 he visited Aaron Burr and the two plotted to establish an independent republic in the West, and shortly afterward he became governor of the Louisiana territory.

There was never any question of Wilkinson's physical courage and at one time he had the confidence of Washington, Adams and Jefferson.

These are only some of the highlights. The question is—how could a man with such outstanding abilities end up in disgrace? And the same question applies to Burr and Arnold.

Wilkinson was born in Calvert County, Maryland, in 1757. After his service in the Revolutionary war and subsequent difficulty, he entered private business and then went west and southwest. Spanish authorities were worried about Col. George Morgan's move to establish a state at New Madrid, and Wilkinson helped to break this up.

After the Louisiana purchase, Jefferson sent Wilkinson, who was still in the Army, to New Orleans to take possession of the vast territory. Wilkinson took over the governor, and sent Zebulon Pike on two expeditions.

With this vast territory under his control, Wilkinson began to suffer delusions of colonial grandeur. He sailed for New York to give President Jefferson an account of the transfer of the Louisiana territory to the United States. In May he arrived in New York and one of his first visitors in his hotel suite was Aaron Burr.

And so began the grand pattern to establish an independent republic in the West.

After the conspiracy with Burr was revealed, Wilkinson turned against him and testified against him. He fought under Mad Anthony Wayne and then quarreled with him and could not get along with President Madison.

Wilkinson had tried to displace George Rogers Clark as the Kentucky territorial commander. He faced court-martial in 1811 and after being cleared fought in the War of 1812.

Even including Burr and Arnold, there probably is no more tragic figure in American treason than James Wilkinson. The tragedy is that he dreamed great dreams but never could anchor them properly. Had he harnessed his tremendous vision in the proper perspective he might have become one of the nation's great men.

March 14, 1970

"SILK MANIA"

The Latin words, Morus Multicaulis, were on the lips of many Missourians 130 to 140 years ago and to some they meant wealth and to others failure.

That particular decade is associated with the "silk mania" in Missouri, and the Morus Multicaulis was a species of mulberry tree whose leaves were much larger than the regular mulberry tree and provided a more rapid growth than the leaves of the black or the Italian white mulberry tree.

Silk was not new in the world. It is supposed to have been started, or discovered, by the Chinese empress, Si Lingshi, about 2,700 years B. C., in the emperor's gardens. She saw a fat white worm, on a mulberry tree, spraying a strand of something that had a shiny gold color.

The empress began to realize the dress and costume potentialities because this unusual filament was two thirds as strong as the same size of iron. She asked the emperor to begin production on a large scale and the Chinese managed to keep production a secret for almost 2,000 years. Then it leaked out.

From France the original trees came to this country. The Cheney brothers of South Manchester, Conn., began production and the mania gradually spread westward.

The Missouri Silk company was organized at St. Louis on February 13, 1839, "to promote the growth and raising of mulberry

269

trees and the making and manufacture of silk and to promote the growth and propagation of the trees."

There were innumerable and fantastic promotion comments. One was that one acre planted in mulberry trees would feed worms sufficient to produce thousands of dollars in silk.

Another story told how a Mr. Atkinson obtained 130 eggs for silkworms and, when hatched, produced 20,000 more eggs and then these hatched 200 000 more eggs.

From several cocoons, one woman is alleged to have "reeled off" 20 skeins of sewing silk.

The Missouri Silk company, after growing thousands of trees, sold many for 75 cents each. They were 2 to 8 feet high and a promotion blurb stated, "We mention these facts to show how admirably our soil and climate are adapted to the culture of Morus Multicauis, and as to the feeding of worms the facts are equally encouraging."

Inflation and investment mania struck the market. The trees in one nursery rose from $4 to $30 per hundred within a short time, during 1834 to 1839. By 1839 some trees were selling for $2 each and in several areas the price went up to from $300 to $500 per hundred.

A national convention held in Washington by "silk culturalists" from several states included much technical talk about the silkworm, the cocoon and the mulberry trees. But this didn't change Missouri soil and weather. The particular variety of mulberry tree needed could not be grown successfully in Missouri.

The Missouri Silk company disappeared and many Missouri farmers went back to raising soil crops, sadder, wiser and in many cases practically penniless.

March 21, 1969

JOSEPH PULITZER

The scrawny lad of 18 pulled the ragged Union uniform jacket around him as a brace against the October winds and stared longingly across the Mississippi river.

He reached into his pockets. Not one penny. The overcoat had been stolen in New York. The lovely and prized silk handkerchief he had sold for 75 cents for food on the slow train to the West.

He was cold. He was hungry. He was forlorn and lonely.

He approached the ferry boat captain and asked if he could do some chores to get across the river.

"Guess you can," the captain replied. "I've lost a stoke. Ever handle a shovel?"

"No, sir."

"Never mind. Get below and start stoking. Whatcher name?"

"Joe."

"Joe what?"

"Joe Pulitzer."

There were no brass bands nor citizen committees in St. Louis to welcome this skinny nondescript lad in 1865, who would, within a single generation, inaugurate a "new journalism" that is still extant today.

Pulitzer, who launched his St. Louis Post-Dispatch in 1878, and William Rockhill Nelson, who established The Star in 1880, both are credited with creating a new format in journalism, but there is nothing in the biographies of either man to indicate they had any exchange of ideas. The amazing similarities apparently are happenstance.

Pulitzer was born in Mako, Hungary, April 10, 1847, the son of a prosperous merchant who was Magyar-Jewish and a mother who was Austrian. The mother was Louise Berger.

The military bug bit the lad early. He tried the Austrian army, the French foreign legion and the British army. Too skinny; eyes not strong—the verdict in all cases.

But the Civil war was on in the United States. Many Germans had gone over at the middle of the century. Now the United States Army recruiter approached skinny Joe and the young man agreed to go to America and fight for the Union. He had wanted to go to America anyway.

Pulitzer served about a year during the later stages of the conflict. He was in the 1st New York cavalry, which had been formed by Carl Schurz, another German immigrant. He served under Custer and Sheridan. One of the battles in which he fought was at Antioch.

Then Appomattox and the skinny immigrant wandered around New York for several months. There are two main gags that biographers repeat and one, at least, is understandable.

Pulitzer's English was "broken" in the Army. He was ridiculed and wanted to go where the "purist" English was spoken. One gagster supposedly suggested St. Louis, knowing there was a strong Germanic element there.

So the skinny lad left for St. Louis with only a silk handkerchief in his pocket after paying the fare.

Pulitzer held many jobs after arriving in St. Louis. He helped to load steamboats, despite his limited physical abilities. He drove hacks

271

JOSEPH PULITZER

and tried being a waiter in a restaurant until he dropped a tray of food on a guest's head.

Chess played an important part in his life. In the Union Army he had been ridiculed by others because of his accent and skinny physique. One day he had enough and slugged a noncommissioned officer. It was a serious offense but a regular officer who had played chess with Pulitzer intervened and nothing happened.

The lad had been in St. Louis now three years. Nobody noticed him. He hung around the Mercantile library where Schurz and his colleague on the newspaper, Emil Preetorius, played chess.

The fact that Pulitzer served in the Schurz regiment didn't mean anything. Schurz was editor of the Westliche Post and an acknowledged leader and spokesman for the German element.

Pulitzer got a job as reporter on the Westliche Post and was ready to move, although not quite certain which way. His English was fluent now, with hardly an accent. He listened to the language, spent hours at night in his room translating German newspaper stories into English and then others back to German.

Pulitzer's jounalistic abilities developed fast. Biographers attribute the second gag to his being elected to the Missouri House of Representatives. When he left a Republican meeting to write a story his name was brought forth as a candidate to run in a heavily Democratic district.

It wasn't funny to Pulitzer. He ran like wildfire and was elected. He took his seat January 5, 1870, and also served as correspondent for the Westliche Post.

The format that was to turn into a "new journalism" began to appear. Pulitzer feared no man. He aimed many of his stories from Jefferson City against corruption in politics, against lobbyists and others. He incurred the wrath of one, Edward Augustine.

Pulitzer shot and wounded Augustine in the leg and the lobbyist whopped the reporter on the head with a derringer, inflicting a scalp wound.

In 1871 Pulitzer bought an interest in the Westliche Post, sold it two years later, then bought the German daily, Staats-Zeitung.

On December 9, 1878, he bought the defunct St. Louis Dispatch and three days later, John Dillon, owner of the St. Louis Post, agreed to a merger.

One year later Pulitzer bought Dillon's interest and in 1883, bought the New York World from Jay Gould. The following year he was elected a congressman from New York but resigned after serving several months.

The scrawny lad of 1865 was now a world figure. He bought two losing newspapers, built them into tremendously profitable enterprises and also initiated the "new journalism."

His eyesight began to fail and in 1887, he went into a semi-retirement, bulwarked by a bevy of secretaries who read the newspapers to him, including the want-ads. He directed his enterprises from his yacht, Liberty, on which he died October 29, 1911, in the Charleston, S. C. harbor.

Leaving behind a journalistic legacy matched only by two or three others, he once said: "Never be afraid to attack wrong, whether predatory plutocracy or predatory poverty."

MONTGOMERY BLAIR

During the recent difficulties the administration had with mail carriers and the Postoffice department, President Nixon should have sneaked a quick look at the biography of Montgomery Blair. Maybe Winton Blount might have studied the Blair story. The high points are these:

When he became President Lincoln's first postmaster general, the department was 10 million dollars in the red and when he left about four years later there was a surplus of $750,000.

During his term he ferreted out waste, increased salaries and launched three innovations that caused many to say he was daft:

One was free delivery of mail in the cities; the second was railway postoffices and the third the money-order plan.

There were other accomplishments in the Postoffice department. In 1863 he called an international conference in Paris to discuss international postal co-operation, and out of this meeting came the mutual agreement on honoring stampprice ratios among the various nations.

On the political side, however, Montgomery Blair was one of the most astute in the latter half of the last century, and he played an important role in nominating and electing Lincoln.

He was born May 10, 1813, in Franklin County, Ky., and was graduated from West Point in 1835. He fought in the Seminole war, studied law at Transylvania University and went to St. Louis in 1837.

His brother, Frank Blair, had carved out an illustrious Civil war record. He and Montgomery joined forces as lawyers and political leaders. The political reputations, however, had been established.

Montgomery Blair was mayor of St. Louis from 1842 to 1843, and then was appointed U. S. district attorney. A short time later he was made judge of the St. Louis Court of Common Pleas. He resigned in 1849 and moved to Maryland in 1853. Two years later he became U. S. solicitor of claims, resigning this post three years later.

Almost all school students have heard about the Dred Scott case but few, if any, know the identity of the slave's chief counsel—Montgomery Blair.

It was about this time that Blair felt he no longer could go along with the Democratic party's stand on slavery, and he switched to the Republican party. He and his brother had met Abraham Lincoln and approved of his stand on slavery. The alliance of the two Blairs and Lincoln was one of the portentous miracles to occur in the political heavens of that day.

The story of Frank Blair has been told. He went to Illinois and helped Lincoln on the campaign trail. Frank Blair manumitted his slaves 12 years before the war.

There was Blair power at the 1860 convention. Edward Bates was a candidate for the nomination and Frank Blair was his floor manager and nominated him.

Bates did not make much of a show but held out for three ballots. Lincoln was nominated when Ohio switched.

Although the Blairs were aggressive, belligerent and sometimes arrogant, they worked hard for Lincoln's election and his re-election.

Montgomery wrote to a friend, "If the South were assured that the Republicans did not advocate white and Negro equality, many Southern states would support them."

In another letter before war started, he wrote, "I am only anxious now to get our people on the aggressive. We are strong enough already to make a progressive movement towards disarming and putting down the vagabonds who fancy they are leading a great movement. It will prove, if dealt with properly, a miserable failure disgracing all concerned with it. The misfortune is that the want of vigor which has so far characterized our movements ever draws some man of character into the secession abyss."

Montgomery Blair was an unreconstructed Unionist. He demanded better re-enforcements at Fort Sumter and when it was taken, fired off an "I told you so."

After the war he spoke against Charles Drake and his Republican radicals of Missouri, as well as against Thaddeus Stevens.

The radicals began to work on Blair. They demanded his resignation. Lincoln said "no" emphatically—but Blair saw the hand-

MONT BLAIR

writing. He was told that Lincoln could not be re-elected unless Blair quit. This ultimatum for a Blair was unusual, but Lincoln's re-election was far too important. Although resigned, he campaigned for Lincoln in 1864.

Blair returned to Maryland, served in the Legislature in 1877 and was defeated for Congress in 1882. He died at Silver Spring, Md., July 27, 1883.

April 4, 1970

CHARLES DANIEL DRAKE

Charles Daniel Drake was one of the most controversial figures during and after the Civil war in Missouri and outside of the odious test oath he contributed far more on the constructive side than many historians suppose.

He was born in Cincinnati 159 years ago today. He attended schools there and in Kentucky and Connecticut, and in 1827 entered naval training as a midshipman aboard the USS Delaware in a Mediterranean convoy. Three years later he decided not to pursue this profession.

He studied law, moved to St. Louis, worked as a collection lawyer in St. Louis for Eastern clients, served briefly as city attorney, dabbled in Whig politics and was one of the founders of the St. Louis Law Library association. His legal business declined in the 1840s and he returned to Cincinnati. His two children died, he failed to get a political appointment and he returned to St. Louis about 1850.

He attracted attention from the legal profession when, in 1854, he published "A Treatise on the Law of Suits by Attachment in the United States," which soon became a standard work in the profession.

From 1850 to 1860, while practicing law in St. Louis, he became indecisive about his involvement with the Whig, the Democratic and the Know-Nothing parties. The Civil war seemed to give him some direction.

He served a short time in 1859 in the Missouri House of Representatives, filling a vacancy, but veered over to the Republicans about the time war started. By 1863 he was the leader of the so-called radical faction of that party. The party's main points were immediate emancipation of the slaves, the adoption of a new constitution and disenfranchisement of all disloyal Missourians.

His faction won a victory in 1864 and the constitutional convention met in St. Louis on Janurary 6, 1865. Six days later the con-

CHARLES DRAKE Credit: State Historical Society of Mo.

vention adopted the ordinance of immediate emancipation, almost one year before adoption of the 13th amendment.

There were 66 delegates and, although Arnold Krekel of St. Louis was elected president, they looked mainly to Drake for leadership.

Drake had carefully studied the present Constitution as well as those recently adopted in other states. He also appeared to have a feeling for the times, especially regarding the South, secession and slavery.

He irritated some of the German elements in St. Louis, was bitterly assailed by Southern supporters when he advocated that Missouri stand by the Union. He was vice-president of the convention, more of a driver than a leader, an excellent debater and speaker and sometimes arrogant and overbearing.

Although Drake zig-zagged for a while, once he drew his bead on slavery, his shooting was straight. He allegedly defended slavery, then tolerated it, then stood for gradual emancipation and finally for immediate emancipation.

One of the clearest and most concise explanations of slavery, emancipation and secession was made by Abe Lincoln when Drake led his Committee of Seventy to Washington.

The rebuff from Lincoln did not deter Drake from his goal. He pursued the abolition of slavery with an aggressiveness seldom seen. He was not willing, however, to grant Negro suffrage; he felt that Negroes were not capable of voting wisely so soon after the war.

Yet he could turn right around and insist the Negro was capable of bearing arms and contributing to the Union strength.

"I have no squeamishness about arming the Negro," he said. "I am no half-breed Unionist, sensitive about seeing white men alongside the American citizen of African descent. No traitor is too good to be killed by a Negro, nor has a traitor the right to insist on being killed by a white man. If, for the sake of slavery, he turns traitor, let former slaves be his executioners; it is a just and fit retribution. Disaffection, if not disloyalty, lurks in him who opposes the arming of the Negro."

It is doubtful if anyone ever uttered stronger words than these about putting Negroes into the Union army. The speech was widely published and broke the ice in many places.

The Kansas City Journal of Commerce on November 5, 1863, following the speech, said, "Everywhere throughout the state the Negroes are coming forward with alacrity to enroll themselves in the service of the government."

Missouri furnished 8,344 Negroes to five regiments of the Union army, 655 being substitutes for whites who had been drafted. Many thousands more Missouri Negroes served because many of those recruited in Kansas, Illinois and Iowa were runaway Missouri blacks.

Almost all of the bitter criticism directed at Drake was on the loyalty oath. Article 2 required that for at least six years every voter, every office-holder, lawyer, clergyman, teacher and juror take an oath by which he swore that he had never been guilty of committing any one of a long list of disloyal acts. Persons who declined the oath could not register to vote.

This stirred up the beehive. George Caleb Bingham, the famous artist known mainly for his polemic painting, "Order No. 11," inveighed against the oath. Frank Blair also struck out sharply, his most memorable speech being at Warrensburg.

The new constitution was known as the "Drake Constitution," and as the "Draconian Code" by Drake's enemies. Drake was elected to the U.S. Senate in 1866 and served four years.

In 1870 Drake accepted an appointment as chief justice of the United States court of claims, holding the post until his retirement in 1885. He died April 1, 1892.

Drake made many valuable contributions to his state and nation and the preservation of the Union. He came on the scene at a time when sharp and aggressive policies were necessary.

Missouri was not a Southern state but had many of the problems of those states. Some historians believe that had it not been for Drake's "radical" policies many of the tragedies and troubles of the reconstruction, that plagued the Southern states, might have erupted in Missouri.

April 11, 1970

STATES NEGROES OVERLOOKED

In music, industry, laboratory research, education, politics, diplomacy and other fields, Missouri Negroes have played important roles, but the names of only a few are widely known today.

George Washington Carver, born on a farm near Diamond, Mo., in Southwest Missouri, and one of the world immortals, is, of course, the best known. In his laboratory he developed 300 products from the peanut, 100 from the sweet potato and 75 from the pecan. He turned cotton into paving blocks, made rugs of okra and contributed to humanity generally in a hundred different ways.

Yes, of course, you know about George Washington Carver. But who were George Washington Ellis, John William Boone, James Milton Turner, Blanche Kelso Bruce and Scott Joplin?

Ellis was born in Weston, Mo., on May 4, 1875. Having earned his law degree from the University of Kansas, he became a lawyer, writer and sociologist. He served with the American legation in Liberia for eight years after attracting the attention of President Theodore Roosevelt.

Few people recognize the name "John William Boone," but say "Blind Boone," and more will know. He was born in Saline County on May 17, 1864. When he was six months old a brain fever caused him to become blind. Yet he went on to become one of the world's outstanding musicians and pianists.

He had a tin whistle and French harp and coaxed melodies from this strange combination. He wandered around Missouri playing for his food. State Sen. Francis M. Cockrell and Thomas Crittenden (later to be governor) sent him to an institute for the blind in St. Louis, where he learned to play the piano. In 1879 he performed in Columbia and John Lange, jr., a Negro contractor, saw his enormous potential and became his manager. Boone was famous for being able to play any tune after hearing it once. He and Lange toured the nation and Europe and Boone composed many songs. He died October 4, 1927, in Warrensburg.

James Milton Turner was born a slave May 16, 1840, in St. Louis County. His father, a veterinarian, used meager savings to buy the lad's freedom from slavery and he enrolled at Oberlin college.

His father died a short time later and young Turner returned home. He did odd jobs and was a bootblack at Camp Jackson at the start of the Civil war. He "enlisted" as a servant to a Union officer and was wounded at Shiloh. The wound caused a permanent limp.

Near the end of the war he sat around a campfire with two white officers and the three agreed that the big hope for Negroes after emancipation was education. They and others collected several thousand dollars from fellow soldiers—black and white—and helped set up Lincoln university in Jefferson City.

Turner was active in politics. He is credited with swinging the majority of Negro votes in Missouri for General Grant's re-election.

Grant appointed him minister to Liberia and Turner proved to be an able envoy. Many nations honored him. So did the prince of Wales. When Turner returned to St. Louis he was besieged with dinners and honors and townspeople vied for the honor of pulling his carriage through the streets during a parade. He died in St. Louis November 1, 1915.

And Blanche Kelso Bruce? He spent a large part of his early life in Missouri and in 1874 was elected United States senator from Mississippi.

JAMES MILTON TURNER

And Scott Joplin? Have you heard of the timeless "Maple Leaf Rag?" He wrote it in Sedalia near the turn of the century. He and other Negro composers, including James Scott of Neosho, Percy Wenrich of Joplin, Scott Hayden of Sedalia and Arthur Marshall of Saline County, are generally credited for creating "rag-time."

And, W. C. Handy and his "St. Louis Blues"!

There are innumerable interesting stories about Negroes in Missouri during the last century but the information must be dug for and panned just as Robert Lewis sought gold in California. He took with him one of his slaves, Jesse Hubbard. They found $15,000 worth of gold and came back to Missouri. Lewis gave Hubbard half the gleanings and his freedom and Hubbard bought a farm and prospered.

COL. ALEXANDER DONIPHAN

There are many historians in this state who feel that one of the truly unsung heroes of the war with Mexico was a Missourian— Alexander Doniphan.

There are many who believe he should have been promoted to a brigadier or major general at the end of the war, during his life or even posthumously. There may be a move starting in Washington to brevet him to a higher rank.

One historian who feels that Doniphan has been slighted is Judge R. Kenneth Elliott of the Clay County Circuit court. Elliott recently addressed the Kansas City Posse of the Westerners on the "Rhetoric of Alexander W. Doniphan" and afterward discussed the matter of military rank with others.

"If any officer in the war with Mexico was entitled to a promotion, even a battlefield promotion, it was Doniphan," Elliott said.

Alexander William Doniphan was born July 9, 1808, in Mason County, Kentucky. HIs father had accompanied Daniel Boone to Kentucky. His ancestors were Irish and English. Alexander Doniphan passed his bar examination in Kentucky and came to Missouri in 1830 practicing three years in Lexington and then going to Liberty where he practiced 30 years before retiring.

As colonel in the Missouri militia he helped to recruit about 1,000 Missouri volunteers for the war with Mexico. They marched overland 3,600 miles in one year and seized the vast area that is now New Mexico and Arizona.

Several towns, including Santa Fe, were taken bloodlessly. The Missourians fought two battles against numerically larger forces, one at

Brazito and the second at Chihuahua where the ragged volunteers faced a Mexican army.

This battle was a complete rout, with 304 Mexicans killed, 500 wounded and 70 captured. The Missouri loss was four killed and several wounded.

The Missourians returned home by water. They received tremendous receptions as they passed through New Orleans, St. Louis and various smaller towns across the state as they returned to their homes. Almost all came from western Missouri

Doniphan was an imposing figure—6 feet, 4 inches tall handsome with piercing hazel eyes and possessing the charm and courtesy of a Southern gentleman.

He remained a colonel the rest of his life. Many military figures who accomplished far less than Doniphan were promoted, some during the war or afterward.

Many historians—among them Judge Elliott—believe that two major points may account for this "oversight".

Doniphan was not a regular (West Point) army man and neither were his volunteers. After Chiihuahua, when the Missourians encamped with regular soldiers awaiting transportation home, the regulars were inclined to look down their noses at the ragged Missourians, and the latter retaliated by pointing out the tremendous victories they had won and territory covered.

In almost all wars involving this nation, there always have been these frequent differences between the regulars and the volunteers as many World War II volunteers may recall.

The second major point is that he incurred the wrath of many Missourians because of his relationship with the Mormons. The Mormons fought other Missourians several times in the Clay County area. Doniphan, a colonel in the militia at the time, was directed to execute the Mormon leaders allegedly responsible for several deaths.

Doniphan flatly refused, but accepted the surrender of Joseph Smith and defended him in court. He was a hero in the eyes of Mormons, but something less in the view of many other Missourians.

His later life was tragic. He had two sons, both of whom died in their teens. His wife, whom he referred to as a "lovely and lively" woman, died in 1872. He began to suffer from many ailments and died in 1887. He was buried in Fairview cemetery in Liberty.

Doniphan was an outstanding courtroom lawyer. His prose soared like poetry, his rhetoric carried the lilt that his Irish ancestors might have possessed. The courtroom was always crowded when he spoke and in public meetings he always drew large crowds.

In his address, Judge Elliott cited many examples of Doniphan's soaring rhetoric. One was from a speech given by Doniphan at West Point:

"And now, my old fellow soldiers, we will never meet again. The green sod grows above many of our loved and honored comrades, and we, too, must soon obey the last call of duty. It is plain that men had a beginning. It is a more grave and startling truth that we can never have an ending. The sun with all its glory must grow dim; the heavens with all their grandeur must pass away, but man is destined to immortal youth under a sun that will never set, and in a world that will never pass away."

OZARK "MOUNTAIN MAID"

Miss Wanda Eve Brewer comments at length on this mysterious Ozark dweller in her recent booklet, "Roaring River Realities" (Lowell Press, Kansas City).

Jean Wallace was known as the "mountain maid." She lived 47 years alone on a mountain top. For most of those years she preferred the cloak of mystery, although she allowed some information to creep out near her death. Also, she permitted some photographs.

The meager facts permitted reveal Jean Wallace was born on an ocean liner on May 17, 1851, followed a nursing profession in New York and then went to the Ozarks in later years.

Jean Wallace preferred solitude in the Ozarks. Solitude and independence are the first laws of the land there.

She loved to stroll the woods at night, surrounded by several cats. She tended a peach orchard with all the meticulous detail of a horticulturist. She chopped her own wood, carried her water from a spring 1½ miles away and obtained what groceries she needed from a general store almost a mile away.

She read the Bible daily and would not permit any killing, even of a snake, on her property. Neither could timber be cut on her land.

Undoubtedly she had some money, judging from the currency used in buying the meager staples. She was friendly to the Ozark people who called on her, but they never obtained any information about her.

She apparently had what has become known in recent years as extrasensory perception. According to Miss Brewer, Miss Wallace quoted on a rare occasion that her Scottish sea captain father once told her, "You have in your eyes the God-given power to see into the future, and you should use it well for the betterment of those who might seek you out."

There are many stories of her using this power. There were tests, too. Several boys hid a saddle and then went to her reporting that it was stolen. Could she help? She told where the saddle was and with a grim smile added, "If you don't hurry back to the spot, the wild hogs are going to have it all chewed up."

While the Volstead act was in effect, revenue agents would visit her and ask her to divulge divinely the location of stills. She usually replied, "That is your business and I don't intend to cause any trouble to my people."

Apparently her nursing background, and the desire to help people, caused her to leave abruptly when World War I erupted. There were no letters or communications of any kind during the war, but a few weeks after the Armistice she was back in her cabin in the Ozarks.

As her fame grew, writers and reporters occasionally visited her. She was always friendly but they never penetrated her anonymity.

To one she said, "My power of seeing into the future was bestowed upon me by an everpresent God, but He did not give me the power to see into my own future. I could use the power only for the betterment of my friends and acquaintances. I am old and feeble. I am quite ready for the summons which I know must come soon."

She died in a fire that destroyed her small cabin. Nobody knows if she had her own extrasensory premonition of death but one week before her death she did agree to photographs.

May 2, 1970

BENJAMIN HOWARD

Benjamin Howard, the first governor of the Territory of Missouri, was an excellent administrator and a military leader with an outstanding record.

Howard County the "mother of counties" in Missouri, was named after him.

Howard was born in Virginia in 1760, received a meager education, moved to Kentucky, fought as a soldier in several Indian wars and in 1795 began the study of law. He served in the Kentucky House of Representatives (1801-02) and in 1807 was elected to Congress from Kentucky.

He was re-elected but resigned in 1810 when President Madison appointed him governor of the Territory of Louisiana, becoming the

MISSOURI COUNTIES

The Approximate Boundaries of the First Five
Counties of Missouri as Described in 1812 and of
Howard County as Described in 1816.

last governor of the Territory of Louisiana and the first governor of the Territory of Missouri.

The War of 1812 was looming on the horizon and Washington began to look westward for military leaders, knowing that the British-led Indian tribes around the Great Lakes region would try a strike at the general St. Louis area just as they did during the Revolutionary war when George Rogers Clark and his band of "Missourians" turned them back.

Howard resigned as governor to accept an appointment as brigadier general in the army. He was charged with working out the defenses of the St. Louis and general Missouri area. Nathan Boone also had considerable military authority and the two mapped out both defensive and offensive measures. Boone, the son of Daniel Boone, trained Missouri Rangers.

The Howard-Boone combination was potent. Howard moved against Fort Madison two days before the British were to attack Missouri and Boone and his Rangers swam upstream in the Mississippi at night to attack British forces from the rear.

Howard ordered a fort erected in Ralls County on the Mississippi. It was named Fort Mason after Lt. John Mason. Another fort was erected in Lincoln County and named Fort Howard, after Benjamin Howard, who by then had command of everything west of the Mississippi river. No other American ever commanded such a vast territory.

On October 1, 1812, he issued a proclamation calling for five counties, 13 territorial delegates to the terrritorial legislature of Missouri and election of the first congressional delegate to Congress.

The state was first divided into five counties—St. Charles, St. Louis, Ste. Genevieve, Cape Girardeau and New Madrid, all south of the Missouri river. In 1816 Howard County was established in honor of Benjamin Howard.

By 1820 seven new counties were carved out of Howard County— Cooper, Lafayette, Saline, Cole, Boone, Chariton and Ray. A short time later, other counties came from Howard, in whole or in part: Randolph, Macon, Schuyler, Miller, Putnam, Sullivan, Linn, Moniteau, Morgan, Camden, Mercer, Grundy, Livingston, Carroll, Pettis, Benton, Harrison, Daviess, Caldwell, Johnson, Henry, St. Clair, Worth, Gentry, DeKalb, Clinton, Clay, Cass, Jackson and Bates.

Howard, embracing 22,000 square miles, became the largest county to be established formally in Missouri. It was larger then than the states of Vermont, Massachusetts, Delaware and Rhode Island.

May 9, 1970

DR. JOHN SAPPINGTON

Dr. John Sappington was born May 15, 1776, at Havre de Grace, Md., and studied medicine in his father's office in Nashville, Tenn. In 1814 he went to Philadelphia and earned his medical degree.

In 1819 he came to Missouri, settled in Howard County and then moved to a farm near Arrow Rock, where he would gain fame by initiating the use of quinine to combat malaria.

Malaria, named for malaria, or bad air, came into Greece from Africa around the fifth century B. C. It quickly spread and over hundreds of years killed thousands throughout Greek-Roman-Mediterranean area. Hippocrates, the father of medicine, and others noted even then that most of the victims lived near swamps or areas of brackish, stagnant water.

In the 16th century a Peruvian soldier, afflicted with the burning fever, crawled to a brackish pool, hung onto a log and drank of the bitter water. Soon his fever left. His companions established a connection with the bark on the log for his recovery. The bark contained quinine.

Progress was slow over the centuries, but in 1820 two French scientists succeeded in isolating quinine. Sappingtion had noted that Missourians, who contracted the burning and sometimes fatal fever also lived near stagnant swamps and that swarms of mosquitoes hovered over them.

Early visitors to Missouri commented on this situation, more than one reporting that the mosquitoes were at least an inch long.

Two towns in Howard and Saline Counties were abandoned because of the prevalence of fevers, or "shaking agues," as they were called. Dr. Sappington, who had an inquiring mind, read everything he could on "Peruvian bark."

Doctors then treated fevers, and many other diseases, by bloodletting, drastic purging, the use of emetics, cold and hot drinks and heavy sedation.

Sappington frowned on these methods and began experimenting with quinine on his patients. In his first 80 cases, all but three recovered and it was doubtful that what ailed those three was malaria.

So in 1832 he determined to make the big leap and began the manufacture of his "Anti-Fever" pills. Each contained one gram of quinine, three-fourths of a grain of licorice, one-fourth grain of myrrh and some sassafras oil to give a pleasant taste. He prescribed one every two hours until the fever broke.

Sappington was a maverick in his profession. He was getting results and worried little about attacks from his colleagues. He was called a "vendor of quack pills" and attacked in many ways. But within a short time there were 25 salesmen covering a large part of the nation selling his pills. Almost daily two or three would ride away from his farm, their saddle bags loaded with the pills.

Sappington had his family rolling pills, put his servants to work and tried to keep up with the market. He bought his quinine from an Easterner, John Farr of Philadelphia was astounded by Sappington's huge orders.

Sappington had patented his process under the medical laws of that era and in 1840 was kicked out of the St. Louis Medical society for advertising his pills.

In 1844 he published a book, "The Theory and Practice of Fevers." and relinquished his proprietary rights to the use of quinine for treatments. In the book he criticized the profession for relying on blood-letting and purges to cure various ailments. To counteract charges that he was trying to get rich by selling his own pills, he suggested that the public buy quinine elsewhere and "roll" their own pills.

Sappington was the father-in-law of Meredith Miles Marmaduke, who became governor in 1844 and of Claiborne Fox Jackson, Missouri's Civil war pro-Southern governor. Meredith Marmaduke was a strong Union man but his son, John S. Marmaduke, who became governor, was a Confederate general.

Jackson wed, one after the other, two of Sappington's daughters, both of whom died. Jackson asked for the hand of a third daughter. Sappington granted it and is supposed to have commented, "But don't come back for the old woman."

Sappington had become wealthy on the sale of his pills. He built an elaborate home, "Fox Castle," near Arrow Rock, and his son, William B. Sappington, built a 14-room mansion nearby in 1840. "Fox Castle" crumbled in later years but the son's "Prairie Park" was bought in 1949 by Dr. and Mrs. John R. Lawrence of Marshall who spent five years and thousands of dollars in restoration. It is now a showplace of mid-Missouri.

Sappington did become a wealthy man and there were innumerable private donations and charitable enterprises in which he was interested. He came to believe that education provided the best basis for a happy and successful life next to love and parental discipline.

He died September 7, 1856, and in his will left $20,000 to help the needy children of Saline County obtain an education. In those days that was a substantial sum.

Sappington wisely realized that the provisions could not be too binding. The child or family, must need financial help to send the youngster to school and he had to be a "reasonably good student".

DR. JOHN SAPPINGTON   Credit: State Historical Soceity of Mo.

There was no limitation on the amount and the help could be repetitive.

For many years the interest piled up on the original $20,000 before it could be used. John P. Huston, now president of the Wood and Huston bank in Marshall, is treasurer of the fund. In 1963 he succeeded the late F. C. Barnhill who had been treasurer almost 60 years.

Huston explained recently that reports are made by the board of trustees every August. Last year a total of 13,471 young persons had been helped and $266,290 spent, and there was a balance of $100,559 in the fund.

These figures might confound amateur financial "experts" but they attest to the wisdom of Huston, Barnhill and the latter's predecessors in investing idle funds. Had few youngsters been helped, the charge might be made they allowed the money to remain idle and built up big surpluses, but over the years aid was given to about 130 annually.

Over the last century little attention has been given to Sappington's educational program, but 20 years after his death the Paris Academy of Sciences began a study of malaria and quinine.

A French physician in Algeria and a British army surgeon started experiments on a large scale. The French couldn't finish the Panama canal partly because of the malarial fevers and American doctors stepped in using many of Sappington's finds.

The lowly mosquito threatened to stop construction of the giant hydroelectric plant in Sao Paulo, Brazil, a few years ago, and again the old Peruvian bark came to the rescue.

NATIVE PROVIDES AUTHENTIC PICTURE

"Don't never have nothing to do with nobody that is ornerier than you are."

That is a gem from a native Ozarkian in a book written by a native of the Ozarks, Douglas Mahnkey of Forsyth, a lawyer and former member of the Missouri House of Representatives.

Mahnkey was born in Taney County, grew up in that area and still lives there. He knows the land well and its people and how to present them interestingly.

The above quotation, as Mahnkey gives it, is from Lum Booth, a blacksmith. Booth is the typical blacksmith of bygone description,

303

leather apron and all muscles, and the writer states, "Many times I watched him, always in complete control of the situation, shoe a wild, mean horse. From his forge and anvil, he made the shoes and then mastered the wild horse and nailed four shoes in place."

The Ozark native will poke fun at himself. Another Booth gem indicates how hard it may be to get ahead of the Ozarkian even though he is not educated.

"Even the half-witted ones are naturally smart," he says.

Then there is the story about "Uncle George" who cashed a check in his bank. The cashier counted out the bills carefully. Uncle George went to a nearby table and counted them twice.

The cashier asked, "What's the matter Uncle George? Didn't I give you enough money?"

Uncle George dead-panned the reply, "Jest barely, jest barely."

Courtroom cases in the Ozarks often provided humor.

One witness had been drinking heavily before going on the stand. He mumbled through answers to a couple of questions, then was stopped by the judge's gavel.

"Mr. Smith, you are intoxicated, are you not?" the judge asked.

"Now, how's that, Jedge?"

"You are intoxicated," said the judge.

"Jedge," whined the witness, "Do you mean, am I drunk?"

"That is exactly what I mean."

The witness shook his head and grinned. "Jedge, that's the best damn decision you've made since you've been on the bench."

And "Doc" Anderson was a Southern gentleman who frequently donned his sartorial best—dark suit, white shirt, panama hat, shiny boots and cane. As he walked past the general store, a loafer asked, "Doc, whar you going to preach?"

And Anderson stiffened and replied, "It is a poor damn town that cannot afford at least one gentleman."

There are innumerable stories from the rustic viewpoint about the "city slicker" asking directions, and Mahnkey narrates one about the "foreigner" asking if he was on the right road to Norfolk dam

"Yep, that's the right road, aw'right," the Ozarkian replied. Then there was a pause, and, "But you're a-going the wrong way."

Mahnkey defines well the important place the rural churches occupied. His simple description could apply to any country area.

"Almost everyone went to church in those early days. Some went, no doubt, because there were not many other places to go, and one always had an opportunity to meet old friends. Many courtships began here. The young people had a chance to spark a little, and many a lad had his first date by waiting at the church house door and asking shyly, 'May I see you home?' "

The writer recalls many unusual names of schools, such as Three Johns, Kentucky Hollow, Loafer's Glory, Ironsides, Possum Trot, Bee Creek and Gobblers' Knob.

Mahnkey recalls several incidents of being afraid in the hills at night and then notes, "As long as your dog and your horse are not frightened in the Ozarks, there is no need to be afraid."

Another famous hill warning: "Look sharp at any man who recommends hisself too highly."

The writer fairly well sums up the situation with this: "Once you have made friends of them, our Ozark folk are splendid companions and become the best of friends, but in the hurry of modern living these easy-going and genial persons are disappearing."

JOHN WOODS HARRIS

Among its leading citizens in the last century, when Missouri still was predominantly an agricultural state, was John Woods Harris.

The Harris lineage in Boone County goes back more than 150 years. The Rev. Anderson Woods and his wife, Elizabeth Harris Woods, came from Madison County, Kentucky, in 1816 and settled on what was known as the Thrall Prairie region, the first permanent settlement in Boone County.

The following year Overton Harris and his wife, with their infant son, John Woods Harris, having heard about the tremendously rich soil and advantages in Missouri, left Madison County and settled in Thrall's Prairie. Shortly afterward, James Harris arrived. James and Overton Harris were brothers-in-law of Mr. Woods. Then came Tyre Harris, a cousin of Overton.

In 1821, the year Missouri officially became a state, Overton Harris bacame the first sheriff of Boone County. The state, county and nation grew and so did John Woods Harris.

He was a good listener and much of the conversation among pioneer families dealt with the proper methods of growing crops and raising healthy livestock. The soil was rich, the prairie grasses were luxuriant and the young man began to dream of the "perfect" farm.

He had learned to work on the family farm and was observant. He also realized that his parents wouldn't just hand him something on the proverbial silver platter.

JOHN WOODS HARRIS

Credit: State Historical Society of Mo.

At 14 he went to work as a clerk in the store owned by Acting Gov. A. J. Williams. After Williams died the boy worked for another storekeeper, William Cornelius. The thrifty lad saved his money and started his own store in Monroe County, saved more and bought a farm, then went into the mercantile business at Rocheport, a thriving community on the overland and river route westward.

In 1855 John Woods Harris married Ann Mary McClure and with his savings bought his father-in-law's farm of 600 acres. A short time later he added 1,200 acres.

The young man now was in farming in a big way. He had educated himself in the academic courses, read everything about farming he could find, talked and listened and over a short span of 15 years the Harris farm became the center of attention.

In 1873 the St. Louis Agricultural and Mechanical society announced a state-wide farm competition for the "model farm." There were hundreds of entries and judges scurried around the state to review the farms and add up the scores.

Harris won the award and for the next several years thousands of persons came from all parts of the nation to see it.

The major crops were wheat, corn and oats. Blooded horses and fine cattle, along with hogs and sheep, were raised. Harris was the first to bring Jersey and Alderney cattle into Missouri.

There were several large barns on the farm, each costing about $5,000, quite a sum for a barn then. There were miles of stake and rail fences. Harris experimented with seeds, grains and fertilizers and brought smiles of ridicule from some of his neighbors when he began crop rotation. But he seldom suffered a crop failure.

There was a 20-acre fenced park with deer and antelope and Harris forbade the firing of a rifle within earshot of the animals for fear of frightening them. This solicitude for animals carried over to his stock A worker was instantly fired for beating an animal.

Harris believed in feeding his family and employees well. He built an ice house large enough so he could supply his neighbors.

Although Harris had Southern sympathies, he did not believe in slavery. His work force varied, but usually there were about 30, both black and white. He had inherited some from McClure, and a few were born afterward, but he never bought a slave.

When Emancipation came Harris placed each Negro family in a separate cabin, or built them if necessary, gave them a cow and tools for cultivation and if they chose to remain with him he paid them wages. He also set up a night school to help educate the Negro children.

The "model farm" did not just spring from the soil. It was the result of hard work and study, attention to detail, experimentation and in all probability due in some measure to the decent treatment accorded his workers, white and black.

Harris served in the Missouri legislature and on the University of Missouri board of curators. He died May 3, 1877, and his agricultural award might also have included "model citizen."

INDEX

30 Jeff City or Osage